EARLY DAYS

BY
SAMUEL BAMFORD
(1788 - 1872)

EDITED, WITH AN INTRODUCTION
BY
HENRY DUNCKLEY
("VERAX")

This Edition
Published 2014

This is a reproduction of an out of copyright book

The OCR of the original has been proof read and then edited into its current form to preserve the original text whilst making it easily available to the modern reader.

The OCR of the original can be found at

The Internet Archive
https://archive.org

© 1849 Expired.
ISBN 978-1-291-95139-4

Published By
www.folkcustoms.co.uk

CONTENTS

	INTRODUCTION	5
I.	BIRTH, PARENTAGE, AND OTHER MATTERS	15
II.	OF MY FOREFATHERS	19
III.	OF MIDDLETON, AT THE TIME I HAVE BEEN WRITING ABOUT	25
IV.	EARLY IMPRESSIONS- MIDDLETON REFORMERS-MEETING AT ROYTON—DENIAL OF JUSTICE	31
V.	FIRST IMPRESSIONS OF MANCHESTER	37
VI.	LIVING BESIDE THE DEAD—A NURSE	43
VII.	A NEW GOVERNESS: PLAYMATES—STRIKING CHARACTERS— DIETARY	47
VIII.	BAD HEALTH-WORSE DOCTORING— A TIMELY RETREAT— SCHOOL, MASTERS—THE FREE GRAMMAR SCHOOL	53
IX.	ANOTHER GREAT CHANGE	61
X.	A NEW LIFE	65
XI.	SCHOOLING—CORRECTION—PRAYER	69
XII.	A HOME-BEARING, A DINNER, AND A MASTER INDEED	73
XIII.	PRAYER MEETINGS—A BOGGART—CHRISTIAN INSTRUCTION	79
XIV.	PASTIMES AND OBSERVANCES	83
XV.	THE WAKES	91
XVI.	BONFIRES—SUPERSTITIONS—APPARITIONS	99
XVII.	LOVE DAWNINGS	105
XVIII.	HOPE STILL DEFERRED— NEW EMPLOYMENTS—NEW BOOKS	113
XIX.	THE WOODLANDS - LIMPIN' BILLY - CATHERINE	119
XX.	OTHER SCENES	125
XXI.	OLD FEELINGS AWAKENED - A VISIT, AND OTHER MATTERS	131
XXII.	SELF-DISPOSAL, BUT NOT SELF-CONTROL—FURTHER DEROGATION AND CONSEQUENT TROUBLE	135
XXIII.	A LONG JOURNEY AND A NEW LIFE	139
XXIV.	JOURNEY PURSUED—ADVENTURES—DIFFICULTIES—HOME	149
XXV.	WAREHOUSE WORK AGAIN— READINGS—CATHERINE	161
XXVI.	ROBERT BURNS—A WEDDING—A RIOT	169
XXVII.	A CRITICISM—MIDDLETON FIGHT—A PARTING—CONCLUSION	175

NOTE

IN revising Bamford's "Early Days" and "Passages in the Life of a Radical," with a view to the present publication, it has been judged desirable to omit some portions which were but of trivial or passing interest, and occasionally to compress the narrative by leaving out formal documents and lists of names, and throwing together a number of short chapters dealing with the same group of facts. A few personal animadversions, which after the lapse of fifty years it was hardly worth while to repeat, are also omitted. But beyond the correction of obvious errors no other change has been made, nor hardly a sentence altered. The works are reproduced exactly as Bamford wrote them. One other point may be mentioned. The "Passages," &c., was published some years before the "Early Days," but in reprinting both as parts of the same publication, it seemed proper to reverse the order. The two together form a continuous piece of autobiography.

INTRODUCTION.

ON the last day of March three-quarters of a century ago a coach drew up at Bow Street conveying a batch of political prisoners from Lancashire. There were eight of them, and one of the number was a young man named Samuel Bamford, a native of Middleton and a weaver by trade, whom we wish to introduce to those of our readers who may not yet have heard of him. It was a time of much excitement throughout the country. The close of the war had not brought with it the blessings which had been expected. There was a sudden stop to Government expenditure on a great scale. The world was impoverised by a twenty years' struggle, and had little left for trade. Our manufacturers were substituting machinery for manual labour, and this meant for the moment the throwing of a large number of "hands" out of employ. There was great distress in the manufacturing districts of the north, and much discontent. The people threw the blame upon the Government; they had no voice in Parliament, and they were persuaded that if they had there would soon be an end to their misery. At any rate a House of Commons which fairly represented the nation would never have passed the infamous Corn Law for keeping up agricultural rents by making broad dear. With or without reason the workpeople in the north looked upon their hardships as wrongs for which the men in power were responsible. They petitioned Parliament, and finding that their petitions were not listened to they began to conspire. Secret meetings were held in almost every town and village. Wild schemes were broached; though ministers turned a deaf ear to the cries of famishing multitudes, they were not beyond the reach of vengeance. A few desperate men might easily make London or Manchester "a second Moscow." It was believed that Government spies were abroad, and that in the furtherance of their trade, in order to have something to disclose, the most violent suggestions came from them. It is certain that the Government were greatly alarmed. Detective measures were set in motion, and the Habeas Corpus Act was suspended to give them free play.

The party who arrived at Bow Street were supposed to have been engaged in these secret meetings, and they had been arrested on suspicion of high treason. They had been travelling since five o'clock of the morning of the day before; they were poorly clad; they were chained to each other, and in this plight most of them, and Bamford for one, made their first acquaintance with London. But they were brimful of Lancashire humour. At an hostelry opposite Bow Street, where they were lodged for the night, they had a heartier meal than had fallen to their share for many a day, and after supper they amused the "King's messengers" and the Bow Street officers in whose charge they were with songs and recitations. The next day they were taken before the Privy Council, where Lord Sidmouth presided, with Lord Castlereagh by his side. After a few questions asked of them separately they were sent by way of detention to Coldbath Fields prison. They were brought up several times before the Privy Council, and at the end of a month their fate was decided. Some of Bamford's companions were more or less implicated in proceedings which might be held to convey a suspicion of treasonable designs. These were sent to distant gaols till the Privy Council might choose to release them. Bamford had not gone so far. He shared their political ideas, but he shrank from acts of violence. He was of an ardent temperament, he could not long brook the monotony of ordinary life, and was always ready for an adventure of any sort. But he was good-natured, kind-hearted, and open as the day. There was nothing of the stuff of a conspirator in him. He was also shrewd enough to see through the itinerant agitators who were taking advantage of the general discontent and endeavouring to instigate the working classes to desperate measures. He had early taken alarm at what he heard; he had warned others against having anything to do with secret meetings, and had kept aloof from them himself. The Privy Council had no doubt plenty of evidence good and bad in their hands, but none of it told against Bamford. His personal appearance, his manner and style of address, appear to have made a favourable impression upon the Council. Naturally frank and fearless, he was not the man to be cowed by the sight of the "green cloth" and of the great people round it. He was rather fond of figuring as a "freeborn Englishman," and of magnifying the prerogatives which belonged to him in that capacity. He questioned their lordships about his right to petition Parliament, and among other favours asked to be allowed the use of pen, ink, and paper, that he might keep a diary. Would they let him have books and a supply of clean linen? Delighting in his native Doric, he could speak fluently in language which had in it something of a literary flavour. Lord Castlereagh eyed him curiously. Lord Sidmouth treated him with perfect courtesy and bestowed some compliments. At his last appearance before the Council Lord Sidmouth said he had great pleasure in restoring him to his family, and, trusting that he would not be seen there again, assured him that he wished him well. Bamford did not appear again before the Privy Council, but two years later he was involved, most undeservedly, in more serious trouble. It was in connection with the famous meeting of Reformers held at St. Peter's Field, Manchester, on the 16th of August, 1819, generally known as "Peterloo." The measures taken by the Government had not put a stop to agitation, but the proceedings were of a more open and public character. Sir Charles Wolseley, Major Cartwright, and Mr. Hunt, were at the head of the movement, and great care was taken to keep it within lawful bounds. Perhaps one of the plans adopted was open to misapprehension. The people were exhorted to drill, not, it was said, with any view to an armed outbreak, but merely that they might appear at public meetings in better order. Drilling went on at Middleton, as at other places, and Bamford was one of the leaders. At nightfall, or in the early mornings, they would betake themselves to the moors, form themselves into companies, march, and face about at the word of command. The day appointed for the Manchester meeting was coming on, a great procession was to set out from Middleton, and all were anxious that they should acquit themselves with credit. When the day came Bamford headed the procession. They carried banners, but no weapons, not even walking sticks. Many of the men had their wives and sweethearts with them. It was a great holiday "turn out," the prevailing merriment being a little subdued by a sense of patriotic aims, and it was moreover a grand thing to march and pause at the sound of the bugle. The magistrates were in a state of alarm. They had communicated with the Government and received instructions. Special constables were sworn in, the Manchester and Cheshire Yeomanry were stationed near the spot where the meeting was to be held, and a company of the 15th Hussars was within call. Everybody knows how the meeting was broken up, and at what cost of violence and bloodshed. A few days after the meeting Bamford, along with Hunt and others, was apprehended. The charge was again one of high treason, and Nadin, an historical personage in the Manchester police, whispered to him that he would certainly be hanged this time. The accused were committed to Lancaster Castle, but the trial was appointed to take place at York, the charge being reduced from high treason to one of seditious assembly. Bamford and three others were found guilty. Sir John Bayley summed up strongly in Bamford's favour, but prejudice carried the day. They were liberated on their recognisances to appear at the Court of King's Bench in the ensuing Easter term to receive judgment, which in Bamford's case was that he should be imprisoned in Lincoln Castle for twelve months, and afterwards give securities for good behaviour.

His year's imprisonment was a turn in Bamford's life. He took it with his usual good humour. He held the verdict to be infamous, but he had done that which a jury found to be a crime, and he had a sort of proud willingness to pay the forfeit. His maxim as a prisoner was to submit himself cheerfully to discipline and pay implicit obedience to orders. He soon became a general favourite. The governor treated him with the utmost kindness. He and an old comrade shared the same room, his political friends supplied him with a moderate allowance of cash, and he was permitted to provide for himself. His only hardship was detention, and this had many alleviations. The visiting justices took an especial interest in his case, and from the conversations they had with him they seem to have come to the conclusion that he was in many ways deserving of respect. It came to be understood that Lincoln Castle had not often opened its gates to a better or more intelligent man. He took with him the reputation of being a poet, and his claim was acknowledged. He could sing his own songs and tell capital stories. Indulgence in his favour was carried to unusual limits. He wished to see his wife, and she was allowed to visit and stay with him, a room being fitted up for them. She stayed with him several months, going in and out as she pleased, and doing her marketing as at home. No wonder that on the day of his discharge he thanked the magistrates for the kindness which had been shown to him. Mr. Scarlett, afterwards Lord Abinger, who had conducted the prosecution, singled him out for special attention. The "King's messengers" who took charge of him on his way to London to appear before the Privy Council, surprised him by their civility. He found that people in the upper ranks and those they employed, whom he had been accustomed to denounce as tyrants and oppressors, were not so bad as he had imagined. The discovery told upon him, and had some permanent results. It modified to a considerable extent the colouring if not the texture of his opinions.

Perhaps the truth is that as a politician Bamford is not to be taken too seriously. His politics were a part of his temperament, and varied with its changing moods. His character was essentially romantic, and he leaned to the sentimental side of everything. The result was a sort of every-day idealism, a dream of something brighter and in every way more desirable than the present moment happened to have brought with it. In his youth he had been left pretty much to himself. There had been an actual lack of discipline, though it is very likely that if the yoke had been forced upon him by parental or other authority, he would have shaken it off. He had fair opportunities for making his way in the world. He had plenty of ability, everybody liked him, and patient application would have enabled him to reach what is usually understood by "a good position." It was certainly his own choice, or the result of a series of voluntary failures, that he took to silk-weaving as a permanent occupation. Who shall say that his choice is to be regretted? Who shall say that he was not on the whole happier and better than if he had kept to the beaten track which leads to success and made a fortune? At any rate, we should have been the poorer. Hundreds of Lancashire men, then and since, starting where he did, and with talents smaller than his, have attained to great wealth, and have passed away without leaving a vestige of anything to remind the next generation that they had lived at all. Bamford escaped a common-place career. He followed the bent of his inclinations. He lived his own life, proud as an aristocrat and gay as a bird. It was not given him to attain to a high place in literature. The wonder is that he found a place in it at all. But he was not without culture. He had read some of the best books, he was fond of poetry, and believed himself to be a poet. In this persuasion he no doubt flattered himself too highly, but he had a gift of versification which was a source of constant delight. In prose he succeeded better. The narrative he has left us of his "Early Days," and his "Passages in the Life of a Radical," need no apology. If allowance be made for some technical defects due to an irregular education, they may be said to reach a high level in point of style. He knows how to use his mother tongue. His diction is copious and unfettered, and not wholly of the homely cast, which might have been expected from the pen of a hand-loom weaver. There is enough of homeliness to give an agreeable flavour, but the more cultivated forms of expression come naturally to him. He is at home in telling a good story, and overflows with humour in describing a grotesque situation, or in painting the foibles of his friends, while his love of nature supplies his imagination with illustrations which err only on being at times perhaps too exuberant. All may read him with pleasure. They will find in his pages such pictures of Lancashire life and manners, of from fifty to a hundred years ago, as are hardly to be met with elsewhere. In the work by which he is best known, Bamford describes himself as "a Radical," and the designation is no doubt correct, especially when used retrospectively. But his political attitude underwent a change after his release from Lincoln Castle. He was not on the best of terms with his old friends, and the fault was probably not wholly theirs. Often modest and even humble in his professions, he nevertheless thought a good deal of himself, and any failure to recognise his claims was noted down and resented. The habit of self-assertion must have made him an inconvenient colleague. He was sensitive and suspicious, apt to take offence where none was intended. He was quick to imagine himself the victim of some intrigue engaged in for the purpose of lowering his credit or impeaching his integrity. By way of reprisal he turned his back upon the offenders, would have no more to do with them, and played the part of a Radical in retreat. In referring to his past experiences, he spoke as one who had been for a time deluded, but whose eyes had been opened and was thenceforth half-repentant. To some extent this was due to his closer acquaintance with Mr. Hunt, the principal figure at the Peterloo meeting, who had been arrested and tried along with him. He had looked up to Hunt as a leader. He was awed by his oratory, and taking him on his own terms, believed him to be a patriot of the loftiest type. On coming to know him better this flattering estimate gave way to disapproval and contempt. Rightly or wrongly, he came to the conclusion that Hunt was a vainglorious, self-seeking demagogue, willing to sell his soul for the cheers of the mob. He resented the deception, and resolved to take good care never to be deceived again. In pursuance of this resolution he extended the inference drawn from the single example of Hunt to all who took a prominent part in agitating for political reforms. He had done with agitators for ever. He fancied that he understood their craft, and he was not going to be victimised a second time. Looking back upon his own exploits, he regarded them in the light of escapades, the outcome of untaught and undisciplined sentiment, and such perhaps they were, though influenced by a good deal of honest feeling. In his own opinion he had grown wiser, and he made it thenceforth a part of his duty to warn others against the false lights which had led him astray.

There was another feature of Bamford's character which helped towards this result. He had an amiable desire to be thought well of by others. He was a good deal less than indifferent to approbation, and he valued it according to the social heights from which it descended. When it was known that he had separated himself from those who were supposed to aim at accomplishing political changes by violent methods, and that he viewed his own past conduct with some degree of reprehension, he became an object of interest to local men of the wealthier class. They praised him for what they naturally described as his moderation and good sense. In turbulent times they pointed him out as a laudable example. If their own workmen, striking perhaps for higher wages and even threatening to break their machines, would only follow the advice of Bamford, everything, it was suggested, would go well. The workpeople did not care to be confronted with such an example, and they gradually came to look upon Bamford as a renegade from the class to which he once belonged. The severance became wider when it was known that he no longer depended for a living upon the work of the loom. His prominence as a politician and his literary talents had been the means of procuring employment on the press. He was the correspondent of a London newspaper, and he acted as occasional reporter for papers in the neighbourhood. He removed to a better house. He could make verses, moreover, and a corner was sometimes found for them in the newspapers. To counsel men not to break machines might well be regarded as easy talk for one who had ceased to weave at all, and to whom, therefore, the question of machinery was a matter of indifference. The outcry against him served only to confirm his isolation, and though he was always the zealous advocate of what he took to be the real interests of the working classes he liked quite as well to play the part of their critic and candid friend. He had no sympathy with the Chartist agitation. The objects aimed at by the Chartists were the same as those for which he had gone to prison; but he denounced them and their leaders with a hearty virulence which would have won the praise of any Tory. When special constables were called out to put down disturbances, he took up the truncheon. If there are any of the Conservative school who may fancy that their time would be thrown away in reading "Passages in the Life of a Radical," they need not be deterred by any such consideration. They will find a good deal in him that is in entire harmony with their own views. The spirit of much that he has written, detached from particular expressions of opinion, can hardly fail to command their sympathy. All this did not disqualify him for the place he held in the ranks of local Liberalism — then rather Whig than Radical — and there can be no doubt that he was sincere and honest throughout.

Bamford took naturally to the press. He was communicative, and, having something to say, he did not rest till he had said it. He published in pamphlet form an account of his first arrest and of the subsequent proceedings connected with it. This was soon followed by a small volume of verses, entitled "The Weaver Boy, or Miscellaneous Poetry." His poetical reputation went with him to York and London on his second arrest. Mr. Scarlett, the prosecuting counsel, had heard of the "Weaver Boy," and asked Bamford to send him a copy. We have said that he was known as "a poet" at Lincoln Castle. That circumstance probably influenced the magistrates in his favour, and procured him more indulgent treatment than he would otherwise have received. The Peterloo meeting was a great event in his personal history. For his share in it he had been, as he believed, unjustly condemned and imprisoned. It was also an event of national importance. It had attracted the attention of the whole country, and had led to animated debates in Parliament. Bamford could not help feeling that the whole affair was the result of a deplorable misunderstanding. The "upper classes" were unacquainted with the condition and wants of the poor; they were badly informed as to the character of their political aspirations; and perhaps the poor were to some extent prejudiced in the view they took of the attitude of the "upper classes" towards them. Bamford was also impressed with what seemed to him a certain hollowness of the agitation on the popular side. He had been brought into close acquaintance with the leaders, and was on the whole disgusted. Here, then, was something to be told. The epic almost demanded a narrator. It seemed to him a duty to give to his countrymen the benefit of his experiences. His first attempt was a failure. He wrote an introduction and sent it to Mr. Tait, of "Tait's Magazine," together with an outline of the proposed work, and offered to supply "copy" monthly. Mr. Tait declined the offer, but gave him advice. He urged him to go on with the work, and when he had finished to submit it to some intelligent and sensible friend — naming Ebenezer Elliott — with full permission to cut out all its redundancies. Mr. Tait's judgment was no doubt correct, but it was based upon an unfortunate specimen. The introduction, which Bamford loved too well to give up, was the worst part of the work as it afterwards appeared, and if the whole had been written in the same high flown style it would have been unreadable. Bamford did not relish the experienced publisher's advice, and abandoned the project for a time.

It was resumed in 1839. The Chartist agitation was then in full swing. The scheme of a "Sacred Month" was proposed, during which all work should be abandoned. A friend had furnished him with a prose translation of Berenger's "La Lyonnaise." This he had thrown into verse, and he now published it as a pamphlet, together with a stirring and eloquent address. It is said to have had some considerable influence in dissuading the working men of the neighbourhood from taking part in the questionable proceedings then contemplated. His former project was now revived. He saw the bookseller's windows filled with numbers of "Pickwick," "Nicholas Nickleby," and " Jack Sheppard." Surely he could do something better than "the trashy, unreal novels which the press deigned to extol." But he could not find a publisher. One to whom he applied would not take the work even with a present of the copyright. It was clear that if it was to be done at all he must assume the sole responsibility. Accordingly he engaged a printer, got five hundred copies of the introduction and the first chapter printed off, and paid for them. His wife stitched them into covers, and then his business was to sell them. By the time the ninth and tenth sheets were published he had twelve hundred subscribers, and the earlier sheets had to be reprinted. The work was a success and the profit it yielded was highly acceptable. It was noticed in the "Athenæum" and the "Quarterly." His friend Ebenezer Elliott sent him warm congratulations. Mr. Scarlett, then Lord Abinger, took copies, and mentioned the work to Lord Campbell, Lord Brougham, the Duke of Buccleuch, and others who showed a warm interest in promoting its circulation. "The head of the great Tory Lowthers," the Earl of Lonsdale, wrote to assure him that he had "read his works with great satisfaction." Bamford speaks rather bitterly of the very different treatment he received from "some Liberals." With the general result he had every reason to be satisfied. He was now a public character. He was appealed to as an authority on working-class politics. His writings were made to furnish lessons of reproof as well as instruction for those who were being led astray by "the wiles of the agitator." The position was in some respects unfortunate, but he had no great difficulty in maintaining the character thus pressed upon him.

In 1848 Bamford published his "Early Days," giving us his own history down to the time of his first arrest, and recollections embracing the whole life of the district as far back as his memory carried him. This is a delightful production, abounding in idyllic pictures and romantic adventures, and in passages of genuine pathos. He had something in the way of ancestry to boast of. His family had long been rooted in the soil, and but for an ancestor's Puritan scruples, he might have been a country squire instead of a hand-loom weaver. A fine opportunity was thrown away when his father took him from the Manchester Grammar School. If he had been permitted to reap the full advantages afforded by that institution, even as it was then, his natural talents would have found their proper scope, though in that case the Peterloo meeting would have missed one of its heroes, and we should not have had the "Passages in the Life of a Radical." Bamford's autobiography has the stamp of truthfulness. He lays his heart open and tells us everything. His youth was wild and stormy, and it must be said that he was anything but exemplary in point of morals. He had to run away from the parish constables to escape the pecuniary consequences of one of his indiscretions. A little girl whom he had loved as a boy, after some temporary transfer of affection on his part, became his wife. But the nuptial knot was tied too late for his reputation. Their only child, then "just beginning to take notice," was placed in his arms with some ceremony at the wedding festival, and he speaks of her constantly as his "love child." But having said this we have said the worst, and never was a wrong more amply atoned for. He was the most faithful of husbands, the most loving of fathers. The three were bound together by the tenderest ties. His wife shared his trials with uncomplaining devotion, and he lavished upon his "Mima" the treasures of a homely but passionate poetry. A more beautiful picture can hardly be imagined than that presented by their domestic life. His narrative is full of interest in other respects. He gives us a graphic portraiture of a state of manners which has passed away. We see modern Lancashire in its first making, before the period of big factories set in, when the weaver fetched his materials from Manchester, wrought them up in his own cottage, and took them back again when the task was finished. Five minutes would take the weaver from his loom into paths that led soon into the loveliest solitudes. He was thus enabled to live in close companionship with nature. Usages which had come down unchanged for centuries were still in full vigour, and life, though laborious, and in hard times pinched with poverty, was nevertheless full of joy. The traditions of a distant time had floated down unbroken. There were stories to be told of Flodden, and the events of '45, when the local Jacobites were blessing the Pretender, seemed a thing of yesterday. All this Bamford gives us in his raciest style and with never-failing humour. The historian who wishes to present us with certain aspects of English life at the beginning of the century can hardly afford to miss his pages.

From some remarks which occur in one of the chapters subsequently added as supplementary to his "Passages in the Life of a Radical," it would seem that a time came when Bamford thought himself entitled to some recognition from the Government. It appears that Mr. (afterwards Sir Benjamin) Hawes said in the House of Commons how desirable it was that "rewards and encouragements" should be bestowed upon those of the working classes "who distinguished themselves by attention to reading and the cultivation of their minds," and that Sir Robert Peel, in expressing his approval of the suggestion, "pointed out a mode by which such individuals might be rewarded without bringing an additional burden upon the country." Bamford's comment is this: "If studious readers, then, and self-cultivators among the working classes are to be distinguished and rewarded, what shall be done to those of the same grade who not only have read a deal and thought a deal, but have also written good books for others to read? Aye, books that mayhap have not only been read by working men with advantage, but also with profit as well as pleasure by some whose robes have brushed the throne, if not by the fair one who sits upon the throne herself; what shall be the reward of these men?" He says a page or two later that he had been led into these remarks by a strong desire to do justice to others rather than to benefit himself. He was "tainted with the irredeemable sin of political leadership," and was "prepared for the consequences." "An independent but unassuming spirit, and contentment with the humblest fare" had rendered him "almost impervious to vicissitude," and had made him the sort of man and his wife the sort of woman "to smile at things and at the want of things which to many would be an affliction." Whatever may have been Bamford's intention, there can be no doubt as to the interpretation which his friends would put upon those professions, and there were some who were in a position to help him. In 1852 he had the offer of an appointment in Somerset House, and it was accepted. It was that of doorkeeper or messenger. He was then sixty-four years of age. The hours were easy and the duties light, but he did not keep it long. It is said that he pined for old scenery and old friends. This may be true, but it is also true that he thought the position beneath him. He was too proud for the place, and he soon gave it up, preferring a precarious livelihood in the midst of his old haunts to a certainty which seemed to him to be associated with some degree of degradation. It was also to some extent the outbreak of a constitutional foible. He had never from the days of his youth been able to endure the monotony of fixed and regular employment.

As time went on Bamford took a sort of historical position among the Liberals of Manchester. Minor incidents were forgotten. He was regarded as a relic of a past around which legends began to gather. His tall and erect form, his rugged and massive features, a flowing beard, and locks of grey hair that were left to fall upon his shoulders made him a conspicuous object everywhere. One could almost fancy him a Druid in modern garb. His friends delighted to do him honour. His portrait hangs in the Manchester Reform Club, along with those of Cobden, Bright, Gladstone, the Duke of Devonshire, and the Earl Grey of the first Reform Bill. At private gatherings he would often be present as the lion of the night, but he was gruff, and often growled at those who tried to stroke him. When his infirmities increased with advancing years a "syndicate" of admirers supplied him with a modest income sufficient for all his wants. He died on April 13, 1872, at the ripe age of 84. A flat stone in Middleton churchyard marks the spot where his remains lie interred, along with those of his wife and daughter. Beneath each of their names is an epitaph in verse of his own composing. Beneath his own is a brief record of what he was and did. A short distance off, where the churchyard hill overhangs the town, a stone obelisk, bearing his effigy in bronze, has been erected to his memory;

but his works will prove a more enduring monument.

CHAPTER I.
BIRTH, PARENTAGE, AND OTHER MATTERS.

MY parents were a worthy and honest couple, residing, when I was born, in the town of Middleton, near Manchester. My father was a weaver of muslin, at that time considered a fine course of work, and requiring a superior hand; whilst my mother found plenty of employment in occasional weaving, in winding bobbins or pins for my father, and in looking after the house and the children, of whom I was the fourth born; and the third then living. I have always been given to understand that I was brought into the world on the 28th day of February, in "the Gallic æra—eighty-eight," when, certainly, many of the world's troubles, as well as my own, had a beginning. My parents were religious, of which further will appear hereafter. My father, for his station in life, was a superior man. He had many talents, both natural and acquired, which in those days were not often possessed by men of his condition in society. He was considerably imbued with book knowledge, particularly of a religious kind; wrote a good hand; understood arithmetic; had some acquaintance with astronomy; was a vocal and instrumental musician, singing from the book and playing on the flute; he had a deep taste for melody, as I can recollect from the tunes he played; he was likewise an occasional composer of music, and introduced several of his pieces amongst the religious body with which he was connected; he was also a writer of verses of no mean order—so that, take him for all in all, he stood far above his rustic acquaintance in the village, and had to endure the usual consequences—envy, and detraction from the meanest of them. During the hot blood of his youth few young men could stand before him, either in the wrestling bout or the battle. I have heard it told that, in those days, notwithstanding his taste for books, and music, and other means for true enjoyment, he at times associated with the wild rough fellows of the neighbourhood at the Church Alehouse, or at the Boar's Head Inn, and drank, danced, or, when nothing less would do, fought with the moodiest or merriest of them. He stood six feet in height, with a good breadth of chest, a powerful arm, a strong, well-formed leg, and a neat, compact foot that could either spring over a five-barred gate, or deal a bone-breaking kick to an adversary. Such, however, was not his wont; when he did fight it was almost certain to be either in self-defence, or in behalf of right which some bully would be trying to domineer over or coerce. At one of these battles, which were forced upon him, the contest took place in a room called "the thrashing-bay," at the Boar's Head, Middleton; it lasted two full hours, up and down fighting, and at the end of that time his adversary, a very powerful man from a neighbouring township, lay helpless on the floor, and had to be carried home by his companions. I mention these feats of my father's youth not in a spirit commendatory of their mere featship; with him, his physical power was never a matter of boast, but rather led him to a pacific guardedness of its use; whilst with me the dominance of mere muscle and bone never was, never will be, held in honour, except when exercised in the repression of other brute forces employed in the perpetration of wrong, or in the maltreatment of right. In such a case I would say, "Let physical power bend the full weight of its vigour to its work, and not give over too soon, not leave off when part done."

But irregularities like these of my father's young days, violent probably in proportion to their unfrequency, could not be indulged in without producing their natural consequences. His health was impaired; he took cold after cold, and disregarded them, and at length a violent fever laid him prostrate at the verge of the grave. On his recovery he was an altered man. His own natural sense, supported by the serious advice of relatives and friends, determined him on endeavouring to lead a different life. Being convinced that the course he had pursued was fraught with evil as well as folly, he sought divine aid in abandoning it, and he joined a society of Methodists, of which his parents and several individuals of the family were already members.

When his health had become re-established, neither his good resolutions nor God's help forsook him. He continued a member of the religious society he had joined; became "a burning and a shining light," as the Methodists term an exemplary young member; and soon afterwards marrying my mother, he set forward, as we may say, on his pilgrimage through this world, and "Zionward." In due time a young family began to sprout about his heels, and, with a view to meet increasing expenditure, he and a brother of his named Thomas adventured a small capital of money in the spinning line, which was then done by jenny, and in weaving their yarns into grey cloth. They succeeded in proportion to their most sanguine expectations, for there was then a market for anything which the spindle or the hand-loom could make, and they were about to realise all they had dared to hope, when a member of their religious body, one of their "brethren in Israel," piqued, as they supposed, by their increasing influence in a religious as well as worldly sense, suddenly called on them for the repayment of a sum which he had lent them for the purpose of commencing their business, and persisting in his demand, they sold off their stock of cloth and machinery, paid every farthing they owed, and closed their concern, my father sitting down to the business of schoolmaster, and my uncle resuming the manual operations of a weaver and small farmer. Difficulties still increased with the wants of our family; my father's school profits were not sufficiently steady to be depended upon, and he relinquished them and returned to the loom. The throes of the French Revolution and the excitement they created in England soon afterwards deranged both money transactions and mercantile affairs. Banks stopped, payments were suspended, and trade was at a stand. Woe to the poor weaver then, with his loom without work, the provision shop without credit, and his wife and weans foodless, and looking at each other, and at him, as if saying—Husband! father! hast thou neither bread nor hope for us?

It was at about such a period as this that my earliest recollections of my parents and our family commence. My father, as I have said, was a huge-framed body of a man, but at that time he was pale, stooping, and attenuated, probably from scanty fare, as well as repeated visitations of sickness. My mother—and I have her image distinctly before me—was a person of very womanly and motherly presence. Tall, upright, active, and cleanly to an excess: her cheeks were fair and ruddy as apples; her dark hair was combed over a roll before and behind, and confined by a mob cap as white as bleached linen could be made; her neck was covered by a handkerchief, over which she wore a bed-gown, and a clean checked apron, with black hose and shoes, completed her every-day attire. Her name was Hannah—a name I shall always love for her sake; she was the youngest daughter of Jeffrey Battersby, a master boot and shoemaker, of whom more hereafter. She had two sisters married, one to a tradesman named Healey, residing at Rochdale, and the other to a woollen-draper living at Manchester; consequently they were both doing comparatively well in the world, whilst my poor mother's dark cloud was ascending and spreading over herself, her husband, and her five children. Small and fitful was the comfort she received from her kindred; but her sister Clemmy (Clementine), at Manchester, treated her with a coolness and indifference which cut my mother to the soul. I perhaps should not have mentioned names in connection with these circumstances had not the recollections of my mother's sufferings divested me of every wish for reserve. Oh! how immeasurably superior was, my poor, but noble-hearted parent, to her proud, mean, sordid sister. I remember as it were but yesterday, after one of her visits to the dwelling of that "fine lady," she had divested herself of her wet bonnet, her soaked shoes, and changing her dripping outer garments, stood leaning with her elbow on the window sill, her hand up to her cheek, her eyes looking on vacancy, and the tears trickling over her fingers. She had been all the weary way to Manchester and back—and it was a long weary road in those days; she had knocked at her "great" sister's door, a servant had admitted her, and, more humane than her mistress, had ventured to ask her to a seat by the kitchen fire, where her proud sister saw her in passing, and scarcely deigned to notice her. The servants, however, in whom the impulses of common humanity had not been suppressed by pride, offered her refreshment; but her heart was too full, and back through the rain, and the wind, and the stormy weather, less inclement than her misnamed relative, did she return to her young and anxiously waiting family, to whose caresses and tender questionings her only reply was, for a while, unrestrained tears.

The recollection of my heart-wounded, but noble-minded and forgiving mother, as she suffered under that trial, is still vividly before me; and never, I believe, will it be obliterated from my memory so long as consciousness remains. Ever since I had the faculty for reasoning on these recollections I have cherished an unmitigable contempt for mere money pride, much of it though there be in the world, and as thorough a contempt have I ever felt for the unfeelingness which mammonish superiority too often produces. Samson said, "Out of the eater came forth meat"; and in application of the parable I may truly say that, out of the unnatural conduct of my mother's sister, arose the very natural and self-sustaining disdain of that mother's son towards all pretension not based on worth, towards all superiority not exalted by goodness. To rank, office, or to station arising from office, suitable concedence would I make; to the man filling that office or station such deference as were commensurate with his known worth would I tender; but to the poor human hull, irrespective of self-desert, would I not concede anything. Before the mere man-husk, however large his money-bag—nay, though he were "plated with gold," not one hair of my head should be abased. Thus the germ of this feeling of repulsion (calculated for evil or for good, according to its right or wrong application) became interwoven with my existence, and part of my being, for all my after life.

CHAPTER II.
OF MY FOREFATHERS.

HAVING thus, as it were, identified myself and my parents, it may not be improper to give some account of my progenitors, especially as two of them were connected with the historical events of their country; and the religious tenacity of a third was said to have decided the fate of his descendants with respect to worldly condition.

It would be about a hundred and thirty-two years since, or the year 1716, that my father's grandfather, James Bamford, lived at Hools Wood, in Thornham, keeping there a small farm, and making cane reeds for weavers of flannel and coarse cotton. Of his children I know not anything, save that he had many sons from whom the Bamfords of Middleton, Alkrington, Tonge, and some other neighbouring places are descended. According to what was handed down in our branch of his posterity, he was the next heir to the estate of Bamford Hall, where he used to visit and be on terms of intimacy with William Bamford, the last male of the old family, who resided at the hall. My ancestor was, it seems, fond of the chase, and on hunting and shooting days, he was frequently at the hall and dined with the other guests. At this time the property was said to be entailed; though for the truth of that I vouch not any more than I do for other traditionary matters which follow. My aunt, who was, I believe, a contemporary of some of the parties, narrated the story to me as I give it. This William Bamford had no offspring save two daughters, and as they could not inherit the property, when he lay on his death-bed, he sent for my ancestor, and by much entreaty, and many solemn promises, backed perhaps by a douceur, he induced my ancestor to forego his claim in favour of the young ladies, on condition that at their decease the property should revert to the next heir in his family. The entail was accordingly cut off; Bamford, of Bamford, made his will and died; and his daughter, "Madam Ann," as she was titled, held the property. The other sister married, and went to reside in Yorkshire; but Madam Ann lived and died a spinster at Bamford Hall. And thus, according to traditionary accounts, were the rightful heirs cut off from the property, which had descended through their ancestors from the time when the Saxon wrested it from the Celt.

My grandfather was Daniel Bamford, the youngest son of James Bamford. He came to reside at Middleton, and was a small farmer and weaver. He married Hannah, the daughter of Samuel Cheetham, who was a watch and clock maker, and was, consequently, considered something better in condition than common in those days. My grandfather had a family of, I believe, six sons and two daughters; and Daniel, my father, was the youngest of his children. The house in which my grandfather lived was situated at Back o'th' Brow. It was an old timber and daub house, with thatched roof, low windows, and a porch. I saw it after it was abandoned and was tottering to its fall. There had been a garden beside it, but the fences were then tore down, the beds trampled, and a few stumps of trees, with sprouts of sweet herbs shooting amongst struggling weeds, marked what it had been. The door of this ruined dwelling was the first that opened at Middleton for the reception of Methodist preachers; and John and Charles Wesley, John Nelson, Thomas Taylor, and many of the first promulgators of their doctrines, had addressed their humble and simple hearers on the floor of that ruined dwelling. The house stood about some three score yards from the arched bridge over the Irk, in the direction towards the Free School, and the cart road now passes over its site. My grandfather and all his family had been strict church-goers, but on their joining the Methodists, their attendance at church was less constant than it had been. The rector one day in conversation with my grandfather expressed his regret at the change, and wondered what made him dissatisfied with his religion. He replied that he was not certified as to the state of his soul, nor with the way in which he was bringing up his family. Why, asked the rector, what did he desire or expect on the score of religion? He came regularly to church; he took the sacrament, and paid all dues and oblations; and what could he do more? He thought that my grandfather would scarcely mend that religion, whatever party he joined. He might consider himself quite as safe in returning to the church, as he would be in remaining with his new friends. No argument, however, could satisfy my grandfather, who had become "convinced of sin, of righteousness, and of a judgment to come;" who felt the necessity of "justification by faith," of "saving grace," and of "being born again." In short, my grandfather exhibited so much of the "new light," that the worthy pastor, dazzled, probably, if not illumined, gave up the attempt at reclamation, and my grandfather and his family remained Methodists.

Whether or not Madam Ann Bamford, the lady before mentioned, had given up all thoughts of marriage, or whether she ever entertained any, does not appear; but, as if she were wishful to do some justice to the ancient stock, she came to my grandfather's house at Middleton, saw his family, and conversed with them. It was even added, that she expressed a particular preference for my father, then a child, and proposed to adopt him, and make him her heir, but that my grandfather, whose views "were not of this world," declined the lady's offer, alleging that the possession of wealth would only lead this child into temptations, and might perhaps cause the loss of his soul eternally. It was after this incident, as was said, that Madam Ann directed her attention to another quarter in search of an heir and successor. Certain it is, that at her death she willed the estate and property to a William Bamford who was not at all of the old stock, but was said to be descended from a family settled in Staffordshire.

My grandmother, in her mature years, acted as a midwife; and herself and another dame at Hollinwood were the only two on this side of the country who then practised the obstetric art. Surgeons were never called to act in those days, except in perilous cases; for wives and mothers of the humble classes had not as yet become reconciled to a custom which one cannot but wish should be repugnant to their private feelings.

My great-grandfather, Samuel Cheetham, was a thorough "King's man." During the troubles in 1745, he loaded his gun, and swore he would blow out the brains of any rebel who interfered with him; and judging from his conduct on several other occasions, there is but small reason for supposing he would not have been as good as his word. On the approach of the Scottish army towards Manchester, the Assheton family at Middleton Hall retired into Yorkshire, leaving my progenitor and one trusty servant to secrete the plate and the other valuables which the family had not had time or convenience for carrying with them. These articles were placed in a chest, and buried by the two confidants in the stable-court at midnight, the place being afterwards paved and strewn over with hay seeds. The Scotch army having entered Manchester, lost not much time in proceeding to ascertain what good things lay within their reach in the surrounding districts. Middleton received a speedy visit. My ancestor and his assistant were on the premises when a party of horsemen entered the hall yard, and the commander, leaping from his steed, flung the reins to the poor waiting-man, who, on receiving them, sighed deeply. "Hoot, mon! wot d'ye sigh for?" asked the Scot, as if he were surprised to hear such an escape of feeling from an English retainer. "It's mi way, sir," replied the servant, meekly taking charge of the steed. The party having searched the hall, without finding either money or plate, which they seemed mostly, to be in pursuit of, they came forth to take their departure, when the officer espying my great- grandfather, demanded of him "Waur's the heed inn in the toon?" "Gullook!" was the immediate reply. Supposing that he had not been understood, the question was repeated more distinctly; "I say, mon, waur's the heed inn in the toon?" "Gullook!" was as promptly replied as before; and in a tone and manner which left no doubt with respect to the feelings of the individual who had been questioned. The officer and his party, however, rode off without stopping to parley with the sturdy Southron.

At this period, and for some time after, party feeling would naturally be in a state of exasperation, and but few opportunities for displaying it would be permitted to pass by the adherents of either the Stuart or the Guelph. If, as we see, during evanescent political squabbles, a bitterness is engendered which would, if it could, give a mortal thrust to its opponent, what must be the deadly hatred of rude minds and stormy hearts alternately suffering and inflicting irreparable wrong, when a population are in a state of civil war, when the sword is made naked avowedly to cut down, to kill, and when neighbourhood and brotherhood are no longer recognised except side by side in camp, or in battle? During such a state of things, many would be the outrages and insults perpetrated by individuals of each party, when one of the other happened to come in their way; and that this zealous forefather of mine was less overbearing than the rudest, I have not much reason to suppose. It was customary in those days for Scotch hawkers to travel slowly and laboriously from town to town, not affecting the gentleman, as they do at present, but carrying huge and weighty packs on their backs, some four feet in length and two or more in depth, as large, in fact, as a family meal ark, and stored with hosiery, drapery, and other necessary articles; tea, coffee, and sugar, not being then in much use amongst the working classes. These packs being securely locked, were generally deposited in some convenient place—the corner of a street, or the side of a friendly door—whilst

the chapman went round to a few customers close at hand. Well, my great-grandfather, one day, ere the exasperation of feeling consequent on the rebellion had subsided, met one of those useful and self-minding tradesmen, crossing over the causeway by the mill-doors, at Middleton; and laying hold of him, demanded that he should say, "Deawn wi'th' Rump" (down with the Rump); an offensive phrase signifying, "Down with the Scottish party." The Scot, of course, would utter nothing of the sort—how was he likely—and he tried to argue with the unreasonable fellow who had him in hand, but to no purpose. "Sithe," said the latter, "ifto dusno say, 'Deawn wi'th' Rump,' theawst goo yed fost into that dam;" pointing to the deep mill-stream just below them. The Scot still would not: my progenitor griped him firmer; and happy should I have been to have recorded that the traveller had soused him into the water head first. But it was otherwise. Might overcame right on that occasion, as it has on others, both before and since; and the traveller, probably calculating on the loss of time and money which a regular contest might cause him, said at length, "Weel, if
it mast be so, it mast be so; doon with the Ramp then." And so he got rid of his pertinacious opponent.

Whilst this surly and stalwart English Saxon was bearding the Scottish officer in the hall yard, as before narrated, my mother's father, Jeffrey Battersby, who was quite his opposite in person, manner, and sentiment, was with the Pretender's party at the Boar's Head, assisting them in the collection of King's taxes, and in the levying of contributions; in which his local knowledge, and his quick perception, would, doubtless, be very useful. He was, when I knew him, a little old man, with sharp features and ruddy complexion. He wore a black coat, of the old-fashioned cut of the time; a waistcoat and small cloths of the same material; with black stockings, and silver buckles at the knees, and on the shoes; on his head he wore a grizzled full-buttoned wig, and a small squareset cocked hat. He walked with a quick short step (toes turned inward), as shoemakers often do; a silver-headed cane steadied his forward gait, his waistcoat was dusted with snuff, and a small leathern apron flapped against him as he tripped on his way.

This quick and lively person, at the time of the appearance of the rebels, would be about twenty-nine years of age; an active, lightsome, free-company keeping young fellow, no doubt. He was a native of Bury, whence he had probably but recently removed to Middleton, and being an excellent hand at his boot-making, he was employed by most of the genteel families in the neighbourhood. The Ashtons of Alkrington; the Asshetons of Middleton; the Radcliffs of Foxdenton; the Hortons of Chadderton; the Hopwoods of Hopwood; the Starkies of Heywood; and the Bamfords of Bamford, were each, at that time, living in their own paternal mansions, and were severally, as their requirements occurred, the patrons and employers of the young craftsman at Middleton. He was, consequently, personally well known to the heads of these old families; with several of them he was on such terms of freedom as we find frequently existed betwixt the old race of gentry and the better sort of their tenants and trades-people. Gentlemen then lived as they ought to live; as real gentlemen will ever be found living; in kindliness with their tenants; in open-handed charity towards the poor; and in hospitality towards all friendly comers. There were no grinding bailiffs and land-stewards in those days, to stand betwixt the gentleman and his labourer, or his tenant; to screw up rents, to screw down livings, and to invent and transact all little meannesses for so much per annum. Mercenaries of this description were not then prevalent on our Lancashire estates. The gentleman transacted his own business; he met his farmer, or his labourer, face to face. When he did that which was wrong, he was told of it in unmistakable language; or, at any rate, he stood a good chance of being so told. When he did that which was right—which was noble-hearted—he got blessings, no doubt, and made friends who stood by him whilst living, and spoke well of him when dead; and that is a kind of speaking of which one does not hear over-much nowadays. There was no racking up of old tenants; no rooting out of old cottiers; no screwing down of servants' or labourers' wages; no cutting off of allowances, either of the beggar at the door, or the visitor at the servants' hall; no grabbing at waste candle-ends, and musty cheese parings. Gentlemen were gentlemen indeed; as ladies were what they pretended to be,—loaf-givers—dispensers of good. If they lived carefully, they were not mean. If they lived sumptuously, their waste was scattered at home—on the spot whence it was derived; and those who toiled to produce it had the benefit of it. The treasure and all the fatness of the land was not carried out of the country, to be wasted and thrown away like dust, in the pride and big-babyism of courtly life, nor in the brothels and gambling hells of London, Paris, or other Babylon of the world.

At such a time, and amongst such a race of English gentlemen, was it the lot of this my grandsire to be cast. He was in agreeable person to converse with; droll, witty, and a rhymster also; and as he had not much disinclination to a pipe and a jack of ale, he was frequently, when he went with his work home, called from the servants' hall into the parlour, where his budget of wit, verse, and country news, made him a welcome guest. It will not be presuming too much, if we suppose that some of the gentry of those days were imbued with Jacobitical principles; and to such, in their moments of conviviality and confidence, the following verse, which I have heard sung as one of my grandfather's productions, would no doubt be responded to.

> "Jammy sits upon the throne;
> He bears the gowden sceptre;
> He is the darlin' of our hearts;
> He is our right protector.
> Ween tak' yon cuckud by his burns,
> An' poo him deawn to Dover;
> An' stuff him full o' turmit-tops,
> Au' pack him to Hanover."

In joining the Pretender, and taking the active part he had done, my grandfather had sinned too far to be slightly passed over. On the retreat of the Scottish army, and the reinstatement of the former authority, he was denounced with many others; was arrested, and placed in Lancaster Castle for trial on a charge of high treason.

Happy was it then for him that he had made friends of some influential persons, and that neither his ready genius nor his friends forsook him. Many of his fellow-prisoners were taken out of their cells for trial; and trial was then almost synonymous with conviction, conviction with death. At last it was his turn to be called, and they called him, but the man was raving mad; and the keepers stood aghast, not knowing what to do with the lunatic. He had been expecting his trial from day to day, and had acted his part accordingly; and on the morning on which he was certified it would take place, he thumped his elbow against the bedstead until his pulse beat a hundred and sixty a-minute and the doctor, on his being sufficiently coerced, and ascertaining that such was his actual condition, declared that he could not be tried. He was consequently passed over, some poor fellow thus meeting his doom before the time, and when the next jail delivery took place, his friends at Middleton and the neighbourhood had so far used their influence that he was amongst those discharged by proclamation. He returned home, probably somewhat wiser for his mad fit, but certainly to take his pipe and potation; to write squibs, satires, and rhymes; and to make the best boots and shoes in the whole country side. Years rolled over him; the blithe young fellow became mellowed down into the more sedate head of a family, though he had always a fund of wit and humour at command. At the age of seventy-eight, he was the little old man I have described; and in the year ninety-six came the finale to all his fancies. He died in the eighty-first year of his age, and was interred in the old yard at Middleton Church. Such were the men and women from whom I derived my being. The rebel blood, it would seem, after all, was the more impulsive; it got the ascendency — and I was born a Radical.

CHAPTER III.
OF MIDDLETON, AT THE TIME
I HAVE BEEN WRITING ABOUT.

READER, having thus described to thee the persons, and conditions, and habits of my forefathers, it may not be going too far from my personal history, if I give thee an idea of the sort of place Middleton was at the time they inhabited it. Beginning with the church, thou must know that externally it was much in the same state as at present. Internally, the chapel of the Asshetons would be somewhat different. The staircase mounting to that piece of "pride " in a place of "humility," the Suffield's pew, did not then cover up and obscure the grave-stone of Colonel Assheton, who commanded the Parliamentary forces of Lancashire during the Civil War of the Commonwealth. The monument of "Old Sir Raphe," the last of the Asshetons of Middleton, was not then in existence, nor were the pennons and flag-staffs, the sword, helmet, and spurs, which always accompany the last of an ancient house to the grave, then suspended in that chapel. Those unsightly things, the pews, more like show-cribs than anything else, a modern invention of sordid pride, lest a poor woman's kirtle should by chance touch a "fine lady's" gown, were not then cumbering and disfiguring either this chapel, or the body of the church. The whole floor was strewn with rushes in winter; and the whole congregation sat on plain oaken benches, the poor and the rich faring alike in the presence of that Being to whom they were taught to pray—"From all blindness of heart; from pride, vainglory, and hypocrisy; from envy, hatred, and malice; Good Lord, deliver us."

The appearance of the chancel was also much different from its present one. A large window with open traceries shed a cheerful and plenteous light on the communion-table, which was surrounded by a curious and quaint-looking oaken railing of spiral staves, carved from the solid piece. The said window then exhibited in its lower compartment, the arms and crests, in stained glass, which now adorn the side windows. Where the benches now stand, were large oaken pews, with carvings and quaint devices. The stalls were in their present state; and the Archer, the Haughton, and the Tetlow monuments, were not on the walls. In a window of the northern aisle was a representation of a band of archers kneeling, each with his bow on his shoulder, his quiver at his breast, and his name above his head; tradition representing them as parishioners who were slain at the battle of Flodden Field, under the command of the Black Knight, who won his spurs that day. This emblazonment is now placed in one of the side windows of the chancel, a situation where it certainly is more likely to be preserved than in its former one. There was not then an organ in the singer's gallery; a tall arch, with zig-zag tracery, sprung from antique pillars at the base of the steeple, and spanned high above the heads of choristers and musicians. A large and bold emblazomnent of the Royal arms, with the initials "A. R." at the two upper corners, and the motto, "Semper eadem," at the bottom, hung in front of the singers' gallery. On the walls betwixt the aisles hung several large tablets containing lists of benefactions to the poor, which have recently been removed to more fitting places. The font then stood beneath the said gallery: the pulpit, a plain oaken one, was placed against the centre pillar on the north side of the middle aisle; and the congregation, as I before said, were arranged on seats, their feet in the rushes; and neither hassocks, nor foot-boards, nor lolling cushions, were then deemed indispensable to a becoming discharge of religious duties. The galleries, on neither side, would probably then be placed; nor would that piece of gim-crackery, the painted and pannelled pew, be stuck out above, more like a garish ball-room than a place for repentance and humiliation. But this has also passed away.

Outside of the yard wall, towards the north, stood an old thatched timber and daub house, which one entered down a step, through a strong low door with a wooden latch. This was "Old Joe Wellins's," the church alehouse, a place particularly resorted to by rough fellows when they had a mind to a private drinking bout. The sacred edifice itself is dedicated to Saint Leonard, the patron of thieves, and whether or not thieves and outlaws felt more assured than common under the wing, as it were, of their saint, it was a current tradition in my younger days, that more than one of "the gentlemen roadsters " who lived by levying contributions on the northern highways, made it his "boozing ken," or place of concealment and repose after their foraging expeditions: Nevison and Turpin were especially mentioned as having frequented this house. When this old building was pulled down several curious antique coins were found; of what date no one who saw them could tell. On the other side of the church, the space which is now occupied as a burial-ground, was a large and excellent bowling-green, which was much frequented by the idle fellows of the village, who preferred ale-bibbing in the sun before confinement on the loom or at the lap-stone. At last it was broken up and the games put a stop to, chiefly, it was said, because the late steward under the Suffields could not, when he resorted to the place, overawe, or keep the rustic frequenters in such respectful bounds as he wished to do: and from this statement I cannot withhold my belief; for it was just such an action as those who knew him would expect from the man.

The bridge over the Irk, at Back-o'th'-Brow, was a wooden one with hand rails. On the other side of the stream, on the right hand, were three or four thatched cottages, in the usual style; a barn and shippon stood on the left; whilst the Irk itself, then a stream like crystal, rippled and dimpled away over a channel of smooth sand beds, and dark gravel mingled with white pebbles which, like drops of unmelted snow, lay shimmering beneath the ripples. Trout were to be found then in the dark old stockholes, where the water was deep and quiet; and loaches lay basking and wallowing their green backs scarcely distinguishable from the dark pebbles.

Owler Bridge, which a little further eastward crosses another branch of the Irk, was to be much dreaded. The field along which the path lay betwixt Back-o'th'-Brow and Owler Bridge, was said to be thronged by spirits, whilst "fairees" were frequently seen dancing and gambolling on the bridge, and the bank of the stream on either side. Woe to the wight or the wean, who had to pass that way on a starless windy night! My father, when a boy, went to take lessons from a wise-man at Hilton-fold, and consequently he had to traverse the haunted field, and to pass the perilous bridge; but he seldom forgot to hum a psalm or hymn tune whilst on his way. It was rumoured that a murder had been committed in that field, and if a strange looking bone was found, it was supposed to have been one belonging to the murdered person. A dreaded place was that.

The Free Grammar School was also a haunted place. The endowment, for those days, was liberal, and the establishment possessed an extensive reputation. Gentlemen's sons, from many parts of the country, were sent to Middleton to receive their education preparatory to going to college. Some, around the neighbourhood, came to school on ponies, which in summer time they turned into the paddock opposite the school, until at night they were again mounted to return home. Some of these youths were wild and reckless, no doubt; and others were said to be more "deeply learned " than the master supposed them to be. On one occasion when they had the school to themselves, they set about raising the devil; and after a due course of conjuration the "dark being" appeared, and stamping a hole into a flag with his foot—the mark of which was shown in my days—he asked what they wanted. The conjurers, being terrified, wished him to retire as quietly as he came, but that he would not do, so they then demanded that he should make a rope out of the sand which lay in the sandbed at the foot of the church-bank, and he was busy at the work, when the head master fortunately came; and with the highest ceremonial dismissed him and saved the scholars whom he fain would have taken, whereupon he became so enraged, that he flew away in a flash of fire, breaking down an entire window, and part of the wall of the school. The school was conducted by a head master and an usher; the former generally teaching at the northern end, and the latter at the southern one. It was also customary for each to reside in a spacious chamber over the part of the school in which he taught, to which chamber access was gained up a flight of wooden stairs, by a door at the back, and through a dark place with which the scholars were wont to associate many superstitious terrors. One of these head masters was a Mr. Dean, a curate, who on a certain day, as the story narrated, on entering his room at the noon-hour of dismissal, met a clergyman in full canonicals, with a book open in his hand as if he were going to read a funeral service. The appearance passed Mr. Dean, who, in great surprise, turned and looked at it. It went out at the door, and apparently towards the stairs, but on Mr. Dean's returning to watch it down, it was not to be seen, nor could anything whatever be heard of any such person having been seen by others about the place. Mr. Dean took it as a warning to himself, and soon afterwards he sickened and died. The school-lane was also haunted by an apparition which came sometimes in one form, and sometimes in another. Two men, it was said, of adverse parties met here during the Civil Wars, when one killed the other, and the deceased's spirit had ever since haunted the place.

Stanicliffe was frequented by a demon which has but very recently quitted his haunt. At an old gloomy looking house, — partly of timber and partly of brick work, — situated on the brow of the hill, and looking, as it were, over the rindle towards Boarshaw, lived, during the Civil Wars, one of the Hopwood retainers, named Blomoley. He would seem to have been a man of ferocious disposition, since his name has been handed down in traditions, the fearfulness of which time has not diminished. Several men he was said to have wantonly put to death with his own hand, during those lawless periods; one he shot on his farm yard, and the bullet, after quitting the man's body, passed through two of his own barn doors. Ever after, until a comparatively recent date, the house and premises he occupied were haunted by "fyerin" (boggarts or apparitions) which came sometimes in the form of a calf, sometimes in that of a huge black dog, and sometimes in the human form, but hideous and terrible. A heavy nailed door, which was hung in such a manner that it shut to with violence, would at times open of itself before a stranger, or one of the family. A dog, or a calf, would at times trot along the passage before a person seeking admittance; the door would open wide; the person would enter the dwelling part, but nothing could be seen or heard of the mysterious appearance. At the dead of night, sounds would be heard as if persons were holding a conversation in whispers; doleful cries would break forth, or a crash would resound as if every piece of crockery in the dwelling was broken, when, in the morning, everything would be found in its place. I am not saying that I credit these accounts, but they were certainly narrated to me by one who had lived in the building during many years: one who could not gain anything by stating that which he did not believe to be true; and whose account was furthermore subsequently corroborated by another of the same family. It was even added, and confirmed in like manner, that other members of the family, besides the narrator, whilst sitting by the fire at night, had seen the cream-mug, or the drink bottle, move from the hearth to the hob, or from the hob to the hearth, without any visible being touching the vessels. Other things in the house were also frequently shifted, but nothing was ever broken; and the noises, appearances, and displacements, at length became so little thought of, that the common observation would be, "Oh! it's nobbut Owd Blomoley;" or, "Th' owd lad's agate agen." The house subsequently underwent some alteration, and about fourteen years ago it was pulled down, and another was rebuilt on its site; since which time, I have not heard of any disturbance at the place. The clough or dingle at the base of the meadow on which the house stood, retains the name of "Blomoley Cloof."

The noticing of these supposed supernatural appearances in, may seem puerile to some readers. The suppositions in themselves may be so; but taken in connection with, and affecting as they did, in a degree, the minds and manners of the rural population of the period, they are of more consequence than may at the first glance be apparent. At all events, in giving an account of a place and its inhabitants in past times, one cannot well refrain from alluding to whatever might have influenced their actions, any more than one can remain silent with respect to the actions themselves. I will, therefore, once for all mention, that but few of the lonely, out-of-the-way places — the wells, the bye-paths, the dark old lanes, the solitary houses — escaped the reputation of being haunted. "Boggarts," "fyerin," "witches," "fairees," "clap-cans," and such like beings of terror, were supposed to be lurking in almost every retired corner, or sombre-looking place; whence they come forth at their permitted hours, to enjoy their nocturnal freedom. Ruffian Lane—the old road to Hopwood Hall—was one of these haunted places: haunted once, as its name would purport, by less harmless beings than "boggarts." A footpath, leading through certain fields belonging to the "Black Bull" public-house, was notoriously the resort of "fyerin" (spirits): and here, indeed, there was reason to be shown why it should be so, since that ominous and awe-creating plant, Saint John's Wort, grew there in its pale, feathery pride. The present road—then a retired one, and overshadowed by a tall hedge and spreading trees—which leads from the bottom of Church Street to the Free School, was then nightly traversed by the appearance of a large four-footed animal, sometimes in the likeness of a dog or a bear, with great glaring eyes; at other times it would start up like a beautiful child, and moving before to a certain place, would disappear. The churchyard could not, of course, be free from supernatural appearances; and of the few who ventured through it after night-fall—the road then leading that way—not many left it whose hair was not standing on end. The path leading from the southern steps of the churchyard, down to the "Gypsy Croft" and the highway, was another haunt of these appearances; whilst the solitary footpath, which led from the same steps along the Warren, beneath the tall elms and sycamores, past the lonely summer-house, and down the wooded bank to the highway, seems to have been a favourite promenade to the beings of another world.

The Rectory was then an old irregular-looking edifice, built partly of brick and partly of stone, with a moat around it, and shot holes in the walls for musketry or cross-bows. The present unsightly brick wall, fronting the highway, was not then in existence. In place of it was a green sod rampart, planted with hawthorns and hedge-shrubs, which were protected by a low neat palisading, so that passengers, whilst walking under the beech trees, could enjoy a look at the fields, and into the shrubberies skirting the garden. Gentlemen in those days were not afraid, it would seem, of the poor man or woman enjoying a look through their hedges, nor catching a sweet wind-waft of their rosebuds, or apple-bloom, as they travelled the droughty dusty high-road.

The old Hall was perhaps one of the finest relics of the sort in the county. It was built of plaster and framework, with panels, carvings, and massy beams of black oak, strong enough for a mill floor. The yard was entered through a low wicket, at a ponderous gate; the interior of the yard was laid with small diamond-shaped flags; a door led on the left into a large and lofty hall, which was hung round with matchlocks, swords, targets, and hunting weapons, intermingled with trophies of the battle-field and the chase. But all disappeared before the spirit of Vandalism which commenced with the Harboard accession to the property, and their transference of power to one whose chief thought seemed to be how he might by any means increase the amount of remittances to his employer. Not a vestige of the edifice now remains. The exact site is at present unoccupied, but is understood to be let for the erection of a cotton-mill. A couple of factories and a gasworks are already close to the spot. The great oaken barn, before mentioned, and a cottage or two, and a remnant of the stabling, are the only vestiges remaining on the place. And so passes the vain stability of this world.

Having thus, as it were, led the reader, not only into the presence of my later ancestors, but also into the country which they inhabited, giving him glimpses of the manners, legends, and superstitions of those days, and thereby enabling him to perceive the great change which has come over the inhabitants of these parts, as well as over the country itself — having thus, in a measure, discharged a duty to some who are no more, and to scenes and things which have departed with them, I may, with a less divided retrospection, take up the narrative of my own life, and to that task — craving the reader's kind indulgence — I now address myself.

CHAPTER IV.
EARLY IMPRESSIONS-
MIDDLETON REFORMERS-
MEETING AT ROYTON—DENIAL OF JUSTICE.

MANY of the earliest of my, impressions were calculated to make me feel, and think, and reflect, and thus I became, imperceptibly, as it were, and amidst all the exuberant lightsomeness of childhood, impressible and observant. The notice I took of my mother's anguish and her tears (as before mentioned), whilst it made me hateful of all wrong — hateful so far as my young heart could be so—disposed me, at the same time, to be pitiful towards all suffering. It was the means of calling into action two of the strongest and most durable impulses of my heart—justice and mercy. Hence I was, in my infantile degree, a friend to every living being that suffered wrong, and an enemy to, or rather a disliker of, every living being that inflicted it. The cause of the unfortunate was mine own cause, from that of the crushed worm, which I put aside from my path, to that of the more noble animals, the dog, the steer, and the horse, when they suffered outrage at the hand of ruthless man. Everything which could not plead its own cause had a pleader in my heart. The horse had an especial one, inasmuch, probably, as whatever pain he might suffer, the expression of it was almost denied to him. The dog could howl, the steer could bellow, but the noble horse was mutely endurant; and these impulses, notwithstanding all that reason, and convenience, and necessity, as we term our palliatives, have at times suggested, and would still suggest, I never could put aside, never could subdue. So in this instance again, "Out of the eater came forth meat"; out of the evil came forth goodness.

The first book which attracted my particular notice was "The Pilgrim's Progress," with rude woodcuts; it excited my curiosity in an extraordinary degree. There was "Christian knocking at the strait gate," his "fight with Apollyon," his "passing near the lions," his "escape from Giant Despair," his perils at "Vanity Fair," his arrival in "the land of Beulah," and his final passage to "Eternal Rest"; all these were matters for the exercise of my feeling and my imagination. And then, when it was explained to me, as it was by my mother and my sister, how that Christian was a godly man, who left his wife, and his children, and all he had in the world, to go forth and seek the blessed land afar off; and that, through many trials, and perils, and hardships, he arrived at that land, and entered another life, never to return; that his wife and family, in hopes of joining him, also left their home and journeyed the same weary and perilous way, my heart was filled with pleasing, yet melancholy impressions. The whole pilgrimage was to me a story mournfully soothing, like that of a light coming from an eclipsed sun.

Others of my early impressions were also of a saddening nature, and I mention them, not because I would be understood to have been less joyous and playsome than were other children of my age — for I was probably quite as much so as the generality of my playmates were — but because, with me, the bright moments are but dimly remembered now, whilst the more sombre impressions remain distinctly present as I now write. The reader, however, need not be afraid of my drawing a totally darksome picture; there may be some strong clouding here and there. There must be if truth and nature are adhered to, and from them we assuredly will not depart.

And now came to myself and my childish playmates strange and alarming rumours of a dreadful war. "The war," we heard, was coming afar off; the French people were bringing it, and "the war" would come to Middleton, and kill all the fathers, and mothers, and children that it could find. This was a sad prospect to me, and I pondered I it over it until I hit on a scheme which I thought would avert the danger. This was that I and all our family, at least, should hide in the wooden coal-shed at the Free Grammar School, and there I was quite certain "the war" could never find us.

One incident of my childhood will serve to show the sort of daily, fireside education which my parents bestowed on their children. I mention it to their honour, and not from a wish to claim any precocity of intellect, which indeed I did not possess. I was probably about three years of age when some one made me a present of a little tin can, as a plaything, and to sup my porridge and milk from. I slept with Sally Owen, a young woman who, having been left an orphan and brought up in my grandfather's family, was now living more as a sister than as a servant with my uncle Thomas. Well, this little tin can nothing could prevail on me to part from, and I was allowed to take it with me to bed. Probably Sally Owen would find it a rather sharp article to turn upon at night. However that were, when I awoke in the morning Sally Owen was gone, and my little bright plaything was gone also. I then cried out, and when the kind-hearted creature came to the bedside, I learned from her replies that she had taken my can, and that if I was not a good boy I must not have it any more. So, looking in her face, I said, "Sally, whot dus Katekiss say?" "Say? why wot dus it say?" asked Sally. "Dus it no say, thou shalt not steal?" "Aye, it dus," replied Sally, "an' wotbi that?" "Well, then," was my rejoinder, "thou shalt not steal my little can." Her tender eyes were brimming full; she snatched me out of bed, gave me my little can, and took me to my mother, who also shed tears of joy when she heard what I had said. "Oh!" she would sometimes ejaculate, "theaw shud habin kess'nt Jeffrey or Daniel."

My father, as before stated, was a reader, and amongst other books which he now read was Paine's "Rights of Man." He also read Paine's "Age of Reason," and his other theological works, but they made not the least alteration in his religious opinions. Both he and my uncle had left the society of Methodists, but to the doctrines of John Wesley they continued adherents so long as they lived. At the commencement of the French Revolution a small band only of readers and inquirers after truth was to be found in Middleton. They were called "Jacobins" and "Painites," and were treated with much obloquy by such of their bigoted neighbours as could not or would not understand that other truths existed in the world than "were dreamt of in their philosophy." This band of thinkers included Edmund Johnson, a druggist and apothecary; Jacob Johnson, his brother, a weaver and herb doctor; Simeon Johnson, another brother, weaver; Samuel Ogden, shoemaker; Thomas Bamford, my uncle; and Daniel, my father. They met at each other's houses to read such of the current publications as their small means allowed them to obtain, and to converse on the affairs of the nation, and other political subjects. They were also supporters of Parliamentary Reform, as it was then advocated by the Duke of Richmond, Mr. Pitt, and other distinguished characters. This notice will explain the rancour which they had to endure, some traits of which I shall proceed to describe.

One Middleton wakes, as I remember, I, a mere child, sat on the steps of my father's dwelling, watching the holiday folks draw their rush-carts towards the church. They went close past our door; very grand and gaudy the drawers and carts were, with ribbons, and streamers, and banners, and garlands, and silver ornaments, and morrice bells, and other music, quite joyous and delightful. At length came a cart more richly decked than others, on the flake of which behind was placed the figure of a man, which I thought was a real living being. A rabble which followed the cart kept throwing stones at the figure, and shouting, "Tum Paine a Jacobin!" "Tum Paine a thief!" "Deawn wi' o' th' Jacobins!" "Deawn wi' th' Painites!" whilst others with guns and pistols kept discharging them at the figure. They took care to stop when they came to the residence of a reformer; the shouting and the firing were renewed, and then they moved on. Poor Paine was thus shot in effigy on Saturday, repaired, re-embellished, and again set upright on Sunday, and "murdered out-and-out" on Monday, being again riddled with shot, and finally burned. I, of course, became a friend of Thomas Paine's. Such was one of the modes of annoyance and persecution to which the few who dared be honest were subjected by the sires and grandsires of the present race of reforming Englishmen. But this was perfect amenity compared with what took place at Royton.

That village was in those days looked upon as the chief resort of Jacobins on that side of Manchester. A few clever, sensible men lived there also, as well as at Middleton, but those of Royton would seem to have taken more active measures for the promotion of reform than did others living in the neighbouring districts. I well remember, in the dolorous days of ninety-two, or three, a small band from Royton perambulating our secluded nook of the town, and singing a piece, one verse of which was as follows:

> "Our Our masters play us roguish pranks;
> Our bankrupt bankers close their banks;
> Which makes our wives and children cry.
> But times shall alter by and by."

One forenoon we were alarmed by the appearance of men armed with thick cudgels and bludgeons, who passed by our house in groups, swearing and threatening what they would do at the "Painites" when they returned. They came from Ringley and Radcliffe, and other places; desperate and ruthless men they seemed, and we children were so terrified that we crept into the hen-roost as a place of the greatest safety. Many eventful hours of anxious expectation succeeded; my father did not remove his family, but I believe he made preparations for self-defence if attacked. The ruffians, however, returned past our house without offering any serious molestation, my father not being a man slightly to be put aside; my uncle also being at hand. Not so, however, did the scoundrels withhold from poor Samuel Ogden; for there they broke open his door, pulled him out of the house, broke his windows and some furniture, and maltreated his person; for none of which outrages did the law ever afford him any satisfaction. The occasion on which these brutes were let loose in the country, was as follows.

On the 31st of April, 1794, a public meeting, for the promotion of Parliamentary Reform, was appointed to be held at Thorpe, near Royton. It was called by a few friends to reform who were correspondents of the society in London;[1] and the purpose of the originators of the meeting was to get a petition adopted, praying Parliament to grant an amendment in the representation of the people. Previous to the commencement of the proceedings, a number of well-wishers to the cause, who had come from a distance, together with several promoters of the meeting, were assembled at "The Light Horseman" public-house, in Royton Lane. They were taking refreshments, and arranging the proceedings, when a mob of several hundred people, led up by one Harrop, of Barrowshaw, an atrocious ruffian, came in front of the house, and with shouts of "Church an' King for ever!" "Deawn wi' th' Jacobins!" began to smash the windows, and break open the doors. As many of the mob were armed with clubs and staves, and there was a supply of stones in the lane, the few inside could neither make effectual resistance to their entrance, nor defend themselves from violence. The mob broke everything down before them. The windows were smashed; the doors and shutters were kicked into splinters. The loyal sign of the old pensioner was torn down; every article of furniture was broken; the glasses, jugs, and other vessels, were dashed on the floor, and trampled under foot; the bar was gutted; the cellars were entered, and the ale and liquors were drunk or poured on the floor; and such being the violence committed on the property, it may be supposed that the obnoxious persons would not be suffered to escape. Oh, no!—this was a real "Church and King mob," and was too faithful to its employers to suffer the "Painites" to escape without punishment. Whilst some of the brutes were guzzling, and others were breaking furniture, others again were beating, and kicking, and maltreating in various ways the persons found in the house. Several of these were lamed; others were seriously crushed and injured in their persons. The constables of the place had been called upon by the peaceably disposed inhabitants to act, but they declined to interfere, and the mob had their own way. Mr. Pickford,

---

[1] The Corresponding Society formed in 1792 for the promotion of Parliamentary Reform.

of Royton Hall, a magistrate, never made his appearance, though he lived within a few score yards of the scene of riot, and was supposed to have been at home all the time during which the outrage was perpetrated. He was afterwards known as Sir Joseph Ratcliffe, of Milnes Brig, in Yorkshire. Such of the Reformers as had the good fortune to escape out of the house, ran for their lives, and sought hiding-places wherever they could be found; whilst the parson of the place, whose name was Berry, standing on an elevated situation, pointed them out to the mob, saying — "There goes one; and there goes one!" "That's a Jacobin; that's another!" and so continued until his services were no longer effectual. A few stout-hearted reformers who had possession of one part of the house would not be beaten like children; they retaliated blow for blow, and kick for kick, until the cowards who assailed them were fain to pause. The strife outside was then nearly over, and these few reformers consented, at length, to go with their assailants before the magistrate above mentioned. About half a score of reformers, in the whole, were conducted as prisoners to Royton Hall, where they were placed in a stable, and treated with every contumely, until the great man was ready to receive them. They were then shown into his presence, and were ultimately held in bail to appear at Lancaster, to answer a charge of rioting. At the August assizes, the case was traversed; and in the spring assizes of 1795, the Grand Jury having "found a true bill," the "rioters" were arraigned; but as the fourth witness for the prosecution was under examination, the judge stopped the trial, and the defendants were discharged. The reformers caused bills of indictment to be presented to the Grand Jury, against a number of the real rioters; but, as in the case of the later affair in Manchester, the same Grand Jury which could find true bills against the unoffending people, could not find any bills against the guilty parties. The persons who had been so shamefully maltreated could not obtain any redress at law; even the poor old soldier, whose house had been broken into and plundered in open sunlight, never received compensation. Everything he had in the world was destroyed or carried away; he was a ruined man, and a ruined man he remained to the end of his days. Such was a specimen of "Justice of the Peace" justicing, of "Church and King Parsons" parsoning; and of "Grand juries" jurying, in the blessed times of 1794! With such an example as this on the records of the county, need we wonder at what took place in 1819?

CHAPTER V.
FIRST IMPRESSIONS OF MANCHESTER

"Straight is the lane that has never a turning:
Long is the joy that has never a mourning."

IT must have been when I was in the sixth year of my age, that one day as I was rolling on the floor with my younger brother and sister, we were surprised and checked by the appearance of a good-looking, fresh complexioned gentleman, who asked for my father. My mother respectfully attended on the visitor, and my father was called up from his loom in the cellar where he was at work. My father, my mother, and the gentleman had some conversation, after which my father put on his better coat and hat, and went out with the gentleman to the place, as I have since understood, where his horse was put up. My father returned, after being absent a short time, and I recollect well, having noticed a change in the look and manner of both my parents, my mother frequently applying her apron to her eyes, whilst my father was quite cheerful. The visitor who had caused this change was one of the churchwardens for the township of Manchester, and his business at our house was to induce my father to undertake the management of a manufactory of cotton goods at the work house for that township. The terms offered were such as my father accepted, and on a day appointed, after appearing before the board of parish officers, and being by them approved of, the agreement was ratified, and my father thenceforward applied sedulously to his new avocation, sleeping at the workhouse, boarding at the governor's table, during the week days, and spending his Saturday evenings and his Sundays with his family at home. He must have discharged the duties of his office in a manner which gave satisfaction, inasmuch as sometime after his appointment, he became governor of the workhouse, and my mother governess; my uncle Thomas at the same time being appointed to succeed my father in the manufactory.

And now, with respect to that beloved relation, let me say a word. He was to all the children of his brother a second father, whilst to their father he was a true brother indeed. A provident counsellor in adversity, what his head advised his hand would assist to effect. In temper he was equable and calm; steadfast in purpose, and unbendingly upright in his dealings. His religion was that of a devout, but unostentatious Christian, and his outward ceremonial of it was that of John Wesley. In stature he was tall, and of a powerful solidity, whilst the clothed appearance of his person and limbs, indicated symmetry united with the fastness of great strength. His features were such as are generally deemed handsome, their expression was indicative of a calm, thoughtful, and benevolent mind. His complexion was that of raven dark; and his black glossy hair hung slightly curling over the front of his shoulders. Reader, hast thou ever beheld a half length "Salvator Mundi," by Bartolozzi? If thou hast—and deem me not impious, for the engraving itself is but the idea of a human genius—if thou hast seen such engraving, then hast thou beheld as good a likeness as could be drawn of the features of my ever-dear uncle Thomas. And, with such a wife as I have described my mother to be; with such a brother as this, and with five healthy, joysome children, did my father wend his way from Middleton, and take up his abode in his new situation at Manchester.

This was to us a vast and surprising change in life. At our little country home, everything was conducted in that plain thrifty way, by means of which a good house-wife renders her cottage so comfortable, and her family so well provided, out of comparatively very small incomings. Our fare was of the simplest kind, and far from profuse, whilst our clothing, though cleanly and well mended, was such as would raise a smile amongst the mothers of these days; big boys, as well as big girls, very frequently wearing their infantile skirts until they became kilts, and those too not of the longest. Then, in summer days, we spent much of our time out of doors, digging holes in the sand, or making little gardens and houses in the hollows amongst the fern, or on the green banks of the Irk where the sweet willows, and the hazels, and gorses formed natural harbours, sheltering us from the passing showers. Or we would form wading parties, and a dozen of us together, big girls and boys, taking the little ones on our backs, would thus go wading up the stream, maybe laying hold of a trout now and then, or bringing up a few loaches: or we would go a bird-nesting, or a moss-gathering, to deck our peace-egg baskets; or a primrose-plucking towards Littlegreen and "Owd Hall-cloof," until, when we turned home—our cheeks brown and ruddy, bare-footed, bare-legged, bareheaded, and bare-necked—our milk and bread, or our meal of solid dumpling, was, to us, a repast so entirely delicious, that of anything more excellent we could not form an idea. Then in schooling, I learned the alphabet from my father at his loom; I afterwards went a short time to the parish clerk at the Free School, but I learned not anything there; I was not, at that age, quick at imbibing instruction. On Sundays I went with the bigger children to the chapel school, which was next door to our house, until another was built on the road to Boarshaw, but neither did I profit by my Sunday tuition. On Sunday evenings we often sang hymns; and we always said our prayers before going to bed. At meals my father never omitted asking a blessing before we partook the food, nor did he omit returning thanks afterwards. Bending reverently forward, and with his hands clasped, he would say, "Merciful God! bless this food to our temporal use, and sanctify our selves to Thy service, for Christ's sake." In returning thanks he would say, "Lord! for the blessing we have received at Thy hands, accept our thanks, for Christ's sake." And these devout customs were continued so long as the family remained together.

But now we had entered a far different scene of life. My parents and the younger part of the family removed first to Manchester, leaving myself and a brother at Middleton until some clothes which the tailor was making were finished. In a few days my father came for us, and leading me by the hand, I went trotting by his side, full of busy imaginings, and asking all kinds of questions about "the great town," and I "the big house," I was going to live at. The sound of the old church[2] bell came booming through the closing day, as we hastened across Smedley fields; and I thought I never heard so deep a tone in all my life. Next we passed over "The Butter-style," and turned on our left, a vast gloom darkening before us as we advanced. Then we heard the rumbling of wheels, and the clang of hammers, and a hubbub of confused sounds from workshops and manufactories. As we approached the "Mile-house," human shouts and cries in the streets became distinguishable; and on the top of Red Bank, the glare of many lights, and faint outlines of buildings in a noisy chaos below, told us we beheld Manchester. We descended the hill, and the lamps which were burning in the Mill-gate excited my attention, whilst the huge pile of the old church—blackest amidst the blackness—inspired me with feelings of disquietude and wonder. The Irwell darkly rolled towards our feet, whilst, on our right, the walls and pinnacles of the old Baron's Hall[3] were dimly visible; and before us, washing the base of the ancient edifice, hurried another stream; my father, pointing towards it, told us it was the same which whimpled so brightly and merrily past our door at Middleton. I looked over the battlement, wishing to behold it as I would a dear companion, but it was lost in the darkness, and a slight murmur was the only response to my fond regret. After proceeding a short distance, we began to ascend a brow. My father knocked at a gate; a bolt was presently shot back, and we proceeded along a flagged walk, until we came to a flight of steps, when my father opening a folding door, we entered a large hall, flashing with light, and before we had time to recover our surprise, my dear mother, my uncle, and the children were enfolding us in their arms.

Here was a theatre for the active habits and kindly feelings of my dear parents and my uncle. A new life, a confiding spirit, was infused into the poor inmates. The men found friendly advisers in all their difficulties and vexations, and there were such even in this sheltering place. They found also encouragers and assistants in the prosecution of every good purpose, as well as power which would be obeyed in whatever was right and necessary. The poor orphans, as well as ourselves, had now a kind father, mother, and uncle; the sick were tenderly nursed and provided for; the aged were treated with indulgent regard, whilst the healthy were put to useful employment, and continued at it day by day. My mother's quick eye was everywhere; her active step was unwearied; no dust, or slop, or sluttishness, would she tolerate: there was a place for everything, and everything would she have in its place. Moving about in a morning in her skirted bed-gown, the long sleeves turned up, and with her milk-white mop-cap fringing the healthy bloom of her cheek, she enforced activity and cleanliness in the servants, and nurses, and attendants; there was a movement to work whenever her step approached; a stirring to industry, whenever her voice was heard.

Thus everything being adjusted, and the routine of management and

---

[2] The present Cathedral.
[3] Purchased in 1654 by the trustees of Humphrey Chetham, for the purpose of founding the Chetham Hospital and Library.

subordination working in regularity, my parents would probably hope that a long day of prosperity was before them. Who can tell the fond anticipations in which they would indulge? Who could estimate the depth of gratitude which in fervent thanks they would endeavour to express towards "the Giver of all good?" He alone to whom those thanks were addressed — He alone could know how truly grateful were my poor parents for this gleam of prosperity. But even now, the fiat which makes mute all joy had gone forth. God would have His own when He would. The death-smell was amongst us; the doomed were moving towards their unseen grave.

Several cases of virulent small-pox broke out amongst the children of the house. My little sister Hannah, then in the fourth year of her age, and as lovely a specimen of child-like beauty as I ever beheld, took the disorder and died; and in twenty-eight days afterwards, my little brother James, then in the second year of his age, followed her to eternity. A few weeks only had passed, when my grandfather Battersby died, at Middleton; and we were mourning, after mourning, three persons of our family and kindred having thus been called to another world. But further trials were yet at hand.

My mother bore up like a Christian heroine; my father submitted in silent resignation; whilst my uncle was probably as much affected as any of the three. Weeks, however, wore away, grief was mitigated, and tears were again almost dried, when a female whose manners and conversation indicated that she had seen better days, was announced to be ill of the fever. Everything was done for her which good nursing and the medical skill of those days could effect, but she continued to get worse and her recovery becoming hopeless, she wished some one to make prayer for her. My uncle, as humane as he was trustful in God, knelt down by her beside, as had been his wont in other cases, and prayed with a solemnity and feeling which softened and comforted her heart, and she begged he would visit her again before she died; he did so, and with thanks on her lips, and an assurance of a joyful hereafter, she expired. In a few days my uncle became unwell; his indisposition increased; the strong man was prostrated by the infecting disorder; and his last words were, "Hannah, I'm coming! Jimmy, I'm coming!"

I slept in the same room with my uncle during the former part of his illness, and I took the disorder, which was now pronounced to be fever of a malignant kind, or what would be called in these days, a typhus of the worst type. My mother would nurse me herself as much as her other pressing duties permitted; at all events, she was determined that I should not suffer from want of attendance during the night, and she had me removed to her own room and her own bed, my father going to sleep in another apartment. She was tenderly assiduous, nursing me as a dove would its young; but I sank and sank, until at last consciousness departed and I knew no more. How long I remained in this condition I have no knowledge, but it must have been during a considerable time, probably a week or two; and when consciousness returned, I was in another bed in the same room, and my mother was delirious and raving in her own bed beside me.

Some days and nights passed in this manner, my mother at times insensible, and at other times praying on behalf of herself and family; my father also frequently knelt at her bedside, praying God, "if it so pleased Him, to let this cup pass away: nevertheless, not his will but God's be done." At length, one night, as I recollect, my father, my brother, my sister, and the nurses stood around my mother's bed. She was conscious of her approaching end, and wished to take leave of us all. That was a solemn time: she would have me wrapt in blankets and brought to her. Every one was in tears. My father besought God to sustain and comfort her now that all human aid had failed; and she invoked blessings on the husband and children she was about to leave. As the nurse held me I stretched out my arms towards my dying parent, when, blessing me with a fervent blessing, she said I should soon be better when she was gone. I remember no more of this sad scene. My father went back to the bed from which he had arisen to take this last farewell; and the next thing that I recollect was my awakening one night, and becoming aware of a terrible stillness. I listened to hear my mother breathing, or praying, but nothing could I hear, and I lay some time in a state of sad foreboding. After gazing long in the darkness, I thought I could perceive that the curtains of my mother's bed were drawn back, and that something white and perfectly still lay there, which I concluded was my mother's corpse, and I began to cry. In a short time there was a light in the next room, and a sound of feet, and doors were opened and shut, and there was much passing and repassing, with the clatter of tea-things; and the persons began to talk, some of them in a very cheerful strain; and they seemed to be sitting down to tea. I then called out and one or two came into the room, and spoke comfortingly to me. They also wrapped me up in blankets and carried me into the room they had come from, and ill passing my mother's bed I saw her lying dead and covered with a sheet.

CHAPTER VI.
LIVING BESIDE THE DEAD—A NURSE.

IN the next room were the nurse and several women, with a young man who, since the death of my uncle, had superintended the manufactory. There was a good fire in the place; the kettle was on the hob, and they were preparing to have "a comfortable cup of tea," with "something in it," previous to washing and laying-out my mother's corpse. I was warmly wrapped up, and placed in as easy a position as my weakness would allow, in a two-armed chair by the fireside. This was another trial to me; the time was midnight, or early morning; the room was the one in which I had been accustomed to meet my father, mother, uncle, and other members of our family. It had been our household room, but none of our family were now present; the voices I heard, the faces I beheld, were mostly those of strangers, and I felt a sense of loneliness such as I never before experienced. The women, stout, hardy working women, who had probably been early and late, toiling in the dangerous task of attending the sick and dying, and more especially my poor mother and father, partook of their refection with a zest and a cheerfulness of conversation, which, however natural it might be in persons of their situation, presented such a contrast to the silence of the other room, and was so little in accordance with my present feelings, that I burst into tears. The kind-hearted creatures no sooner saw my distress than they did everything they could to console me, telling me my mother was now happy, that my father would soon be better, and that I should quickly be able to run about again; and so kind and assiduous were they in their endeavours to mitigate my grief, that at length the feeling of desolateness which had afflicted me passed away. I felt that all friends were not yet lost to me. I thanked them with renewed tears, and with expressions of trustful confidence; and after partaking their refreshment—which their hearty enjoyment of it made me think must be very good—they put me to bed in another room, and went to perform their necessary offices to my mother's dead body. The funeral took place on the day following at the old church; and my father was unconscious of her decease, being himself at the time in a delirium of the fever.

As my mother had foretold, soon after her death I began rapidly to recover, and my father being placed in the same room with me, one nurse attended to both of us during the night. This night-nurse was an elderly female, whose name I will not mention, because, although during years and years afterwards the very word inspired me with horror, it is the distinctive appellation of many worthy persons. She was a tall, brown, bony, hard-featured woman, with long tanned arms, and wearing a dark dingy bed-gown, and with a profusion of snuff on her face and on her soiled cap. She had a callous and unfeeling way of performing whatever offices our situation required; and she was probably assigned to this duty more from a belief of her capability to sustain it than from any other qualification. At first the old hag was very attentive, giving us our medicine, or wine, or whatever was necessary, at their prescribed seasons; soon, however, she became neglectful, and somewhat rude, and my father being delirious and incoherent at times, she overawed and terrified me. At length, one night as I remember, my father being in his better mood, asked her to give him his wine; she said there was none, and when he questioned her as to what had become of it, she straightway opened upon him a torrent of oaths, curses, and abuse, such as I had never heard. She was quite drunk, and he had the strength to tell her audibly that she was "a vile woman"; whereupon she went raving mad, and swore she would murder us both in our beds, and she looked round the place, seemingly for a weapon with which to dash our brains out. I thereupon called as loudly as I could, but it being midnight, and no one being awake in our part of the house, it was a considerable time, or, at least, so it seemed, before any person came to our assistance; and during that interval, the words, looks, and gestures of the old crone were those of a perfect demoniac. She had drunk every drop of the wine we should have had, and when at length the desired help arrived, she was dragged out of the place, and went blaspheming and yelling down the long corridors and passages, doors closing after her one by one, until her howlings were no longer heard.

After this we had very good nurses, and though my father had a crisis almost as perilous as myself had had, he at length gradually recovered, and we both turned, as it were, though wearily and feebly, into a world, oh! how different from the one we found on our first arrival at this once inviting, but now dolorous place. Brother, sister, grandfather, uncle, mother, five persons out of nine, parts, as it were, of our own being, torn from us in the space of a few brief months. What a change we felt! What a void was around us — and what a diminished and unsheltered group we seemed to be! Surely "the bitterness of death" is in the lonesome desolation of the living; and this bitterness, notwithstanding my naturally cheerful temper and all which kindness could do to console me; was long my portion, until it began to be feared whether or not I should ever be called from "the valley of the shadow of eternity." We had our sympathisers, however, and though they were of the humblest station of their race, their friendship was probably not the least sincere, nor, consequently, ought it to be the least regarded. When I got strong enough to falter into the yard, I was surrounded by the pleased countenances of children who accompanied me with every demonstration of joy, singing at times a rude rhyme somewhat like the following:

> "Here's a health to Daniel Bamford,
> Who is so kind and true;
> When he gets better we'll write him a letter,
> And send it to Middleton too."

The mature and elderly paupers also would stop, look at me and walk away invoking blessings on "the poor motherless boy."

When my father had completely recovered, he was grieved that my mother had not been buried at Middleton, with her children, as it was her expressed desire to be. He accordingly took measures with a view to having her wish complied with, but Doctor Ashton, who was at the time rector of Middleton and warden of the Collegiate Church at Manchester, refused to grant permission for the removal of her remains, alleging as his reason—and that perhaps a proper one—that the infection of which she died might be communicated to persons attending the ceremony. She therefore remained in her grave, on the north side of the steeple at the Collegiate Church, where my father caused a stone to be placed, with a suitable inscription; but in the alterations which some years ago were made in the churchyard, my mother's gravestone, like many others, disappeared.

CHAPTER VII.
A NEW GOVERNESS: PLAYMATES— STRIKING CHARACTERS— DIETARY.

WHILST my father was recovering from his illness, a new governess was appointed in the place of my deceased mother. She was the wife of a Mr. Rose, who had been recently unfortunate in the grocery business. She was a tall, fat, heavy-footed woman, about fifty years of age, I should think, and had once, no doubt, been a fine-looking person. She was well acquainted with all kinds of cookery, and was industrious and managing enough in her way, but that way was quite a different one from the simple housewifery of my mother. She was, however, I believe, good at heart, since she was generally kind and considerate towards us children, whose waywardness at times would probably be quite sufficient to try even a mother's temper, much more that of a mere friendly stranger. When her husband's affairs were arranged, he took the situation of schoolmaster in the house, and as such had his meals at the governor's table with his wife, my father, the superintendent of the manufactory, the apothecary or dispenser of medicine, and sometimes the governor's three children. Mr. Rose was a quiet, mild, elderly person, inclined to corpulence, and apparently satisfied with an easy life. The dispenser of medicine was a little cheerful old man, dressed in black, with thin grey hairs on his head, a white cravat, and a dusting of snuff on his waistcoat; his walk was almost a kind of dance, it was so lightsome, and he went tripping round to his patients, as he called them, every morning, with a small saying or a cheerful word for every one. He was a native of London, and had moved there in a respectable mercantile sphere, but being suddenly ruined and abandoned by those on whom he thought he had claims of gratitude, he left the place in disgust of mankind, and almost of life, and having, scarcely knowing how or why, wandered into Lancashire, he took a humble situation in a tea warehouse at Manchester, when, his health failing, he was transferred to the workhouse, and on his recovery became the attendant on the physician, and a kind of house apothecary, in which situation, having a small salary and comfortable maintenance, the old gentleman seemed to have become quite happy, and forgetful of his former condition, seldom indeed even alluding to it. The superintendent of the manufactory was the young man I have before mentioned, a native of Middleton, and on his leaving after a short stay, the place was filled by John Haworth, a native of the Forest of Rossendale, who, having in the hey-day of his youth enlisted into the dragoons, had spent the best part of his life as a soldier in the Flanders wars. John was quite an original in his way; he was huge in stature, massively bony, with but a small portion of fleshy texture to round off the sharp points of his frame. He was very serious and staid in his manners, superstitious in his notions about witches, apparitions, and beings of another world, and equally sincere and credulous in his religious opinions. Yet at times, when something very adverse and unexpected amongst the workmen tried his patience, he would rap out a round regimental oath, and as instantly call it back, as it were, with a "Lord, help us!" "God, forgimmi!" and then he seemed to suppose all was right again. Poor John — he was a true specimen of the fearless, sword-hewing English dragoon, engrafted on the simple, credulous, ineradicable rusticity of the old Lancashire moorlander before the hill-streams were poisoned by dye-vats, and the valleys were studded with smoke funnels. Besides the persons I have noticed who formed my father's more immediate associates, he had a stout assistant also, who helped him in the management of the lunatics, and the refractory paupers, when there were any; and who also brewed, and did the other cellar and porter's work of the house; so that on the governor's side there was no lack of power for coercion when lien it was necessary, but that was seldom the case, except with the unfortunate insane.

My father's health having been re-established, he resumed the duties of his situation, and the management of the house was carried on with regularity and mutual satisfaction betwixt my father and the governess, who was very kind and attentive to me. I continued in a weakly and a feeble state, and that was probably the reason why I was more indulged than I otherwise should have been, and certainly more than was conducive to my quick recovery. I was allowed to run about the place, almost when and where I chose, and I was not long in selecting a few especial playmates from amongst the pauper children. The big boys carried me on their backs; with the girls I played at ball, or at hide-and-seek, or the old-fashioned game of "Blackthorne;" and when a group of girls came around me as I sat to recover breath, the conversation would often be allusive to my mother, and then to parents generally, and next to such parents or relatives of the children as had died, or had deserted them, or were unknown. And thus we often chatted in our childish way until our young hearts got too full, and, forgetful of our play, we sat in tears. With these poor children I was an immense favourite; a kind of little brother to those who had none other in the world. Besides, I always divided amongst them any trifle or choice bit of delicacy which I happened to be pampered with at the time. Pip Brown, who was my big horse, thus got my toasted cheese; Bill Jordan, who ran races, and leaped furthest, had my buttered toast; little Nelly, whose father had been pressed and sent to sea, came in for my pie crust or my currant dumpling; whilst the pale and desolate-looking Alice, who was always alone, and who had not a relation in the world, was often cheered by my kind word, and was sure to get a share of my custard or my plum cake. The women also would confide to me some little message to Mrs. Rose when they wanted a trifling favour: the old men would get me to mention their being without clogs, or their want of a new doublet for the winter time, whilst if any punishment was to be inflicted, any penance undergone, I was ever a pleader for the suffering party, and was often in some degree successful; perceived that neither my father nor Mrs. Rose were displeased with my interference; and I had, consequently, friends in every part of the house. The old women would tell me strange stories of ghosts and hobgoblins; the old men narrated shipwrecks and battles, or they would chant the song of the famous outlaw, how

> "He blew so loud and shrill;
> Till a hundred and ten,
> Of Robin Hood's men,
> Came tripping over the hill."

And I was quite delighted with the idea of a free life in " the merrie green-wood."

Even amongst the lunatics, where I would sometimes prevail upon the keeper to let me accompany him, unknown to my father, I felt very little apprehension, and had several acquaintance. Some who were fierce and dangerous towards all others would permit me to approach them, and seemed pleased by my confidence. Others would be entirely mollified and disarmed of their frenzy by a trifling kindness, or a soothing word; and for such as these I generally had secreted some little present, such as a pinch or two of snuff, a quid of tobacco; or for the women some female ornament, with a word or two of hope and persuasion that they would soon return to their friends. Some were unmitigably mad, and untamed as wild beasts; and from these I was kept at a proper distance. One who had been an extensive trader in Manchester, but was ruined by gross dissipation, was loathsome to behold, and frightful to hear; whilst another, old Sally T., whose sons were then in business, and have since retired with princely fortunes, was invariably lamenting, and shedding tears; she was beyond the reach of consolation in this world. But there was one who, having been once seen, was not soon to be forgotten. She was a young girl, an Irish girl I think, of perhaps seventeen years of age. Whilst her features were of the most beautiful outline, her person appeared to be of faultless symmetry, and whilst her face and neck were pale without a streak, her hair, which hung over her bosom and shoulders, was black as jet; her head, and the upper part of her bust, were mostly bare; and at first glance, she looked like one who had come amongst us from some unknown sphere — so strange, so unearthly, so hopeless, so deathful, seemed the very life within her. Her features were immovable as the marble from which they seemed to have been chiselled. If pressed into a seat, she sat, if lifted to her feet, she stood, mute and motionless from sunrise to sunset would she have so remained if permitted. No tear fell from her eye, no sigh broke from her heart, no word escaped from her lips, save once, and that was "Edward!" the name of him who had betrayed and abandoned her. The poor thing lingered in this state some weeks, taking no food except when compelled to do so. All the natural functions were suspended, and at length the only indication of life which she had retained ceased also, and she no longer breathed.

Amongst the harmless lunatics who were suffered to go about the yards, was one who imagined himself to be the Duke of York. My father rather humoured his innocent whim, and he soon appeared in a cocked hat, and with various coloured stripes and shreds on his shoulders and across his breast, to the great amusement of the boys, whom he enlisted, and formed into a regiment to conquer the French; a business almost as feasible and wise as some of those in which the real Duke was at the same time engaged. Paddy Hamilton was another lunatic, who, though not so entirely harmless as "the Duke," was allowed the run of the yards. The boys used to tease and irritate him, when he would sometimes turn upon and chase them, striking such as he caught unmercifully, and as they durst not complain, for fear of further punishment, my father was kept in ignorance of these proceedings. On one of these occasions, the boys had teased the poor young fellow until he seemed to have become all at once conscious of his wretched condition, and instead of throwing stones, or running after the children, he sat down on the edge of the stone pump trough and burst into tears. We were all surprised to see him sitting so quiet—for I was one of the party —and on going near cautiously, we found him weeping bitterly, and exclaiming, "Why did you do this, boys?" "Oh, what did I do to you, that you thus ill-use me?" The other lads stood around, some laughing, some inclined to be sorry; but as for me, my heart smote me instantly; I felt that I had been committing a great wrong, and going up to the poor fellow, I took his hand, and cried with him for company, telling him we would never do so any more, inducing also the other boys to promise the same; and to make the peace lasting, and somewhat satisfactory to my own conscience, I went into the kitchen and asked for some bread and cheese, as if for myself, and coming out again I gave the whole to Paddy. Ever after that I was Paddy's protector, and he was my devoted friend.

Such was the sort of life which I passed amongst these poor children and poor people. It is true I saw and heard some things of which it perhaps would not have been any disadvantage had I remained ignorant for the time. But my heart was never corrupted, never beguiled of its childish simplicity. Nor did any of these poor people, and I will do them the justice to state it, ever by word or deed, throw in my way an inducement that might lead to vice.

The great mass of the poor and unfortunate are not, in my opinion, so vicious as by the "well-to-do" multitude of the world they are supposed to be; and judging from what I have seen of them, from my childhood to the present time, which has not been a little, I should say they are more entitled to pity than condemnation. Some, we know, are thoroughly vicious and debased; but that the main body of them, struggling as they do, daily and hourly, with want on one hand and the allurements to vice on the other, still lean, nay, hold strongly, by "virtue's side," and cast from them temptations of which those who judge them severely know nothing, appears to me a truth so undeniable, that although my humble testimony may increase its acceptance, I cannot expect that it will add to its force.

I may, before closing this chapter, observe that the dietary of the paupers, according to my best recollection, was water porridge and milk for breakfast, and sometimes drink porridge: boiled beef and vegetables, broth, hash, pea-soup, stew, and bread for dinner; the dishes in succession, of course, or as convenience might require—the bread at dinner always. The suppers were water porridge and milk, or drink porridge, except on Sunday evenings, when each adult had a pint of good ale, with a slice round a loaf and a decent lump of cheese, served to them. The sick and very aged and infirm had bread and butter, or buttered toast, with tea or coffee, morning and evening; their dinners were cut from the neat on the governor's table. The spade-men working in the grounds had bread and cheese and ale every afternoon, and the smokers and snuff-takers were each gratified every Friday with an allowance of their favourite luxury. Married couples did not live together; they were separated; they could not be otherwise, unless a separate apartment could have been found for each family, and that was out of all question. The men, therefore, lived in the men's ward, and the women in that of the women, taking with them infants at the breast, and perhaps one of the very youngest of the children, if they had a number. The men and their wives might see and converse with each other in the day time, especially when going to or returning from their meals in the public eating room; it was not considered an offence to do so; they were not, however, to remain conversing, but to depart to their respective wards, or avocations, when the other paupers did the same.

CHAPTER VIII.
BAD HEALTH-WORSE DOCTORING—
A TIMELY RETREAT— SCHOOL, MASTERS—
THE FREE GRAMMAR SCHOOL.

I CONTINUED in a very lingering condition, and my health having been consigned to the care of the worthy apothecary, who undertook my cure with the utmost confidence, he almost finished me by continual doses of a nauseous and sickly drug, called syrup of buckthorn, which the cheerful old gentleman, whom I almost began to hate, prevailed on me by coaxing or threats to gulp down every other morning. I scarcely need to say I got no better; the physic I took, such was my disgust towards it, would have made me ill had I been in health. I had a feeling of tightness or weight upon the chest, with a lowness and weariness of mind and body, which increased as it continued; I had also an ever-present wish to be at Middleton, an earnest longing to return to what I considered my true home, and to play once more with my earliest comrades. This longing, no doubt, had more to do with my illness than either my father or the apothecary had ever dreamt of; it was, in fact, the "home-sickness" which has carried multitudes to the grave. On one fine Sunday afternoon, as I well remember, my father took me to have a walk in the country. Our course was up Strangeways, and across Cheetwood to Cheetham Hill, where, with a relish I had not experienced for a long time, I partook of bottled porter and biscuit and butter. After having rested, my father would have returned through another part of Cheetwood, but learning that the highway we were upon led to Middleton, and that the field-road to that place turned off a little further down, I prevailed on him to go past that spot, that I might once more behold the path that led to my Paradise on earth. We accordingly returned by the end of Smedley Lane, past the "Eagle and Child"—I hobbling as well as I could—and coming to Butter Stile, I prevailed on my father to go over it, and let me rest on the sweet green grass of those meadows, which to me appeared more brilliantly green than any I had seen during a long time. Here I luxuriated amongst the buttercups and daisies, and the glent of a little peeping primrose or two cast a whole stream of sunny thoughts and pleasant feelings into that happy moment. The trees seemed to wave a broader and richer foliage; the air was balmy and refreshing; the sun itself was more life-fraught than when I felt it shining against the high walls and the flagged yards of the workhouse. Here, also, were birds the very same in appearance with those I had seen at Middleton; the bonny white wren, whose nest I so often found; the golden wagtail, and the lark too, singing just as he used to do during the field rambles of myself and play mates. I was now in a happy mood, and I made known to my father how very agreeable this country walk was to me; how much better I already felt, and that I was sure I should soon be well if I might only go to Middleton for a short time. My indulgent parent listened with attention: he seemed struck for the first time, with an idea of one cause, at least, of my illness, and he promised that I should go to Middleton, as soon as he could make arrangements for my reception in the family of his sister, or that of his nephew. Blithely then did I rise from the grass, though sadly tired, and very weak. My father was not forgetful of what he had learned with respect to my illness, and the Saturday following I was committed to the care of Betty o' Booth, an old neighbour of ours who kept a shop at Middleton; she took me to the apple market, and stowed me away in a manner which, above all others, I should have chosen, namely, on a cart, amid hampers of apples, pears, and other fruit, which to me was not forbidden. By her I was safely delivered into the hands of my relatives, one of whom, a second mother, was more dear to me than all the rest, and this was Sally Owen, who had become the wife of my cousin William, before we left Middleton.

I need not dwell longer on this passage of my life than to say that the habits of this family were strictly regular, my cousin was a Methodist of the old primitive earnest cast. Every morning a portion of Scripture was read, after which followed extempore prayer. Blessing was asked and thanks returned at every meal; and the day closed with another prayer. Other concerns were transacted with the same regularity which governed the devotions; and though the family was a rather large one, everything was carried on with the exactitude of clockwork, I alone being allowed some indulgence with respect to my incomings and outgoings, for as I had a home at Betty o' Booth's, as well as here, and only the brook divided them, there was less need of my keeping a strict attention to the meal times. But though I was happy myself, enjoying former scenes and associations with relish, I found I did not inspire others with the pleasure I hoped to have done. My "trindled shirt," which lay all white and nice with the collar and ruffles on my shoulders, was a cause of envy to one or two of my comrades. Neither did my speech, which during my twelve-months' absence had become a little polished, entirely meet with their approval. "Yerthe," I could hear them whispering to each other, "Yerthe, he ses yis, an' no." Some shyness was at first caused by my altered appearance and speech, but we soon became friends, and after a month of unrestricted freedom, and of continual action in the open air, with a diet at once simple and nourishing, I returned to Manchester with roses on my cheeks and quite restored to health.

I was now sent to school, and my first essay was with a master in Hanover Street, from whom I learned nothing, save a knowledge of the severe chastisement to which he subjected his unhappy scholars when they chanced to arouse his ungoverned anger. John Holt, who kept a school near to the Methodist Chapel, in Oldham Street, was my next tutor. He was a Methodist local preacher, and opened school every morning with singing and prayer; he was a person of low stature and quick action, and wore a full-bottomed grey wig, and a "cock and pinch'd hat." I attended his instructions a considerable time, without much advancement, for, notwithstanding all he could do — and he was an industrious and ingenious teacher — I only got to spelling and reading words of one syllable; in fact, I must either have been very dull, or so taken up with play, with objects of mere feeling and impulse, that the faculty of thought and attention had remained inactive. After a time I was sent to the Free Grammar School, with the almost forlorn hope that at a place of such high repute something would be done, or would accidentally occur, to awaken my dormant faculties, if faculties at all for the acquirement of book knowledge I had. The house apothecary, who could assume a most polished address, undertook to introduce me to the respected master of the lower school, at this venerable and useful institution. All the rules and customs of such occasions the old gentleman would, of course, be careful to observe. He first, therefore, took me to a confectioner's shop in Smithy Door, where, having purchased a couple of pounds of the best gingerbread, he toddled, and I after him, across the churchyard and down Long Mill Gate, to the school; and having gained admittance, he respectfully presented me to the master, with a request, on behalf of my father, that he would be so kind as to afford me the benefit of his instruction. The master, receiving us courteously, asked what were my present requirements, also my name, age, and place of residence, which latter replies he entered in a book; and my conductor, depositing the gingerbread in a parcel on the table, together with a shilling, bowed and withdrew, leaving me abashed and confused amid the gaze and observation of the scholars, which I did not expect would be much in my favour, as I was weakly and ill-looking enough, and the more so from wearing a white linen cap, which tied under my chin. On a sign from the master a boy approached, and, taking me with one hand and the packet of gingerbread with the other, he led me to his class, which was that of the spellers, into which I was joyfully received. The boy who led me hither, and who was the head one of his class, now went round and delivered to each boy of the class sitting in his place a cake of the gingerbread, and continued so doing until the whole I had brought was distributed. This was a very acceptable introduction to the boys; it was the invariable custom of the lower school, and was always productive of a friendly greeting towards the fresh comer; for my part, in five minutes I had a score or two of new acquaintance, asking questions, giving me information, and ready to lend me a helping hand in anything, especially so long as my gingerbread was sweet in their mouths. Such was my introduction to, and thus I became the lowest scholar in the lowest class of, the Free Grammar School.

My present instructor was a gentleman of probably thirty years of age, well-formed, above the middle height, with his powdered hair turned back from his free open countenance, and his face somewhat coloured by irruptions. His dress was such as became his station, that of a curate of the Church. His coat, vest, and breeches were of fine black cloth, the latter article of dress being held below the knee by a brace of small silver buckles, his stockings were dark grey speckled, his shoes were also fastened with silver buckles, and his cravat and linen were neatly adjusted, and very white. Thus did the Reverend John Gaskell appear on that well-remembered morning when he took me under his care; such was also his general mode of dress on other ordinary occasions. The school was a large room of an oblong form, extending north and south, and well lighted by large windows. At the northern end was a fireplace, with a red cheerful fire glowing in the grate. The master's custom was to sit in an armed chair, with his right towards the fire and his left arm resting on a square oaken table, on which lay a newspaper or two, a magazine or other publication, a couple of canes with the ends split, and a medley of boy's playthings, such as tops, whips, marbles, apple-scrapers, nut-crackers, dragon banding, and such like articles. The scholars were divided into six classes, namely, accidence, or introduction to Latin, higher Bible, middle Bible, lower Bible, Testament, and spelling classes: the accidence class sat opposite the master's face, and the higher Bible one was at his back. Each class sat on a strong oaken bench, backed by a panel of the same, placed against the wall, with a narrow desk in front, so that all sat around the school in regular gradation. The spellers only had not a desk, they sat on forms outside the desk of the higher Bible class, they being considered as children amongst the boys. The boys of each class were placed according to their proficiency, and the first and second boys of the class exercised considerable authority over the others. The school hours were from seven to half-past eight at morning, from half-past nine to twelve at noon, and from two till five afternoon. The master was seldom more than five minutes beyond the time, and on coming in, he first pulled off his hat, and his extra coat or handkerchief, if he brought such; he would then probably give his hands a warming at the fire, stamp the wet from his shoes, and turning his back to the pleasant warmth, he would take a survey of the muster already arrived. Every boy who now entered the school was bound to go up to the table and present his shoulders for a correction, and they in general got off with a slight cut or two of the cane, except frequent defaulters, and those were hit more severely, being often sent to their class writhing, to the amusement of their more orderly comrades. The mustering and flogging being over, the classes were severally called up, arranged round the table, and went through their lessons, the boy who in spelling or reading could readiest make out a word when those above him were at fault, moving up to their places, and thus the quickest spellers and readers were always towards the upper end of their class. When a boy had been at the head of his class some time, and especially if he happened to have some acquaintance amongst those of the next class above him, and they wished to have him amongst them, their head boy would take him by the hand, and leading him to the master, would say, "If you please, sir, must — (mentioning the surname) go into my class?" when a brief intimation, as a nod, a "yes," or "no," would decide the application, and the parties withdrew either elated with success or abashed by failure. The boys of the accidence class had a singular, I may say an anomalous, privilege at this school. Betwixt their lessons, and when, as one might suppose they should have been, studying their books for another lesson, they were allowed, two or three at a time, to perambulate round the school, in front of the other boys, when if they saw any one playing with a top or a ball, or other trifle, or showing one to a comrade, the privileged scholar would seize it and deposit it on the master's table; or if the boy who had it were more than a match for the other, he would inform the master that so and so was at play with a top, or other thing, when the offender would be called up, compelled to lay down the toy, and would perhaps get a cut or two with the cane for his contumacy. These articles of plunder lay on the master's table until the school broke up, when, the moment the master put on his hat and stepped towards the door, the boys being previously all ready for a start, a rush was made from every corner of the school, a regular scramble ensued, and he who could fasten on a prize and keep it had it for his pains. Thursday and Saturday afternoons were play-times, and at Easter, Whitsuntide, and Christmas we had holidays of longer duration. Such were the customs of the lower department of the Free Grammar School, and the manner of conducting it at that time. What were the systems of the middle and upper schools—which were in other parts of the same building—I never knew, and consequently cannot describe. I may as well say, however, that it was understood amongst the scholars that the system of the lower school, with all its irregularities, was such as had prevailed a long time, and that our instructor was not at liberty to depart from it in any material degree.

At that time the Rev. Joshua Brookes[4] lived at the house adjoining the school. He was not a very great favourite with the scholars, or with any one that I ever heard tell of, though, excepting a little uncontrollable irritability of temper, I never knew why he should not have been so. His father, however, was still less esteemed than himself.[5] He was a little old deformed cripple, with his features as crumpled and knitted as if he were a living alegar cruet. His up-cast face was a clear healthy brown, and on his head he wore a little old round hat, with a broad girdle and buckle in front of it. His knees were rigid, and his legs were doubled backward, so that when he stood upright he was on his knees; and in that posture, with a pair of short crutches under his arms, his knees protected by thick leathern sockets, and the toes of his buckled shoes by plates of brass, he used to hobble about the streets, dragging his feet after him. On fine sunny days he would often be sitting at his son's door, when woe to the boy at play who chanced unthinkingly to get within the reach of his crutch, especially if at any former time the youth had not treated him with that respect which he thought was his due.

My especial companions amid the varied crowd of these scholars were John Pilkington, son to the clerk at the old church; Jim Torkington, whose parents kept a hat shop in Church Street; Dick France, whose father kept the "Sir John Falstaff," in the Market Place; Henry Woodhouse, whose father kept the "Bull's Head"; and Dick Lyon, the occupation of whose father I have forgotten. Jim Torkington I respected because I had beaten him once and he did not get me flogged as he might have done. Henry Woodhouse was agreeable, being always willing to do as the others did. Dick Lyon, with his bold, honest face, would undertake anything, and stand by any cause that I did. He it was also who first got me advanced in the school by "asking" me from the spelling into the Testament class; and poor Dick France I was partial to because I thought he was rather severely treated, being flogged more than any other boy in the school, not because he was more vicious than other boys, but because he was more thoughtless and unlucky — inattentive, not having the power to be

---

[4] An eccentric but learned divine and chaplain of the "Old Church," in which capacity he is said to have baptised, married, and buried more persons than any other clergyman in the kingdom.

[5] An eccentric but learned divine and chaplain of the "Old Church," in which capacity he is said to have baptised, married, and buried more persons than any other clergyman in the kingdom.

otherwise, and continually in scrapes for which others deserved the punishment. He was a fine, good-looking lad, however, as brave as he was thoughtless, and as kind-hearted as he was brave. Many and many were the rambles I took with this gang on our holiday afternoons. Cheetwood, Kersall, Crumpsall, and Broughton, were most frequently the see scenes of our wanton frolics — our runnings, and leapings, and tumblings, and boxings. For in those hilarious outbreaks we were all life, laughter, and kindly joke. The sweet breath of the earth, coming up through the sod, we felt and inhaled, as we rolled over each other amongst the flowers: then the gusty wind blew our wild hair into each other's faces; when the sun broke we sung aloud; when the rain came we uncovered our dewy foreheads to cool them with the welcome drops. Then there was bird's-nesting to be done, and stick-cutting, and flower-culling, and earth-nut digging, and cress-gathering, — and when gnawing hunger came, as it did full soon, we sat down by the first clear rindle or dimpling spring that fell in our way, and each one pulling out his store of eatables, we fell to and feasted as joyously as if our fathers were the kings of those sweet solitudes.

Sometimes I and my companions would visit the "Giant's Castle" at Castle Field, after which we generally made the afternoon away by watching the boats on the Duke's Canal, or rambling around Hulme Hall, or on the dangerous brink of the Irwell, leaping like young kids. The remains of the ancient fortress at Castle Field embraced a level plot of ground almost of a circular form: the turf was quite smooth, and the grass where not trodden was very green. The centre of the plot was lower than the circuit, along which, here and there, might be seen grey stones and lumps of mortar. In one part of the area was a spot elevated above the rest, a small green mount, and around this also at intervals, foundations and ruins were seen jutting above the surface. But even these small remains of old Mancenion, hoary in tradition of untold years, are not now to be found.

Sometimes we would spend an hour or two in going through the College (the Old Baron's Hall), in playing in the pump-yard above the Irk, here all sadly metamorphosed and defiled; and in ever-recurring astonishment at the vast length and bulk which the fish must have been, which opened and shut — awful idea — the huge jaw-bones which spanned the arch of the eastern gateway. Or we would climb the tower of the old church when the bells were ringing a peal, and the more daring would grasp a comrade's hand and stand upon the edge of the parapet, the steeple vibrating at the time almost like a stout oak in a breeze. This feat was done by more than one of our party; and in truth, if there were a place to which we ought not to have gone, or a feat we ought not to have attempted, to that place we were nearly sure to stray, and that exploit was almost certain to be tried.

And now, as is often the case, for the most important thing last, namely, my progress in learning at this celebrated school. When I entered the school, as already stated, I was one of the spelling class, and when the day for, general promotion came at Christmas I was the first scholar in the first Bible-class, and consequently was the first English speller and reader in the school. I first discovered that I had made some progress in learning one Sunday morning at home, when conning, as usual, a chapter in the Testament, I unexpectedly found that I could read slowly verse after verse, almost without spelling a word. This was a joyful event to me; I read to my father when he came into the room; I read to the old apothecary, and the latter, patting me on the head, gave me a silver sixpence, and encouraged me to get on with my learning. I had some time before made myself master of the awful tale of "Brown, Jones, and Robinson," in the spelling-book, but then I had only got through it by the help of numerous spellings; whereas, now, being able to read, I had almost continually the Testament in my hand. I read all the wondrous accounts in the Revelation, and my father, not a little pleased, would at times sit down, and in his way explain the meaning of the strange things about which I read. After I had gone through the Revelation, I began with the Gospel of St. Matthew, and was deeply interested by the miracles, sufferings, and death of our Lord. The New Testament was now my story book, and I read it all through and through, but more for the interest the marvellous passages excited, than from any religious impression which they created. The gentle and benign character of Christ filled me with admiration and awe: His sufferings excited my deepest sympathy, His persecutors my strongest hatred, and I only wished that Peter had chopped off one side of Judas's head, instead of merely cropping "the servant of the high priest's" ear.

And now a wider range was opened to my assiduous quest after the wonderful. At the corner of Hanging Bridge, near the old Church yard, was a book shop kept by one Swindells, a printer. In the spacious windows of this shop, which is now "The Wedding-Ring" coffee-house, were exhibited numerous songs, ballads, tales, and other publications, with horrid and awful-looking woodcuts at the head; which publications, with their cuts, had a strong command on my attention. Every farthing I could scrape together was now spent in purchasing histories of "Jack the Giant Killer," "Saint George and the Dragon," "Tom Hickathrift," "Jack and the Beanstalk," "The Seven Champions of Christendom," tale of "Fair Rosamond," "History of Friar Bacon," "Account of the Lancashire Witches," "The Witches of the Woodlands," and such like romances, whilst my metrical collections embraced but few pieces besides "Robin Hood's Songs" and "The Ballad of Chevy Chase." Of all these tales and ballads I was soon master, and they formed the subjects of many a long study to me, and of many a wonder-creating story for my acquaintance both at the workhouse and elsewhere. For my part I implicitly believed them all, and when told by my father or others that they were "trash" and "nonsense," and "could not be true," I, innocently enough, contrasted their probability with that of other wondrous things which I had read in books that "it were a sin to disbelieve." So I continued reading, and doubting nothing which I read, until many years after, when a more extended acquaintance with men and books taught me how better to discriminate betwixt reason and unreason, truth and falsehood. When I first plunged, as it were, into the blessed habit of reading, faculties which had hitherto given but small intimation of existence, suddenly sprung into vigorous action. My mind was ever desiring more of the silent but exciting conversation with books, and of whatever was conveyed to it from that source, small was the portion that did not remain. My attention was quick, and my memory was very retentive of what I read.

Whilst I thus made myself acquainted with the New Testament, the Bible, and all the other books that fell in my way, the day had come round when, previous to the Christmas holidays, a general promotion took place of such scholars as were qualified for higher classes, and I being the first boy in the first English class, should have been promoted to the "accidence." But, alas! when called upon I could only inform the master, with blushes on my cheeks and tears in my eyes, that my father did not wish me to go into the Latin class at present, but desired that I might remain in the class to which I then belonged. My master, I can recollect, looked at me incredulously; studied, questioned me again, and, with an expression of disappointment, motioned that I should return to my place. This was a sore humiliation to me. My comrades Pilkington, Woodhouse, and others, passed over to the Latin side, whilst I remained in a class lower than theirs, and consequently stood in a situation inferior to that of those whom I had been in the habit of leading. Henceforward I thought meanly of my position, and never glanced at my former comrades without a feeling which lowered the zest of my future school-life.

This as it regarded my welfare was probably the most momentous and ill-advised step which my father could have determined upon. Had the threshold of the classics been once crossed by me, great must have been the difficulties indeed which would have prevented me from making the whole of that ancient lore my own. I was just at the right age, and in the right frame of mind, with faculties as it were newly come to life, and with an instructor who I have since had many reasons for supposing would have done all he could towards helping me forward into the upper schools; and, had I once got fairly introduced to the learning of the ancients I should not have stopped short on this side of the university I think. But my father had more humble views, founded on serious and conscientious reasons I have no doubt. He said Latin should be learned by such only as were intended to become doctors, or lawyers, or parsons; and as I should never be any of these, the time spent in learning it would only be thrown away. A knowledge of English grammar, he said, was worth more than Greek or Latin to an Englishman, and he wondered why, in the name of goodness, English grammar was not taught at this English grammar school; and so he concluded he would not buy me an "accidence." Such were the homely views and the determination resulting from them, which kept me at my English rudiments another year, and thrust me from that portal of knowledge which I never afterwards had an opportunity of approaching. Had my mother been living, such would probably not have been the case, and a course of life, far different from the one I have pursued, would have been marked out before me.

CHAPTER IX.
ANOTHER GREAT CHANGE.

MEANTIME Mr. Rose, the schoolmaster at the workhouse, died, and his place was filled by a Mr. Pickering, who, like his predecessor, had been in business and failed. Mr. Pickering was about fifty years of age, a quick and rather haughty kind of man, who endeavoured to maintain a remnant of the authoritative manner of his former state, though it was greatly out of place in the situation he then occupied. My father, I recollect, was under the necessity of setting him right once or twice, after which, as he came round to understand his position better, he was not an unpleasant associate. His wife had died some time before, leaving him two children, a son and a daughter, to provide for. The latter, who was a sweet-looking, affectionate young woman, probably from sixteen to eighteen years of age, lived in the family of a Mr. Richardson, who kept a large glass and china shop at the top of Smithy Door: and the son, Samuel, who was a fine lad about my own age, and had a great resemblance of his sister, came to live with his father at the workhouse. Sam and I were, of course, inseparable companions; we ate together, and when not at school, played together from morning to night. He was as great a blockhead in books as I had ever been, and in our walks outside the gates, which were not unfrequent, I read to him my twopenny histories, and narrated all my stories, until he was as great an enthusiast as myself. At length, "Robinson Crusoe," that ever exciting day-dream of boys, fell in our way. I read it to him, as I had done the others, and for a long time both Sam's ideas and mine were awed and fascinated by the descriptions of sea-dangers, shipwrecks, and lone islands with savages, and far-off countries teeming with riches and plenty. In a field close to the gates was a large and deep reservoir of water which accumulated from a small rindle which came through the wood I have before mentioned, and supplied the extensive brewery below, which afterwards belonged to Messrs. Fray, Hole, and Potter. In one part of this reservoir was a small island covered with willows and other shrubs, and Sam and I had often explored this island when the water was sufficiently low for us to wade it — our reward being sometimes a couple or so of duck-eggs. We had also taken a goodly number of fish, chiefly perch and bream, with which we stored a circular pond in the garden of the workhouse. Now, however, we assumed other characters than those of mere idling schoolboys: we were henceforth "Robinson Crusoe," and his "Man Friday." The cock-clod was our "desert island"; the brushwood was our means of concealment; the duck-eggs and the fish were as much our lawful right as was anything which Crusoe possessed in his place of solitude; we had "savages" also, whose "footprints" made us pause and look around; those savages being the men from the brewery, who sometimes discovering us when they came up to let off the water, gave us chase and made us carry our heels quickly towards the wood. Nor were we without our perils and "shipwrecks"; for getting some old planks and a split board or two, we made a raft, on which, whenever we found it necessary to "go on a voyage," we paddled the length or breadth of this our "ocean," often getting ashore, only just at the time when our timbers were dispersing, and our craft was "a total wreck." Poor Sam! I had a great affection for him. I sometimes went with him to see his sister; and I could perceive that she was not at ease, for her employer looked very crusty when he found her otherways employed than in dusting glasses or arranging china. Both Sam and his sister often shed tears at parting after their brief interviews. He stopped not long at the workhouse; his father, I think, sickened and died there. But however it was, Sam went to sea, and in a voyage or two news came that he was lost. I was years and could not believe that he was dead. I had a notion that he had been sold to slavery in some foreign land, and would certainly return. But poor Sam never came back again; he was lost sure enough.

It must have been about this time that I was taken to see that unfortunate youth, George Russel, pass through Manchester, on his way to the place of execution at Newton Heath. The impression left by that sad spectacle will never be eradicated from my mind, unless reason fail.[6]

My father, judging it expedient, as I suppose, to enter again into the married state, took to wife a widow with four children, who earned a frugal livelihood by doing needlework for saddlers. Her children were three sons and one daughter, and the oldest son was at sea in the African slave trade. After this event, the business of the workhouse was conducted in a less agreeable manner than it had heretofore been betwixt my father and the governess. It is only reasonable to suppose that my father had been induced to take this decided step by the persuasion that his wife would fill the situation held by Mrs. Rose; he probably had some grounds for a supposition of that kind; promises and pledges to that effect were probably given by the parish officers, or some influential portion of them, but however that might be, disagreements betwixt my father and the governess became of almost daily occurrence. Crimination and recrimination followed; the parish officers became partizans in the dispute; we children were sent away—my sister to a friend in town, and I and my brother to our relations at Middleton. From that time I never resided with my father, and soon after both he and Mrs. Rose were discharged from their situations.

My father had lost a wife, a brother, two children, and nearly his own life and that of a third child, in the service of the township of Manchester; and though, as I have good reasons for supposing, no valid impeachment was made against either his capacity or his integrity, he got nothing by way of "indemnity," when a party in the town's office thought fit to dispense with his services. There was no "retiring pension" for him; no "compensation" for his irreparable losses. If this was scarcely just towards himself, as an individual, it was still less so towards his children who were turned into the world, "shorn to the quick"; fatherless now, as well as motherless; for in most essential matters he was no longer a guardian to them. Two

---

[6] See "Passages in the Life of a Radical."

of the three never afterwards had a home under the same roof with him.

It was a cold winter's afternoon when my brother and I, with our bundles under our arms, took our way up Red Bank on the road to Middleton. We had been instructed to keep on the high road, for there had been a heavy fall of snow followed by a strong wind, and the snow was now drifting in clouds. Over Cheetham Hill we hobbled along, knocking the thick snow-clogs from our shoes, our hands thrust into our pockets, and our jackets buttoned up to the chin. Coming to the summit of Bowker Bank, where the wind swept fast and cold, I asked my brother why he kept wiping his eyes? He said it was only the snow he was wiping off, but I knew better, and though not exactly in a joyous mood myself, I endeavoured to rally him out of his gloomy bodings of the future.

It was towards the close of the day when we arrived at the house of my uncle William, which was in High Street in the town mentioned. We presented a letter from my father, and were received with kindness by the worthy couple, whilst their three children looked on us with a bashful and pleased reserve. We joined the circle at their homely meal, and my uncle and aunt not having convenience for lodging us, we were accommodated temporarily at the house of another relative.

The row of houses in which my uncle lived faced the morning sun; a neatly paved footpath, and a causey for carts, lay in front of the houses from one end of the row to the other; and separated from the houses by the causey and footpath was a large green, used as a playground. My uncle's domicile, like all the others, consisted of one principal room called "the house"; on the same floor with this was a loom-shop capable of containing four looms, and in the rear of the house on the same floor, were a small kitchen and a buttery. Over the house and loom-shop were chambers; and over the kitchen and buttery was another small apartment, and a flight of stairs. The whole of the rooms were lighted by windows of small square panes, framed in lead, in good condition; those in the front being protected by shutters. The interior of this dwelling showed that cleanly and comfortable appearance which is always to be seen where a managing Englishwoman is present. There were a dozen good rush-bottomed chairs, the backs and rails bright with wax and rubbing; a handsome clock in mahogany case; a good chest of oaken drawers; a mahogany snap-table; a mahogany corner cupboard, all well polished; besides tables, weather-glass, cornice, and ornaments; pictures illustrative of Joseph and his Brethren, and various other articles indicative of a regard for convenience as well as ornament. And though last enumerated, not the least to be regarded by a hungry youth of my age, was a large bread-flake well stored with oaten cakes.

My uncle's family consisted of himself, my aunt (Elizabeth), their son Thomas, and their two daughters Hannah and Dolly. Thomas was a rather thoughtful and clever lad, a year or two older than myself; Hannah was a neat, good-looking girl of my own age; and Dolly was a fair, delicate, and sadly spoiled child. My aunt, that sister of my father whom I have before mentioned, was rather tall for a woman; dark complexioned, middle aged, somewhat corpulent, fresh coloured, intelligent looking, and with an arch and penetrating manner of conversation. She took snuff, wore a mob-cap, a bed-gown, a stiff pair of stays which stood out at the bosom, a warm woollen petticoat, white knitted hose, and shoes with patten clogs to keep her feet warm. She was asthmatical; and consequently often in delicate health, but as her chief employment was to sit at the wheel winding bobbins for the weavers, her complaint was less embarrassing than it would have been had she been necessitated to do the heavy drudgery of the house, much of which her daughter Hannah performed. My uncle was of the middle height, rather corpulent, about fifty years of age, good looking, a quiet, sententious, equable tempered man, who took his work, his meals, his pipe, and his repose regularly, and seldom troubled himself about affairs out of his own house. Not but he had opinions and wishes, both religious and political, and they were all on the right liberal side, but he did not make a parade of them. He was both in theory and practice a Christian patriot of the old, simple, unpretending class, who not being gifted with a multiplicity of words, gave lessons to his family by example. His mind was, I believe, as intentionless of wilful offence as that of an infant; but he possessed a sturdy resistance to wrong or menace, which would have verily held him to be martyred sooner than give way. This worthy couple were Methodists of the old John Wesley caste, which prevailed in those days; their children were brought up in the same religious tenets, and with this family of humble but respectable condition my lot was cast thus once more in the place of my birth.

CHAPTER X.
A NEW LIFE.

MY brother was now set down to the loom at once, whilst my employment was to fetch milk every morning, to run to the well for water when wanted, to go errands generally, and to assist my aunt at times in the bobbin-winding department—all of which suited my disposition and habits most pleasingly, except the latter piece of bondage, which on account of its monotonous confinement soon became abhorrent to my feelings; and had not my frequent escapades in the way of errand running allowed me many sweet snatches of freedom my situation would have been far from happy.

In the performance of my task of fetching home the milk every morning I soon became acquainted with several children of my own age who attended the same place on the same errand. During my loitering perambulations to and from Hollin Lane, where the milk-house was, I had sometimes the attendance of two or three such companions, who caught every word I spoke, as I described the strange things to be seen at Manchester, and the still more wondrous ones of which I had read, and which accounts I was quite sure were true. But soon my most constant attendant on these occasions was a little smiling, rosy-cheeked child, who was almost certain to be found standing alone by the highway side, or loitering slowly until I appeared. I took not any particular notice of the girl; I was a tall, straight, pale-looking boy, whilst she appeared to me nothing more than a kind of little human cherry-bud, who was always the first to join my company, and the last to leave it.

At the milk-house we often found an assemblage of a dozen married women, two or three young ones, an old man or two, and some half-score or so of children, all come on the like errand as ourselves, and waiting until the milk arrived. Meantime there would be some snatches of scandal turned over—sly insinuations respecting "this body's character" and "that body's conduct." Some would treat themselves and neighbours to snuff; others would take a whiff or so of tobacco, "just to keep the wind off," whilst the woman of the house, "Owd Beet wife," sat croning at her wheel, and her daughter, a flashy lass, was on her loom weaving napkins, and singing love ditties like a nightingale. When the milk arrived, all the persons waiting surrounded it, and there was much pressing and entreating to be served early by those who were impatient; at such times I was often useful to my little cherry-bud, and my other youthful companions, in making a way for them through the crowd, and when they had got served with milk they would retire, and wait until I joined them; and then we all returned together, interchanging our childish observations as before. But the little cherry-bud was nearly always on the road with me, going and coming, whilst I had the company of the others only incidentally.

Her name was Jemima, but I knew her only by that of Mima, and by that alone shall I distinguish her. Like myself she lived with an uncle and aunt, who had taken charge of her when only an infant. What I was virtually also, she was in reality, an orphan, and when I became aware of her condition in that respect, I felt a greater interest in whatever concerned her — I was more desirous of pleasing her, and of rendering her any little service which lay in my power. Nor was she indifferent to anything which affected me; when in moments of sadness I sometimes reverted to my mother's well-remembered fondness, or the kindness of my uncle Thomas, or to my father's tender regard, whose absence I deeply felt, and whom I now seldom saw, she, who had never known either father or mother, would often be moved until her full heart overflowed from her eyes. She became a very agreeable and always welcome companion on the road — a child to whom, because she had no parents, I felt bound to be kind, but nothing more.

The mode of living at my uncle's was of the simplest country style. At breakfast, a brown earthen dish being placed on a low beaufet[7] near the middle of the floor, a boiling of water porridge was poured into the dish, hot from the pan. A messpot of the same material as the dish was placed for each one about to partake of the breakfast, a quantity of milk and a spoon were placed in each pot, my uncle took a seat and asked a blessing, each of the children of the family standing around; we then took our several messes of milk, and helped ourselves to the steaming porridge as quickly as we chose, and mixing and eating in the manner we liked best, not a word being spoken all the time. The porridge being scraped up, which they[8] in general were rather quickly, each would take a piece of hard oaten cake and eat it to the remainder of his milk, after which a little butter, or a small piece of cheese, with more oaten bread, would finish the meal, and in a few minutes work was resumed. My aunt would shortly after make her appearance, her face red, and herself distressed with coughing; the kettle would then be set on for her, and when the asthmatic paroxysm had sufficiently abated she took her breakfast and sat down to her wheel. Our dinners consisted generally of butcher's meat and potatoes, or potato-pie, or meat and broth, or barm dumplings, or drink porridge, or hasty pudding, and in each case the food was partaken in the same primitive manner. When we had meat and potatoes each had an allowance of the meat on a piece of oat-cake, and the potatoes being poured into a dish placed on the beaufet as before, we all stood round, and with spoon or knife, as we chose, ate from the dish so long as the potatoes lasted, after which we stole out to play, eating our remnant of butcher's meat and cake the while. There was not a word heard until we got out of doors, and then we were as noisy as others. When we had potato-pie for dinner an allowance of the crust was given to each; the potatoes were then eaten out of the dish as before, and the crust, as being the most dainty, was eaten afterwards. When we had broth each received a mess for himself, to which he added as much oaten cake as he chose; the potatoes were eaten out of the dish, and the meat being served in portions, each ate it with cake at his leisure. When we had dumplings they were

---

[7] A low three-legged stool, called in the north buffet-stool.
[8] Porridge used to be described in the plural number.

set on the beaufet in the same brown dish, or one of the sort; a little dip was made from the water the dumplings had been boiled in, a lump of butter and a little sugar or treacle being added; the dip was then poured upon the dumplings, and we fell to and ate as we liked, the only restriction being that there was not to be any talking at meat. How different was this sententious and becoming manner at table from the one which now prevails around fashionable boards, where, if a person cannot, or will not, both gabble and gobble at the same time, he is looked upon as vulgar, and where the highest test of good breeding is to keep both chin and tongue — the latter especially — in motion, it matters not on what subject if it only elicit not a thought. Such is one of the puerilities by which insane pride seeks to be distinguished from the thoughtful and earnest portion of society. Our bagging, or afternoon lunch, consisted of half an oaten cake, with butter, treacle, cheese, or milk, as circumstances rendered most convenient, and our supper was generally the same as breakfast. On Sunday mornings we had mint or balm tea, sweetened with treacle, and oaten cake and butter; on Sunday afternoons we had tea of the same kind, and a slice of buttered loaf was added, which was an especial dainty.

CHAPTER XI.
SCHOOLING—CORRECTION—PRAYER.

AT this time the Methodists of Middleton kept a Sunday school in their chapel at Bottom of Barrowfields, and this school we young folks all attended. I was probably a far better speller and reader than any teacher in the place, and I had not gone there very long when I was set to writing. I soon mastered the rudimental lines, and quitting "pot-hooks and ladles," as they were called, I commenced writing "large-hand." For the real old Arminian Methodists, the immediate descendants of the Wesleys, the Nelsons, and the Taylors, thought it no desecration of the Sabbath to enable the rising generation on that day to write the Word of God as well as to read it. Had the views and very commendable practice of these old fathers been continued in Sunday schools generally, the reproach would not have been cast upon our labouring population, as it was on the publication of the census of 1841, that a greater proportion of the working classes of Lancashire were unable to write their names than were to be found in several counties less favoured by means of instruction. The modern Methodists may boast of this feat as their especial work. The Church party never undertook to instruct in writing on Sundays; the old Arminian Wesleyans did undertake it, and succeeded wonderfully, but the Conferential Methodists put a stop to it; other religious bodies, if I am not mistaken, did the same, and in 1841 it was a matter of surprise to many that our working population was behind that of other counties in the capability of writing names. Let the honour of this stoppage be assumed by those who have earned it, by the "ministers of religion," so called, generally, and by those of the Conferential Methodists especially.

Every Sunday morning at half-past eight o'clock was this old Methodists school open for the instruction of whatever child crossed its threshold. A hymn was first led out and sung by the scholars and teachers. An extempore prayer followed, all the scholars and teachers kneeling at their places; the classes, ranging from those of the spelling-book to those of the Bible, then commenced their lessons, girls in the gallery above, and boys below. Desks which could either be moved up or down, like the leaf of a table, were arranged all round the school, against the walls of the gallery, as well as against those below, and at measured distances the walls were numbered. Whilst the Bible and Testament classes were reading their first lesson the desks were got ready, inkstands and copy-books numbered, containing copies and pens, were placed opposite corresponding numbers on the wall; and when the lesson was concluded the writers took their places, each at his own number, and so continued their instruction. When the copy was finished, the book was shut and left on the desk, a lesson of spelling was gone through, and at twelve o'clock singing and prayer again took place, and the scholars were dismissed. At one o'clock there was service in the chapel, and soon after two the school reassembled, girls now occupying the writing desks, as boys had done in the forenoon, and at four or half-past the scholars were sent home for the week.

My readers will expect hearing that the school was well attended, and it was so, not only by children and youths of the immediate neighbourhood, but by young men and women from distant localities. Big collier lads and their sisters from Siddal Moor were regular in their attendance. From the borders of Whittle, from Bowlee, from the White Moss, from Jumbo, and Chadderton, and Thornham, came groups of boys and girls with their substantial dinners tied in clean napkins, and the little chapel was so crowded that when the teachers moved they had to wade, as it were, through the close-ranked youngsters.

My father having been appointed to the situation of governor of the workhouse of Salford, with his wife as governess, I was placed as a half-day scholar under the tuition of the Rev. James Archer, at the Middleton Free Grammar School. I soon began to improve in writing. This indulgence of schooling lasted, however, only during a very brief space, for my aunt, in consequence of her own ill-health, becoming more and more exacting in the hateful drudgery of the bobbin-wheel, I was not able to perform my allotted task in time for school attendance, which, therefore, soon became irregular, and was next discontinued.

As before intimated, my connection with this school was brief, and then, with the exception of Bible lessons at the Sunday school, all my reading was done at home, after the daily task was finished. When not strongly tempted to play I was almost certain to be reading by the summer's twilight, or by the red embers of the winter's fire, my books being chiefly " Wesley's Journals," and " The Arminian Magazine," wherein I found "Maundrell's Travels from Aleppo to Jerusalem," which I was very much interested by; "An Account of the Inquisition in Spain," which filled me with a dislike of Popery; "The Drummer of Tedworth;" "Some Account of the Disturbances at Glenluce;" "An Account of the Apparition of the Laird of Cool"— and other most marvellous narratives, which excited my attention, and held me poring over the ashes until the light was either gone or I was sent to bed. I also got hold of an old superstitious doctoring book, which gave me some unexpected information relative to the human frame, and equally surprised me as to the occult powers of certain herbs and simples, when prepared under supposed planetary aspects. A copy of Cocker's Arithmetic soon after set me to writing figures and casting accounts, in which I made but slow progress; and part of a small volume of "The History of England," which I found in rummaging an old meal ark, gave me the first insight into the chronicles of my native country.

Whilst my life at the bobbin-wheel was wretched on account of the confinement, my poor old aunt had generally a sad time with me. It was scarcely to be expected that a tall, straight, round-limbed young ruffian like myself, with bare legs and feet, bare neck, and a head equally denuded, save by a crop of thick coarse hair, should sit day by day twirling a wheel and guiding a thread; his long limbs cramped and doubled under a low wooden stool. For I may observe that the clothes with which I left Manchester having been worn out, I went in the week-days of summer time never hosed, and but scantily draped, except Sundays, when a decent suit was at my service. I accordingly at times, from a sheer inability to sit still, played all kind of pranks, and threw myself into all kinds of attitudes, keeping my wheel going the while, lest my aunt should have it to say I was playing and neglecting my task. I generally sat near her at work, and I must confess that I sometimes exhibited these antics from a wish to provoke rather than amuse my observant and somewhat irritable overseer. On these occasions I frequently got a rap on the head from a weaver's rod which my aunt would have beside her, whereupon I would move out of her reach and continue "marlockin" until I got either more correction, or was despatched on an errand, or banished into the "loom-house " amongst the weavers. Then, when my uncle went into the house to smoke his pipe, which he generally did in the forenoon and afternoon, my aunt half diverted, half provoked, would give him the history of my pranks and my "flitting," as she would call it, when he would laugh until tears filled his eyes, or his pipe snapped in twain — for he used to sit quite at his ease, with the tube pendant from his mouth — and on his returning to his loom, he would admonish me sharply, or more commonly would question me as to the cause of the rupture — pretending not to know about it, — and would conclude by advising me to be submissive to my aunt, and by all means to keep on good terms with the Mistress of the house wherever I dwelt. I was certainly so good tempered and cheerful they scarcely could be long displeased with me for all my faults, and so these little darkenings passed like cloud spots, and presently all was bright again. The most serious rupture which I had with my aunt was occasioned by an act of wilful disobedience on my part. She dealt out to me a certain number of hanks and cops which I was to have wound by "bagging-time," in the afternoon, or beaten I certainly should be. I sat at my wheel and made not any reply, determining not to wind them, as I thought the task unreasonable, and that she was, in this instance, acting arbitrarily. I continued, therefore, to turn the wheel very deliberately, indeed, rather carelessly, until the time appointed had expired, when my aunt, laying hold of a stout rod, began to lay it upon my back and across my shoulders, which she did until she was spent for breath, I but little flinching all the time; she seemed rather puzzled by my coolness, whilst I was equally diverted by her embarrassment; at length, being quite exhausted, she stood looking at me with an air of vexation, and suddenly began to hit me on the legs, which set me a capering, and made me run out of the house, and remain away until the storm was blown over. With a determination to incur the beating, and a knowledge that I should have it, I had got two thin boards, part of an orange box, which I put under my waistcoat, so as to cover each shoulder blade, and buttoning waistcoat and jacket over them, I was well encased against my poor aunt's weak blows, so long as they were applied to the defended parts. My comical expedient caused more suppressed laughter in the family than anger; and when I returned into the house again, looking rather dolorous of course, I could perceive that my aunt had got quite enough of the beating as well as myself, whilst my uncle at his next smoking bout, — I being banished as usual into the loom-shop, where I could see but not hear him, — sat and laughed until his corpulent frame shook as if he would have fallen out of his chair, and then he came to his work without reprimanding me.

About this time I had a sincere desire to become religious; and I earnestly prayed, in my way, that God would awaken me to a strong sense of my "sinful and lost state," and would make me cry out as in agony for my "manifold transgressions"— amongst which losing my Bible once, when I went a bee-hunting instead of coming home from school, covert disobedience to my uncle and aunt, and carelessness after prayer, were to me the most prominent. I wished, like Saul, to be convinced and converted whether or not; to be "arrested in my career " by an irresistible arm, for I felt almost certain that if I never forsook sin until I did so voluntarily, and from my very heart, there was great danger of my never doing so. I was as sincere, however, as I could be—as I well knew how to be, and often I expected to have "a call," like my name-sake of old, when I would reply, "Lord! Thy servant heareth." But there was no call for me; my obdurate heart remained "unbroken by the hammer of the word," and somehow it happened that my longest and most fervent prayers were made on my visits to the little chamber upstairs, when instead of being on my knees, I ought to have been looking out cops and hanks to wind for my weavers. Thus it was, I would have either sung, or prayed, or I believe, I should have done any other thing, sinful or devout, that would have kept me from the hated wheel. I came to the conclusion that God never did nor ever would take the trouble to convince one of my condition, and that there was no religion in the world that could ever make a bobbin-winder content with his lot; — and so ended, at that time, my efforts for obtaining grace.

CHAPTER XII.
A HOME-BEARING, A DINNER, AND
A MASTER INDEED.

AS I was getting rather too unmanageable for my aunt at the bobbin-wheel, fortunately in this respect for both her and myself, my brother went to reside at Manchester, and a vacancy thus occurring on one of the looms, I was transferred to it, and became a weaver. At the Sunday school also I was promoted from being a scholar to a ruler of copybooks, a cutter of pens, and an attendant generally on the writers; one of whom being Mima, "the little cherry-bud," I took care she should always have a clean copy and a new pen. She had become a frequent visitor at our house, and a close companion to my cousin Hannah, who for some time had slept with her at her uncle's. Having now become an active lad, and, from my good temper and willingness to perform any service, now that the abhorrent wheel was not in the way, had made some advances into the kindly feelings of my aunt and uncle, I was at times chosen to assist the latter when he took the work home to Manchester. The family were, at that time, chiefly employed by Messrs. Samuel and James Broadbent, of Cannon Street, and as the work was for the most part "pollicat" and " "romoll" handkerchiefs, with a finer reed, occasionally, of silk and cotton "garments," or handkerchiefs, the "bearing-home wallet" was often both bulky and heavy; and when it happened to be too much so for one person to carry, a neighbour's wallet would be borrowed, the burden divided into two, and I would go with one part over my shoulder, behind or before my uncle. He being, as already stated, rather heavy in person would walk deliberately, with a stick in his hand, his green woollen apron twisted round his waist, his clean shirt showing at the open breast of his waistcoat, his brown silk handkerchief wrapped round his neck, a quid of tobacco in his mouth, and a broad and rather slouched hat on his head. So would he appear when setting out on a "bearing-home" journey; whilst I, with my smaller wallet, with my rough jacket, my knee breeches, my strong stockings and shoes, my open collared shirt, and pleasure and glee in my heart and countenance, footed the way as lightsomely as a young colt.

The warehouse of Messrs. Broadbent was nearly at the top of Cannon Street, on the right-hand side. We mounted some steps, went along a covered passage, and up a height or two of stairs, to a landing place, one side of which was railed off by the bannister, and the other furnished with a seat for weavers to rest upon when they arrived. Here we should probably find some half-dozen weavers and winders, waiting for their turn to deliver in their work and to receive fresh material; and the business betwixt workman and putter-out was generally done in an amicable, reasonable way. No captious faultfinding, no bullying, no arbitrary abatement, which have been too common since, were then practised. If the work were really faulty, the weaver was shown the fault, and if it were not a serious one he was only cautioned against repeating it; if the length or the weight was not what it should be, he was told of it, and would be expected to set it right, or account for it, at his next bearing-home, and if he were a frequent defaulter he was no longer employed. But very rarely indeed did it happen that any transaction bearing the appearance of an advantage being taken against the workman by the putter-out was heard of in those days.

It would sometimes happen that warp or weft would not be ready until after dinner, and on such occasions, my uncle having left his wallet in care of the putter-out, would go downstairs and get paid at the counting-house, and from thence go to the public-house where we lunched on bread and cheese, or cold meat and bread, with ale, to which my uncle added his ever-favourite pipe of tobacco. This house, which was the "Hope and Anchor," in the old churchyard, was also frequented by other weavers; the putter-out at Broadbents generally dined there in the parlour, and when he had dined he would come and take a glass of ale, smoke his pipe, and chat with the weavers, after which, my uncle would again go to the warehouse, and getting what material he wanted, would buy a few groceries and tobacco in the town, or probably, as we returned through the apple market, to go down Long Mill Gate, he would purchase a peck of apples, and giving them to me to carry, we wended towards home, I, by permission, making pretty free with the apples by the way. Before leaving the town my uncle would probably call at the "Queen Anne," in Long Mill Gate, to see if there were any suitable company going our way; if there were, we took a glass until all were ready, and then we walked on together. Another calling house was Schofield's, at Scotland Bridge, and the last in the town was the "Flower Pot," on Red Bank. In winter time, and especially when day was closing, the weavers preferred thus returning in groups, for the road was not altogether free of foot-pads any more than at present. In hot summer weather, the weavers would sometimes indulge themselves by a ride in a cart, or they would leave their heavy burdens at the "Three Crowns," in Cock Gates, to be forwarded by Abraham Lees, the Middleton carrier. When a party of weavers returned in company, they would generally make a halt at Blackley, either at the "White Lion," or at Travis's, the "Golden Lion," over the way. There the wallets, or "pokes" as they were mostly called, were piled in a heap, ale was ordered, seats drawn round the fire, pipes were soon lighted, news interchanged with the host or some of his company; half an hour, or sometimes more, was thus spent, when the shot being called and paid, the travellers took their wallets and climbing the Hill lane, were soon at home. Such was "a bearing-home day" to Manchester in those times.

But even those days, advantageous as they certainly were when compared with the present ones which are devoted to a similar errand, were considered as being greatly altered for the worse since the days which could be spoken of from remembrance. The two classes of workmen and employer were already at too great a distance from each other, and it was a subject of observation that the masters were becoming more and more proud and uplifted each day. Some had seen the time when, on taking their work home, and material not being ready, a dialogue like the following would take place.

>   *Master.*—Well, William, there will be no piece for thee till afternoon.
>   *Weaver.*—Very well, I'll wait for it then; wot time munni come, think'n yo ?
>   *Master.*— Why, it's nearly dinner time now, and if thou'll go an' have a bit o' dinner wi' me, th' work will, mayhap, be ready when we come back.
>   *Weaver.*—Thank yo, mester, I'll goo wi' yo then.

So master and man would walk together to some decent-looking house, in some decent, quiet street, where the master, his wife, his children, and the guest, would sit down to a plain, substantial dinner of broth most likely, with dumpling and meat, or roast beef and baked pudding, or a steaming potato-pie; after which, master and workman would sit with their ale and pipes, talking about whatever most concerned themselves; and it were no undue stretch of imagination to suppose that a conversation somewhat like the following would take place—the lady of the house also being present with her knitting.

>   *Master.*—Well, William, an' how are you going on at your side o' th' country?
>   *Weaver.*— Pratty weel, mester, only they're begun a screwin op rents, and ar reyther niblin' at wages.
>   *Master.*—Aye ; who's screwin' up rents?
>   *Weaver.*—You new felley ats comn to th' Hoe ses he mun ha' three shillin' a acre moor fro his Middlet'n tennants th' next hawve yer.
>   *Master.*— That's a bad beginnin'; but I always thought yon Norfolk landlord would alter th' strip of old Sir Raphe's cloth. An' what do the tenants say about that?
>   *Weaver.*— Wot con the say? they're ill enoof obeawt it yomay besure. They grumbln confoundedly, an' sen iv Lady Mary had nobbut wed Sir Asht'n isted o' yon Sir Hury Byert, Middlet'n had nere ha lookt behind it agen.
>   *Master.*—And who has been nibblin' at wages, as thou wert saying?
>   *Weaver.* — Why, Snidgers yonder, at th' Hedgelone. They sen, at-te bated a hawpenny a peawnd th' last Setturday, at ther broad-ribb'd fustian; an' Hook-thum an' Son, o' Hollinwood, bated sixpence a cut th' Monday afore.
>   *Master.*—These are two very bad moves i'th' way o' business, and I hope the examples will not be followed, William; it's not the way to "live an' let live," which ought to be the rule always betwixt master and workman.
>   *Weaver.*—It ought so to be, indeed, mestur ; yo sen true, an' I only wish at o' mesters wurn o' yore mind; th' warkman wud then be sure o' havin' a just consideration for his wark. An' iv th' mesturs did'n but know wot a peawer they han for makin' bad things an' marrin' good uns, they'dn stop,

an' look afore 'em, ere they gan way to sitch a grabbin' o' money.

Master.—What thou says is right; William; and I am glad to hear that one of my weavers has so much good thought in him. "Live an' let live," is accordin' to Jesus Christ's rule, and whatever master gets his money by a rule different from that-rich, beyond measure, though he become — happy he never can be either in this world or the next; an' that is an awful consideration, is it not, William ?

Weaver. — It is, mester ; it's awful to think that a mon shall be tryeadin' o' carpets an' ridin' in coaches to-day, an' tryeadin' o' brimstone an' rowlin' i' hell foyer to-morn.

Master.—And yet it must be so, with unjust employers, or truth in God's Holy Word there is none. Hitherto, however, we cotton masters and our workmen have gone nearly hand in hand together. There have been blamable characters on both sides certainly, but generally speaking, they have acted pretty fairly towards each other. Has it not been so, William?

Weaver.—It has bin mostly as yo sen, mester.

Master. — And I do greatly wish it may so continue. But I am afraid, William — I am afraid this insatiable thirst after money and power, which is now making great progress amongst mankind, will, in the end, divide the masters and workmen of this country, making the former into a set of tyrants, and the latter into a fearful multitude of moody, hateful slaves:

Weaver.—I hope thattle not be i' yore days, nor mine noather, mester.

Master.—I hope it will not come to pass soon, William; but I fear it will come eventually. I hear almost every day a new dogma quoted, namely, that the great principle of commerce is "to buy at the cheapest, and sell at the dearest, market." I cannot act upon it. It is not honest — it is not Christian like—it is not wise. Let us try this vaunted principle, William, by the test of honesty — by the test of "Do thou unto others as thou wouldest they should do unto thee" and there is no better test of right and wrong under heaven. Suppose thou and thy family were distressed from want of employment; and thou came to me asking for work, and I, knowing thy situation, purchased thy labour "at the cheapest rate at which I could get it," and sold it again at the dearest, putting the profit screwed out of thy necessities into my pocket — suppose I did so — should I be acting like a Christian? like an honest, conscientious man?

Mistress.—Dear Thomas, I know you will never act in that manner: it would cover us with self-reproach; and neither you, nor I, nor the children, would ever become rich in the true riches of contentment, whatever were the wealth in gold, which we obtained by such unworthy means.

Weaver. — Kind Madam, yo're very good and considerate tord us worchin' fokes, and God will, I hope, bless yo and yores, for the worthy use 'at yo mak'n o' yore prosperity.

Mistress.—Thank you, William; come take a little more ale, and help yourself to tobacco. I assure you, I am always glad to see a honest working man or woman at my table.

Weaver.—Yore good yealth, main; and yore good yealth, sir; an' happiness to yursels an o' yur family.

Master.—Thank you, William; and the same to you and your family.

Weaver.—I'm oblig'd t'yo, sir. An' neaw I'm thinkin', Suppos', as yo sed'n afore, 'at yo bought'n my necessitous labour at th' lowest price 'at yo cud'n get it at, an' sowd'n it at th' heeist, an' isted o' puttin' o' th' profit i' yore own pocket, yo gan me th' tone hawve on it—wudno that doo?

Master (laughing). — Why, yes, William, that would do very well, I should think; but then thou knows, the principle of " buying at the cheapest," would be in that case given up, and I should be paying thee more for thy labour; than I bargained for, and there would be an end of the vaunted dogma of trade which we have been talking about. There are other dogmas, however, William, which, though they are not so plausible, nor so much in vogue as the one we have been discussing, are, in my opinion, quite as practicable, and far more just.

Weaver.—I shudbe fain to yer 'em explaint, sir.

Master. — We will say at once, then, that "the labourer should be deemed worthy of his hire," and that he should I have it also.

Weaver.—Good, sir.

Master. — That the hire of the labourer should never be less than what was sufficient to feed him, to clothe him, and to furnish him with the necessaries of a comfortable existence. This should be an inevitable condition of all labour.

Weaver.—Very good.

Master.—The cost of labour being thus immutably determined, all other costs would depend on supply and demand. With this condition, trade would be an honest and respectable vocation. Without this condition, fair trade cannot exist, for it ceases to be trade, and becomes spoliation, ruin, and dishonour.

Weaver.—That's graidly true. A trade 'at dusno pay th' warkmon for his wark is no trade at o, but a robbery an' a disgrace to th' country.

Master.—Just so. When, therefore, our commercial men talk about "buying in the cheapest, and selling in the dearest, market," they should always except human labour in their calculation. It is the bread and the means of existence of our fellow-beings, and it ought not, under any circumstances, to be placed in competition with mere money making, nor wantonly exposed to vicissitude. Sacredly inviolable it ought ever to be held. It is the source of all wealth, of all national strength and vitality, and the least price that should ever be given for it ought to be an ample sufficiency of all the necessaries of life. "Thou shalt not muzzle the ox that treadeth out the corn." Now, William, thou knowest what my "cheapest market " for wages will ever be; for if it happens that I can no longer give my workpeople the means for a comfortable subsistence in return for their labour, I will cease to employ them.

Weaver.—I wud 'at that mornin' may never oppen it een, at ony rate.

Master.—Now we will go back to the warehouse; and I will find thee a warp and weft at the old price.

Mistress. — Farewell, William, and give my respects to your good-wife at home.

Weaver.—I will, Madam. An' mony thanks for yur kyndniss.

CHAPTER XIII.
PRAYER MEETINGS—A BOGGART—
CHRISTIAN INSTRUCTION.

MY companions at this time were about half a dozen of as wild and gamesome beings as could be found in our neighbourhood. Very demure and reserved were we whilst under the eyes of our guardians or parents, but the moment we were beyond their ken our license for gambol and mirth was as great as had been our restraint. At Sunday school we were regular attendants, and each went away with his crumb of instruction. At the sermons we were frequently present, but from those meetings we generally departed as unregenerate as we came. What could our young heads or hearts make of the mysteries and creeds of the pulpit? They were strange, certainly; wonderfully incomprehensible were these matters which the preachers tried to impress on us; undeniable also as the fact of our own existence appeared to our unreasoning minds--the certainty that we must be either "born again," or damned eternally. So we sang when others sang, we prayed when others prayed, we sat out the sermon, sang and prayed again, when, hungry and impatient, we ran home to our meals, and then stole out to play. Sometimes the religious observances of the Methodists were sought by us as opportunities for rude sport. One place was in particular a favourite resort of ours. About once a month, a number of the most gifted members of the Methodists' society went over from Middleton to hold a prayer meeting at the house of Samuel Hamer, in Grunsha Lane. Mr. Hamer was a small farmer possessing some little property; he and his wife had recently become converts to Methodism. That respectable and very loving couple, with their only child, a son, were constant attendants at the chapel at Middleton, and were as exemplary in their duties as they were zealous in the propagation of their new religion. Mrs. Hamer was a clever, talented, good-looking woman; one likely to be influential, for she had an uncommon "gift of prayer," and as the house in Grunsha Lane was in a district bordering on Tonge, Alkrington, and Chadderton, where "Satan had as yet many strongholds," these prayers were looked on as so many assaults on "the powers of the Prince of the Air." The leaders of the meeting generally assembled at Samuel Smith's, who lived at the corner of Union Street, Middleton. There would perhaps be half-a-dozen of men, a woman or two, and a party of us lads. With coats buttoned up, lanthorns lighted, and sticks in hand, the men led the way, the women following, and the boys hovering sometimes before, sometimes behind. When, however, we were fairly in the fields, one of our party of lads would be missing; a whistle would be heard through the darkness, and loitering behind until the men and women were at a distance, we would set off as we could, helter-skelter, over hedge and ditch in quest of the whistler. This, especially on dark gusty nights, when we could scarcely hear each other's voices, and often became lost for a time, was fine, exciting sport. A low yell, like that of a hound, would occasionally recall us to the pack, or to some comrade thrown out of the way like one's self. Then there were particular places where one did not like to be quite alone; lest we fell in with company other than mortal. Such were Babylon Brow, going up to the heights of Tonge, and Tonge Wood, a thick dark plantation, and Tonge Springs, fairy-haunted, and its brook-bubbling sounds, like human words. On fine moonlight nights also, during the chase, things would be sometimes seen, and sounds heard, which one could not exactly make out; and as these added to the spirit of adventure, and were seldom of a decidedly terrific character, they served but to increase our excitement and relish of the pastime. When at the meeting, a hymn having been sung, and a prayer or two made, on a signal being given, we would slip out without exciting notice, and have another hunt over the fields and across the hedges, after which we returned; joined in the concluding devotions, and came home, our good guardians little dreaming of the sinful manner in which we had spent the holy Sabbath evening. On one of these night adventures I was certainly rather startled by what took place. My comrades had set out and left me behind, and in order to overtake them, I began to run, and had not run far, when I saw one before me running also, whom I seemed to be gaining ground upon fast. I soon made him out to be a lad of our party whom I knew I could easily outrun, and I chuckled at the idea of mortifying him by passing him at full speed, as I intended to do. When I got nearer I called out, but he still kept onward, making no answer. When close behind him I shouted, "Bill! Bill! why so fast?" but there was no notice--no reply--which I thought rather strange, and when I came abreast of him, I said in a tone of defiance, "Come on, then; and see whot theawrt short of," and darting past him like an arrow, I turned my head with an air of triumph, and saw a face--not Bill's, but that of one who had been dead many years. I now ran in earnest to get rid of him; but on looking back, saw he was within a few yards of my heels. He seemed almost to sweep the ground, whilst I passed the low fields betwixt Tonge Springs and Grunsha Lane, I know not how, but at an incredibly swift pace. In the lane he was still close behind me, and when I turned towards the door of the meeting-house, there was nothing to be seen or heard, save the tone of one in earnest prayer, and the frequent responses of "Amen, Amen." The lad whom I had set out to run against was inside on his knees, and I crept beside him and prayed more really in earnest that night than I had done during a long time before. I never mentioned the circumstance to my comrades lest I should get laughed at by them, or be seriously questioned and admonished by the elder Methodists if it came to their knowledge. Poor Bill was afterwards killed at Talavera; as good a specimen of dogged straight-forward John Bullism was he, as ever left England. Mr. Hamer died suddenly in the hayfield; his widow, on a rather short courtship, became the wife of our friend Samuel Smith; and her young son in process of time became a leading character amongst the Methodists, and is now, I believe, one of their travelling preachers.

Methinks I hear one Sanctimonia exclaim--"And a pretty way of bringing up the rising generation was that of the old Methodists at Middleton."

To which I reply by asking: "How would you bring them up better?"

"Oh," says Sanctimonia, "parents or guardians should always accompany their youthful charge to places of public worship, or should commit them to the care of vigilant elders who would reprehend every indication of levity or inattention."

"But could you govern the eye? Could you restrain the wanderings of the mind or of the heart?"

"No, but the bodily positions could be regulated, leaving the rest to God."

"You would exact 'the outward and visible sign,' then, whether or not I 'the inward and spiritual grace' were present?"

"I would."

"A very easy method that, of manufacturing devotees, but let me say that, in my opinion, you would begin at the wrong end, and that the article after all would be spurious. We have plenty of it nowadays, and I believe it is produced by a process very much like that which you recommend."

"What sort of an article, as you call it, would you produce?"

"I would, with God's help, try to produce a genuine one, a true Jesus Christ's own Christianity."

"And how would you set about it?"

"In every heart there is at least one germ of goodness. I would cultivate that by every gentle, and kind, and appropriate means; making its practice and development become a plea sure, not less than a duty. For instance, a child may be very impatient or drowsy over a sermon, whose heart would leap, and whose eyes would gush with tears on being addressed with words of kindness, or on seeing a fellow-creature or a dumb beast unworthily treated. Another who is less susceptible of tender feelings would colour with indignation on witnessing an act of dishonesty or ingratitude. Another would perish sooner than be guilty of an untruth. A fourth shall battle for the weak in right, against the strong in might, whilst his neighbour shall be lion-brave in the endurance of injuries. So one is merciful--cultivate that mercy, and other virtues will arise with it. Another is just--by all means encourage that spirit of justice, and mercy shall be thereby impartially dispensed. Another shall be indignant of wrong--nurture that young heroism, and both justice and mercy will grow up with it. A fourth shall be nobly magnanimous, and is he not so far a Christian? I would, with God's help, train up the tender-hearted child to be just, the just one to be merciful, the veracious one to add graciousness to truth, the heroic one to be moderate in triumph, and the magnanimous one to be powerful as well as endurant. In every assemblage of youth, all these good qualities are to be found, like gems strewed in darkness. Why should they be left to be lost? Precious emanations are they of God's own being. Let us worship God by deeming His gifts worthy of our care--most solicitous care. Children would understand this kind of religion better; they would love it better, they would imbibe it sooner, than the present one

> "Of sermonising and catechising,
> And bell-ringing, and drone-singing,
> And knee-bowing, and pride-showing,
> Of vain finery, and mock shinery."

I would not have it all lip-worship, and form-worship; but heart-worship, coming from the heart, and heart-penetrative, wherever it was introduced. I would, in fact, have less of priestianity, and more of Christ's own Christianity; less of creeds and dogmas, and more of the living faith which bringeth forth works, testifying to the reality of a true belief.

CHAPTER XIV.
PASTIMES AND OBSERVANCES.

AS my wish is to give a true description of the life which I led in my early days, and consequently of the manners and customs to which that life would be conformable, I shall only be proceeding with the proper end in view, if I give an account of the games, pastimes, and observances, which were prevalent amongst both the youthful and the more mature classes of the working population of my neighbourhood at the time I am writing about; and this may be considered as less irrelevant, inasmuch as that most of the pastimes and diversions which I shall describe are no longer practised—some of them not even known—by the youthful population of the manufacturing districts at the present day. Thus we are enabled distinctly to perceive the great change which, in a few years, has taken place in the tastes and habits of the working classes. And, seeing these alterations clearly set forth, we shall be better able to determine whether or not the labouring classes have been advancing in, or retrograding from that state of mind, and that bodily habit, which are meant by the term, Civilisation.

It was always a custom with the Methodists to hold a public prayer-meeting or "watch-night" at the chapel, and to continue in prayer or singing from the eve of Christmas day to the following morning; when the leaders, and such of the attendants as chose to accompany them, perambulated the town, singing hymns and carols, and stopping to sing before the dwellings of individuals of their own society, or of any other individual who was of their congregation, or who was generally respected. On the forenoon of the following day, they also generally held another prayer-meeting, unless there was service at the chapel, whilst in the evening there was generally a full service. On New Year's Eve there was a prayer-meeting again. And these were the chief Christmas observances of the religious body with which I was associated in worldly matters.

Some two or three weeks before Christmas it was the custom in families to apportion to each boy or girl weaver a certain quantity of work, which was to be done ere his or her holidays commenced. An extra quantity was generally undertaken to be performed, and the conditions of the performance were such indulgences and gratuities as were agreeable to the working parties. In most families, a peck or a strike of malt would be brewed; spiced bread or potato custard would be made, and probably an extra piece of beef, and some good old cheese would be laid in store, not to be touched until the work was done. The work then went on merrily. Play hours were nearly given up, and whole nights would be spent at the loom, the weavers occasionally striking up a hymn or Christmas carol in chorus. A few hours of the late morning would perhaps be given to rest; work would be then resumed, and the singing and rattle of shuttles would be almost incessant during the day. In my uncle's family we were all singers, and seldom a day passed on which several hymns were not sung. Before Christmas we frequently sung to keep ourselves from sleep, and we chorused "Christians, awake," when we ourselves were almost gone in sleep.

I recollect, on one of these occasions, my aunt had a very nice brew of ale in the buttery, and as we were working extra hours, I suggested that an allowance of it should be served to us whilst so working, instead of its being reserved until the work was done, when we should no longer require it. My aunt, however, would not give way; not a drop must be tasted until the work was finished. I determined, therefore, on helping myself, deeming it no dishonesty to obtain a part of my good fare when it was most wanted. I got a hollow straw, therefore, and whenever I went into the buttery, which was not unusual with any of us, I introduced my tube into the bung hole and sucked until I was satisfied for that time. This was repeated on several other occasions, and at last I heard my aunt say to my uncle that she thought the ale was not working so well as she could wish it to do. He told her to fill it up, and it would be prime ale, no doubt. So she filled it up, and I sucked it down; she filled it again, and again the barn, was below the bung-hole. I, chuckling with mischievous glee at my poor aunt's embarrassment, who no doubt began to have surmises that something not exactly "of this world" might have interfered with it, at last one day, as I was having a most refreshing draw, a bump on the back drove my nose into the barm, and there stood my aunt, crying out, "Ah, I've catch'd him! I've catch'd him i' th' fact!" She brought me forth, and narrated my trick to my uncle, who sat smoking, and though he endeavoured to look angry, could not help laughing until tears ran down his face.

Christmas holidays always commenced at Middleton on the first Monday after New Year's Day. By that day every one was expected to have his work finished. That being done, the cuts were next carefully picked and plated, and made up for the warehouse, and they having been despatched, the loom-house was swept and put in order; the house was cleaned, the furniture rubbed, and the holidays then commenced. The ale was tapped, the currant-loaf was sliced out, and lad and lass went to play as each liked best; the boys generally at football, and both boys and girls at sliding, when there was ice on the ground. In wet weather we should have a swinging rope in the loom-house, or should spend the day in going from house to house amongst our playmates, and finishing at night by assembling in parties of a dozen or a score, boys and girls, where on some warm, comfortable hearth we sat singing carols and hymns, playing at " forfeits," proposing riddles, and telling " fyerin tales," until our hair began to stiffen, and when we broke up we scampered homeward, not venturing to look behind lest the " old one" himself should be seen at our heels.

At this season also it was the custom for the sexton of the church, and the ringers to go from house to house wishing their neighbours "a merry Christmas," when they were generally invited to sit down, and were presented with a jug of ale and a present in money. This was done at most of the houses, especially if trade was going well; dissenters as well as church people gave, for religious differences had not so far divided the people into sects as to make them forget good neighbourship. It must have been a very furor of religion indeed which could have made my kind and simple-hearted uncle entertain one disparaging feeling towards his fellow townsmen of any party. Nor were the hard-working colliers shut out from the Christmas festivities. They also made it a custom to visit their neighbours, and were treated with ale or money, or both, as the circumstances of the family permitted. The poor sympathised with the poor, their sympathy not being of that description which in these times froths out in rabid speeches to starving multitudes, but was expressed by action as well as by word. "Come, Jim, have a slice of my loaf. Now, Bill, tak' a cup of my ale. Thou deservest what ever thou canst get. I live and work here in cheerful day and sunlight; thou spendest thy life in constant danger, and in little dark cells under ground. Come, don't need inviting. Thou art heartily welcome, and thou canst never be too greatly paid for thy labour." Thus the weaver and the collier would reciprocate their good wishes, which is better after all, more manly, and more in the old English way—more respectfully kind than the vaunted French mode of fraternisation.

At Shrove-tide we had always a holiday on Tuesday, when we went to each other's houses to turn our pancakes, and "stang" such as incurred the penalty by not having eaten their cake before the next cake was ready. The person to be stanged was placed on a pole, and being held on each side, was carried by others to middin and there deposited, amid the laughter and jokes of all present. On one of these occasions my little companion Mima, having to be stanged, and there being no poles at hand, I lifted her like a child and carried her towards the appointed place, she struggling and making a great show of resistance the while, which caused her to fold her arms round my neck, and to hold so closely, that had I not discovered that she had the sweetest breath as well as the prettiest cheek in Middleton, I must have been a blockhead indeed.

Midlent Sunday, with us called "Cymbalin Sunday," was another of our feasts, when it was customary to eat cymbalin cake,[9] and drink mulled ale. This was more particularly the custom at Bury than at any other town in our neighbourhood. Latterly the inhabitants of Heywood and Royton have set up as special observers of this day, though on what pretence I know not, except it be with the view of bringing strangers to their town, whereby shopkeepers may get purchasers of their cake, and publicans of their ale. I know not how to account for the origin of this ancient observance, except by supposing that it is in some way or other derived from the

---

[9] Usually known as "Simnel Cake" and "Simnel Sunday." Bamford wrote the name as he heard it pronounced. It occurs in Herrick's ' "Hesperides" (1647)—

>"I'll to thee a simnel bring
>'Gainst thou go a-mothering,"

Mid-Lent being Mothering Sunday.

heathen "feast of cymbals." That it has in its very name and manner an allusion to the instrumental cymbal, there can scarcely be a doubt; the name itself, which I here spell as it is pronounced, directly points to such meaning, whilst the form of the cake—the cymbalin—is a more positive indication of its origin. A cymbalin is not a merely round spiced cake—such an one would be a spiced cake only, and would be so termed—but let the maker raise a lump in the middle, like the ball of a cymbal, and turn up the edges like those of the instrument, and any native of South Lancashire will call it a cymbalin. There have been many disputations and surmises about the orthography and derivation of the name—some of those by persons who probably did not know a cymbalin from a cake; but this definition, I think, may be allowed to set the matter at rest. The name is Cymbalin; the form is exactly that of a cymbal: but when or by what means this custom, so directly allusive to a musical instrument, became connected with a Christian observance in our part of the country, some one more learned than myself must determine, if it can be determined at all.

Easter was a more important holiday time at Middleton. On Good Friday children took little baskets neatly trimmed with moss, and went "a peace-egging," and received at some places eggs, at some places spiced loaf, and at others halfpennies, which they carried home to their mothers, who would feel proud that their children had been so much respected. On Easter Monday, companies of young men grotesquely dressed, led up by a fiddler, and with one or two in female attire, would go from house to house on the same errand of "peace-egging." At some places they would dance, at others they would recite quaint verses, and at the houses of the more sedate inhabitants, they would merely request a "peace-egg." Money or ale would in general be presented to them, which they afterwards divided and spent. Meantime, the holiday having fairly commenced, all work was abandoned, good eating, good drinking, and new clothing were the order of the day. Men thronged to the ale-houses, and there was much folly, intemperance, and quarrelling amidst the prevailing good humour. On Tuesday night, some unlucky fellow who had got so far intoxicated as not to be able to take care of himself, would be selected to fill the post of lord mayor for the year ensuing, and as—for the sake of the drink and the sport which it afforded—there were always parties on the look-out ready to secure some one suitable for their purpose, the town was seldom at a loss for a lord mayor. Their mode of election, most certainly, was not of so courteous nor so grave a character as are the proceedings of mayoral elections in some of the recently created neighbouring boroughs, but "the Middleton Charter" having been in existence "time out of mind," granted no doubt by some king or lordly ruler, whose very name is lost in remote antiquity, the electors were not very strictly circumscribed in their operations, and they generally went to work without consulting either town's-books, town-clerk, statute, or charter. The individual pitched upon would generally be found in the nook of some ale-house, in the state which has been before described, or if by a more lucky accident he were picked up from the gutter, he would be conveyed to some friendly tap, where the necessary preparations could be carried on without interruption. The electors who undertook this important duty for "the good of the town" would be mostly of that class of "free burgesses" who, on festive occasions, are always the first at the ale-house and the last to leave it; the first to leave work, and the last to return to it; such as weavers who, disdaining slavery and being for the Charter, are always at leisure to look after their favourite pints, with a determination to get, by hook or by crook, as many toward the six[10] as they can;—cobblers, "Souter Johnnies," "droughty cronies," who'd

> "Rather be a hobble in,
> Than bend to their cobblin';"

hedge joiners, whose chief hedging is that which edges towards the drink mug; and dusty-throated colliers, who for of all the working classes, have the greatest apology for a good wash-down of ale. Such being the electors, what might be the mode of election?

First of all, then, if the candidate happened to have a somewhat decent coat on his back, it was stripped and given into the care of the landlord, or his equally obliging wife. The face of the candidate was next well daubed with soot and grease, his hair would be dusted with both soot and flour, a pig-tail made from a dish-clout would be appended behind, a woman's kirtle, a cap, a hat without crown, an old jacket, an old sack, or any other shred of dress which the imagination of his lordship's robers could construe either into an article of adornment or deformity, would be placed upon him so as to have its greatest effect. He would then be taken into the street, placed on a chair, or in an armchair if too far gone to sit upright, and proclaimed "Lord Mayor of Middleton," with every demonstration of drunken and mischievous glee. If the landlord, for reasons best known to himself, declined the honour of furnishing one of his old chairs for the procession, as most likely he would do, his lordship would probably be hoisted on a pole, with attendants balancing him on each side; or he might be laid upon a ladder, or mounted upon some poor strayed donkey; and so, amid shouts, laughter, yells, and oaths, would be conducted through the streets and lanes of his new dominions. It was generally somewhat past midnight ere his lordship commenced this his first survey, and the noise which accompanied his approach was such as permitted but few of his subjects to remain in repose. A loud knocking would be heard at every door, whilst many voices called out, "Come deawn, milord wants his dues," " Milord wants his dues." If the window were opened and one within said, "Well, yo' met'n make a less din, an' behange'd to yo'; heer's tuppence, an' be off wi' yo';" the response would be, "Hurrey! milord's gett'n his dues; come, let's try this next dur. Hur-rey! Hur-rey!" And so was chosen, elected, installed, and paraded, the lord mayor of Middleton.

On the forenoon of the following day his lordship might perhaps be seen, half washed and not yet awaken, on the form of the noisiest tap-room of the town. His conductors of the over-night drinking, smoking, dancing, and singing, in the same place. Some having been fighting, some ready to fight, some with black eyes, others with torn and bloody clothes, some with scarcely any clothes at all, whilst

---

[10] Written in 1848, when the Chartist agitation collapsed. The charter consisted of "six points."

anon, constables would be peering about and making inquiries as to who it was that kicked open such a door? who smashed such a window? who stole this body's can? who broke that body's mug? and a woful reckoning being promised for next week, some of the marauders would look serious. And, in truth, if the affair got over without some damages having to be made good, some law having to be hushed up, it was considered a very peaceable and exemplary election, and the "free burgesses" were in good heart for a repetition next year.

This custom was analogous to one which prevailed at Ashton-under-Lyne on Easter Monday, and which was called "Riding the Black Lad." At Ashton, however, the ceremony took place in the day time, when the figure of a man dressed in black was paraded through the streets, mounted on a horse, or a sorry nag of any kind. The origin of these customs is involved in obscurity. Both customs seem to have had one origin, and to have been held in derisive commemoration of some member of the Assheton family, as no such custom prevailed except in the two townships connected with the Asshetons. At Ashton the figure was ignominiously paraded in the day-time; at Middleton, as we see, "The Lord Mayor," all blackened and soiled, and, in fact, disguised, was paraded at midnight, and with mock authority demanded "his dues." The ceremony at Ashton would seem to be expressive of hatred and contempt, that of Middleton to indicate the cause of it, namely, severe and arbitrary exaction. Another supposition also arises, namely, that the Ashton ceremonial would scarcely have been allowed to take place, had the object of it been on the spot in the person of a powerful chief; and we may thence infer that he was gone thence to some other place. At Middleton, however, the ceremony was performed at midnight, in comparative secrecy and obscurity; and on the night but one following the day exhibition at Ashton. And this circumstance seems to indicate that the object of distaste was present at the latter place, with the power as well as the will to punish those who incurred his displeasure; hence it might be that the ceremonial took place at midnight. Ralph Assheton, Esquire, a son of Sir John Assheton, Knt. of Ashton-under-Lyne, having married a daughter of Richard Barton, Esquire of Middleton, in 1438, became lord of the manor of Middleton, and left Ashton to reside at the latter place. He was called the "Black Knight," and tradition points to him as the original of the "Black Lad."

On Easter Wednesday, what was called "The White Apron Fair," was held at Middleton. It was merely an occasion for the young wives and mothers, with their children, and also for the young marriageable damsels, to walk out to display their finery and to get conducted by their husbands, or their sweethearts, to the ale-house, where they generally finished by a dance, and their inamoratos by a battle or two, and their consequences, bruised hides and torn clothes.

The night of the 1st of May was "Mischief-neet," when, as "there is a time for all things," any one having a grudge against a neighbour was at liberty to indulge it, provided he kept his own counsel. On these occasions it was lawful to throw a neighbour's gate off the angles, to pull up his fence, to trample his garden, to upset a cart that might be found at hand, to set cattle astray, or to perform any other freak, whether in the street, house-yard, or fields, which might suggest itself or be suggested. The general observation in the morning would be, " Oh, it's nobbut th' mischief-neet." If a young fellow wished to cast a slur on a lass, he would hang a rag containing salt at her parents' door, or he would cast some of the same material on her doorstep, as indicative of gross inclinations. If he remained unknown he escaped punishment, but if he were detected, or his secret became divulged, he generally got thrashed, as he deserved, by a brother, or some favoured swain, or he might get his face channelled by the fair one's nails the next time she met him, or a mop slapped against his cheek, or a vessel of odorous liquid poured on his clothes as he passed the desecrated threshold; all or any of which retaliations would earn for him but small sympathy with his neighbours—the men chuckling or laughing and saying nothing: and the women all agreeing, "Aye, it sarves him quite reet, th' wastril." A gorse bush indicated a woman notoriously immodest; and a holly bush, one loved in secret; a tup's horn intimated that man or woman was faithless to marriage; a branch of sapling, truth in love; and a sprig of birch, a pretty girl. If a house floor wanted cleaning, a mop would be left for that purpose; and if a dame was notorious for her neglect of needle-work, a ragged garment of some sort would be hung at her door. The morning after "mischief-neet" was generally prolific of gossip and some laughter, as it generally became known by breakfast-time what "lumber" (mischief) farmer So-and-so had had done, and what this young girl, or that young widower, found at their doors when they opened them.

The feast of Whitsuntide was not attended by any particular local customs, except the relics of the old "Whitsun ales," which consisted in what were termed "main brews" of ale; a number clubbing to purchase malt which was brewed by one selected from the party, and drunk at one of the houses. Dances and ale-house fuddles were also common, and latterly races attracted vast crowds to the scene of their operations. Sticks were indispensable to pedestrians on these occasions, and hazel or holly sticks, with the peel taken off in a spiral form, were considered the very example of a country "somebody." Oldham pedestrians went to the races by hundreds, and were designated as "Owdham Brewis;" whilst Rochdale folks, still more numerous, were known as "Ratchda Roofyeds." The inhabitants of Blackley were "Blackley Lions," perhaps from the circumstance of their having lions for the signs of their two public-houses; people who come from Bowlee were "Bowlee Tups"; whilst the inhabitants of Middleton were retaliated upon as "Middleton Moons," a term indicative of a notion that, with all their wit, they were not more wise than their neighbours.

CHAPTER XV.
THE WAKES.

BUT "The Rush-bearing" was the great feast of the year, and was held on the anniversary of the dedication of the church. At Middleton it is held on the third Saturday in August, or if there be five Saturdays in the month, it falls on the fourth. From tradition, as well as from custom itself, we may conclude that at first it was a simple offering towards making the church floor comfortable during the winter services. Every family having then its separate bench to sit upon, some one or two of them would at first strew their own floors with rushes to promote the warmth of their feet during the stormy months. Others perceiving how snugly and cosily their neighbours sat, would follow the example. Probably the priest would encourage the new luxury, and it would soon become common. Thus Nan and Dick, and Bob and Bet, would be seen carrying bundles of rushes to the church at the feast of the dedication, and the church would be littered for the winter. Next, families forming small hamlets of the parish would unite, and pitching each their quota of rushes into a cart, would send down a load. Some of these hamlets in order, probably, to ingratiate themselves with the priest, by rendering extra homage to the church, would arrange and decorate their rushes with green boughs; others would excel them; and a rivalry as to which hamlet could bring the neatest formed and the most finely decorated load of rushes would ensue, and thus the present quaint and graceful "rush-cart" would be in time produced. Music, dancing, and personal finery would accompany and keep pace with the increasing display; the feast would become a spectacle for all the surrounding districts, and the little wood-shadowed village, would annually become a scene of a joyous gathering and a hospitable festivity; and thus, the wakes, as they existed in my early days, would be gradually produced.

The folds or hamlets which mostly sent "rush-carts" to Middleton, were Boarshaw, Thornham, Hopwood, Birch, Bowlee, and Tonge. About a month or six weeks before the wakes, the young men of the hamlets, as well as those of the town, would meet at their respective rendezvous, which was some ale-house, where the names of such as wished to join the party during the wakes were given in, and the first instalment of money was paid. These meetings were called "enterings," and they always took place on Sunday evenings, when each one paid a certain sum towards a general fund, and a trifle more for drink at their meetings. It was the interest of these young fellows to raise as strong a party as they could, not only with a view to a plenteous fund, but also in order to repel—if necessary—aggression from other parties; for as these little communities were seldom without a few old grudges to fall back upon should an opportunity offer, it was very extraordinary indeed if a quarrel did not take place amongst some of them, and half-a-dozen battles were not foughten before the wakes ended. It was consequently an object with each to get as numerous' a party and as heavily bodied an one as they could, agility and science not being so requisite in Lancashire battles as weight, strength, and endurance. These young fellows, therefore, mustered as imposingly as they could, and if one or two of the young women of the place happened to have sweethearts who came from a distance — and especially if they were likely to clear their way in a row — the courters would probably be found joined with the brothers and friends of their fair ones. Well, the "enterings" having been formed, and the subscriptions duly paid, a rush-cart would be determined upon. Such a farmer's broad-wheeled cart was to be bespoke. Then, lads and lasses would at all spare hours be engaged in some preparation for the feast. New clothes would be ordered; and their quantity and quality would probably depend on the amount of money saved during the year, or on the work performed in a certain time before the wakes. Jack would obtain, if he could, "a bran new suit, wi' trindl't shurt," and Bess would have her "geawn made wi' tucks an' fleawnces; new shoon wi' ston op heels; new stockin's wi' clocks; a tippit wi' frills o reawnd; monny a streng o necklaces; an' a bonnit made by th' new mantymaker, the prattyist 'at ever wur seen, wi' a skyoy blue underside, an' pink ribbins." By "day skrike" in a morning, or by "neetgloom" in the evening, the jingle of morrice bells would be heard along the lanes and field roads; for the lads having borrowed each his collar of bells at neighbouring farmhouses, would hang them on their necks and come jingling them home, waking all the echoes in the deep lanes, and the meadow nooks, and the old grey solitary places, until the very air was clamorous of the bell tingle and the musical roll of the crotal.[11] Ropes and stretchers would also be borrowed, and the rushes growing in certain waste pieces having been marked out, and when necessary bargained for with the owner of the land, mowers were appointed, and a day or two before the commencement of the wakes the rushes were cut down. An old experienced hand was generally engaged to "make the cart," that is, to lay on, and build up, and trim the rushes, according to the design which is always adopted in such constructions. The girls meanwhile would all be employed at over-hours getting their own finery and that of their brothers or sweethearts ready for the great event. Tinsel was purchased, hats were trimmed with ribbons and fanciful devices; shirts were washed, bleached snow-white, and neatly pleated; tassels and garlands, and wreaths of coloured paper, tinsel, and ribbon were designed and constructed, and a grand piece of ingenuity and splendour, a kind of concentration of the riches and the pomp of the party was displayed in the arrangements and setting forth of "the sheet." This was exclusively the work of the girls and women, and in proportion as it was happily designed and fitly put together or otherwise, was their praise or disparagement meted out by the public, a point on which they would probably be not a little sensitive. The sheet was a piece of very white linen, generally a good bed sheet, and on it were arrayed pretty rosettes, and quaint compartments and borderings of all colours and hues which either paper, tinsel, or ribbons, or natural flowers could supply. In these compartments were arrayed silver watches, trays, spoons, sugar-tongs, tea-pots, snuffers, or other fitting articles of ornament and value, and the more numerous and precious the articles were the greater was the deference which the party which

---

[11] A kind of cymbal.

displayed them expected from the wondering crowd. Musicians were also secured in good time; a fiddler for the chamber dancing always, and never less than a couple of fifers and a drummer to play before the cart. But if the funds would allow, and especially in later times, a band of instrumentalists would be engaged, often a sorry affair certainly, but still "a band" to swear to, and that would be a great thing for the ears of the multitude. All true church-goers were duly apprised of the wakes, as its date was cried by the bellman in the churchyard whilst the congregation were leaving the church, on three Sunday afternoons previous to its commencement. The morning of the great day comes, and every one is in a state of bustle and anxiety. Heads of families are bundling up their work and hastening off to town in order to be back in time for the opening of the wakes. And now, the rushes having been mown are carted to the place where the cart is to be made. The maker with his assistants are all present; the wheels are sunken in holes; and the cart is well propped to make it steady; the peeled rods and binders are set up so as to make the structure steady, and to give the proper form as it advances; ale is poured out and drunk liberally; numerous youngsters are playing and rolling about on the rush-heap, whilst others are making of them small sheaves bound at each end, and being cut in the middle with a scythe-blade are called "bowts" (bolts); others again are culling the finest of the rushes and making them into "bowts" of a superior description wherewith to form a neat edging to the front and back of the structure. And so they keep binding and cutting and piling up until "the cart" is completed, which now presents the form almost of a flattened bee-hive, with the ends also flattened, and ornamented with a projecting edging of rushbolts, which gives them a quaint and trim appearance. The sheet, before described, is displayed with all its wonder-exciting treasures in front of the cart; sometimes another sheet less costly is exhibited behind, and when that is not the case, letters and various devices in flowers are generally found there. The top of the cart, or rush-heap, is stuck with green boughs which wave and nod like plumes, and amongst them one or two of the young men who have been the latest married take their seats astride the load. The drawers, all donned in ribbon finery and tinsel, now begin to make their appearance; some dozen or so of the leaders having bells around their necks. The drum is beating, the music is blowing and snorting and screaming, the gay tinkling of morrice bells is floating and waking up the echoes. The children are wild with joyful expectation, or astonished by the wondrous fairy scene. The girls bepranked in their new pumps, kirtles, and bonnets, now add beauty to the spectacle; and on the arm of each may be noticed the best Sunday coat and doublet of her brother, or her sweetheart. The ropes are attached, the stretchers noosed fast at proper distances; all is ready. The music strikes up louder; the driver clears the way with his long whip, making it give a loud and clear crack at every stroke—that being his feat—the word is "Neaw, lads," and at one strong pull, and a heave of the shafts, the wheels are dislodged from their socket holes, and the cart is slowly drawn up to the level sward, amid the loud shouts of the admiring gazers; and so, with music-clangour, and bell-jingle, and laughter, and words of caution, as, "Howd on, lads," "Gently, lads," the quaint and romantically fantastic spectacle moves towards the village of its destination.

If the party can go to the expense of having a set of morrice dancers, and feel inclined to undertake the trouble, some score or two of young men, with hats trimmed, and decked out as before described, precede the drawers, dancing in couples to various simple country tunes, one of which may be measured by this stanza:—

> My new shoon they are so good,
> I cou'd doance morrice if I wou'd;
> An' if hat an' sark be drest,
> I will doance morrice wi' the best.

In some later instances there have been processions of banner and garland bearers, with all beautiful flowers, artificial or real, and apt and ingenious devices. A choice beauty of the village may also, on some occasions, be induced to personate the Queen of the Wake, walking under a bower borne by four of her companions, and preceded by dancers and the other pageants described. But these spectacles I should rather suppose to be of comparatively modern introduction in this part of Lancashire.

Arrived at the village, other parties similar to their own will be found parading their cart on the high road. The neighbouring folds and hamlets, having been nearly deserted by their inhabitants, all are there concentrated seeing the wakes and partaking in the universal enjoyment. The highway is thronged by visitors in gay attire, whilst shows, nut stalls, flying-boxes, merry-go-rounds, and other means of amusement are rife on every hand. Should two carts meet, and there be a grudge on either side, a wrangle, and probably a battle or two, settles the question, and they each move on; if the parties are in amity, they salute each other with friendly hurras, the drawers holding their stretchers above their heads until they have passed. Each cart stops at the door of every public-house, which the leaders enter tumultuously, jumping, jingling their bells, and imitating the neighing of horses. A can of ale is then generally brought to the door and distributed to the drawers and attendants; those who ride on the top not forgetting to claim their share. When the whole town or village has been thus perambulated, the cart is drawn to the green near the church, where the rushes are deposited — or should be — though latterly, since the introduction of pews in the church, they have generally been sold to the best bidder. The moment the first cart arrives on the green the church bells strike up a merry round peal in honour of those who have thus been alert to testify their devotion; but as the rushes are now seldom left at the church, so neither is the ringing so strictly performed as it wont to be; and, in fact, though the name and the form are in some degree retained, it is evident that attachment to our venerable state-worship has far less influence in the matter than it had in the days of my early life.

After disposing of their rushes, either by gift to the church in which case they became the perquisite of the sexton—or by sale to the best bidder, the lads and their friends, sweethearts, and helpers repaired to the public-house at which they put up for the wakes, and there spent the night in drinking and dancing. On Sunday some of the principal banners and garlands, which had been paraded the day before, were displayed in the church; and on Sunday night the lads and lasses again met at the public-house, where they drank, smoked, and treated their neighbours and friendly visitors from other public-houses. Sunday was also the great day for hospitality. Relations living at a distance, old friends and acquaintances, being generally invited to the wakes, considerable numbers of well-dressed people would be seen in the forenoon entering the town from all quarters. Then, the very best dinner which could be provided was set out, the ale was tapped, and the guests were helped with a profusion of whatever the host could command. It was a duty at the wakes to be hospitable, and he who at that time was not liberal according to his means, was set down as a very mean person. Even decent strangers who apparently had no fixed place of visitation, would be frequently called in as they passed the open door and invited to partake with the family and other guests, and would be made entirely welcome to whatever the house afforded. This was not the custom at Middleton only, but at all wakes holidays in that neighbourhood, and at none was it carried out with more genuine and hearty welcome than at Oldham. The town would, during the afternoon of this Sunday, be thronged with visitors; private houses were mostly occupied, and the public-houses were crowded, whilst dealers in nuts, oranges, and Eccles cakes vended their wares from basket or stall, and shows, flying-boxes, and whirligigs stood there, mute and still, as if in admonition of the vain, restless, and wearying crowd which floated around them. Monday was the day for hard drinking, and for settling such disputes and determining such battles as had not come off on Saturday. Tuesday was again a drinking day, with occasional race-running, and more battles at night. Wednesday would be spent in a similar manner. On Thursday the dregs of the wakes-keepers only would be seen staggering about. On Friday a few of the dregs of the dregs might be met with; Saturday was woful, and on Sunday all would be over, and sobered people, going to church or chapel again, would make good resolutions against a repetition of their week's folly. And thus would have passed away the great feast of "The Wakes."

From this time, as days began to shorten fast, candles were lighted up in the loom-houses, and what was called "wakin' time " commenced—not so termed from the keeping of the wakes, but from the lighting up—the waking with candles.

When the fine clear nights of late August came, many were the joyous gatherings of lad and lass on the broad open green in front of the houses of Barrowfields. Two or three score of wild, nimble, gleesome beings would assemble there, running, leaping, wrestling, singing, and laughing, in that unalloyed mirthfulness which is the especial blessing of innocent youth. After the various groups had for a while pursued their several sports, some one would call out — "Come neaw, lads an' wenches, let's play together." Immediately the games would cease, and all would be called together, and when they had determined on what they should play at, dispositions would be made accordingly. If it were "Hitch-hatch," all would lay hold of hands, a lad and lass alternately, and a ring be formed, the couples standing at arm's length, and making as large a one as they could. One of the maids then went round on the outside of the ring, with a handkerchief in her hand, which she applied to every pair of hands, an d then took away again, repeating as she went round—

> "Hitch-hatch, hitch-hatch,
> I've a chicken undermi lap;
> Heer I brew, an' heer I bake,
> An' beer I lay mi clap-cake"

laying the handkerchief at the same time on the arm of some youth or maiden, and running away, in and out, across the ring and round about, the one on whose arm the handkerchief was left, following as quick as possible to catch her, and if he or she succeeded in doing so, she must begin and perambulate again, until she can contrive to slip into the vacant space left by her pursuer, when she keeps the station and her pursuer goes round as she did. This, of course, gives an opportunity for a good deal of running and chasing and laughter, and of endeavours to escape when overtaken; which again necessitates a pretty close hold to be had of the captive — not an unpleasant one often—and much merriment until the play proceeds.

If the play was "Bull-i'th'-Barn," a lad chosen to enact the bull stood within a ring formed as before, and tried to break through by running with all his force against the clasped hands without using his hands to dissever them. The ring would often give way without being broken, and his disappointment would be hailed by shouts of laughter. Again he would survey the ring, and choosing what he considered to be a weak place, he would perhaps break through and take to his heels, when the ring broke up and the whole followed him helter-skelter, and after a smart run and a deal of hauling and fun, he would be brought back captive, and either placed in the ring again, or another be placed instead of him.

"Sheppey," or "Blackthorne," was another of our youthful plays. Two or three of the best runners having been selected, they took their station at one end of the green, whilst the main body of their companions were at the other end. The runners then shouted

> "Blackthorne,"

which was answered—

> "Buttermilk and barleycorn."

Runners—

> "Heaw mony geese han yo' to-day?"

Answer—

> "Moor nor yo' can oather catch or carry away."

The two parties approached each other at a swift pace, and the runners made as many of the others prisoners as they could, taking them back to the place from whence they started, when they also took part with the runners in the subsequent game. Thus they kept running and taking prisoners until the whole of the geese party were secured, when they divide, as at first, and the play was renewed.

Other games used by the boys alone were leapfrog, running races, leaping, and wrestling, which expanded our lungs with fresh air and filled our veins with new, life-fraught blood, we continuing our play untired until parents or guardians standing at their doors called us to bed, and to an oblivious healthful repose.

CHAPTER XVI.
BONFIRES—SUPERSTITIONS—APPARITIONS.

THE next holiday was on the Fifth of November, the anniversary of the discovery of Gunpowder Plot. Most people ceased from working in the afternoon, and children went from house to house begging coal to make a bonfire, a distich of the following words being their form of application:

> "The Fifth o' November, I'd hayo remember;
> A stick an' a stake for King George's sake;
> Pray, dame, gimmi a cob-coal,
> To make a leet i' Lunnun cellar hole."

In addition to these contributions gates and fences suffered, and whatever timber was obtainable from the woods and plantations was considered fair game "for King George's sake." At night the country would be lighted up by bonfires, or as pronounced in Lancashire, "bunfoyers;" tharcake and toffy were distributed to the younger members of families, whilst the elder clubbed their pence and at night had "a joynin'" in some convenient dwelling. The lord of the manor made the young men a present of a good two-horse load of coal, with which a huge fire was lighted on The Bank near the church, and kept burning all night and most of the day following. The young fellows also joined at ale from the public-house, and with drinking, singing, and exploding of firearms, they amused themselves pretty well, especially if the weather was favourable. Such were the principal games, pastimes, and observances of the rural population of Middleton and its vicinity when I was a youth. There were other observances, however, which were supposed to relate to the immaterial world, to give an account of which would perhaps be considered too much out of the line of my narrative. I will, however, briefly describe two of them.

A young woman who wished to have a sight of her future husband would walk three times round the church at midnight, sprinkling hemp-seed, and repeating as she went:

> "Hemp-seed I sow, hemp-seed I sow,
> And he that must my true love be—
> Come after me and mow."

When the spirit of the young man she was destined to marry would appear and come mowing at her heels, and if she stopped to scrutinise him over much she was in danger of being cut down. So much for the gallantry of spirit mowers.

We know that according to old legends the two nights of All Saints and All Souls were especially set apart for spiritual appearances. That on the night of All Saints the spirits of the blessed who in the course of the year should depart within the parish were visible in their human forms at the parish church, and that on the night of All Souls the spirits of all those who should die, whether sinner or saint, were also certain to appear in bodily shape. On one of these yearly recurrences Old Johnny Johnson, who was then the sexton, had an irrepressible curiosity to know which of his neighbours should die, as well as to ascertain the amount of grave and other fees and perquisites he was to receive during the next twelve months, so, on the night of All Souls, he concealed himself in the church, and watched the ghostly visitants come in and go out and walk about the place, and a decent number he had already counted up, which at the usual fee per head would amount to a goodly sum. Still they kept dribbling in one by one, and sometimes in couples,

> "Old and young,
> Weak and strong,
> Rosy—pale—
> Faint and hale
> Come and go,
> Passing slow;
> Life in death,
> Not a breath,
> Not a wail."

There sat old Johnny, chuckling and counting up his gains, when at last a little old man made his appearance, and Johnny at the first look knew him to be himself. He had then seen enough, and with all speed he hastened to his home, became very thoughtful, soon after sickened, and within the twelve months he died.

As for the Parish Church of Middleton, every one in those days admitted that there was not a rood of earth around it which was not redolent of supernatural associations. My poor aunt Elizabeth no more doubted these things than she did the truth of every word betwixt the two backs of her Bible. Often when on a winter's night we youngsters were seated round the hearth, and my uncle was engaged elsewhere, would she set her wheel aside, take a pinch of snuff, hutch her chair towards the other hob, and excite our curiosity and wonder by strange and fearful tales of witches, spirits, and apparitions, whilst we listened in silence and awe, and scarcely breathing, contemplated in imagination the visions of an unseen world which her narratives conjured up before us. Often she would tell—for these tales were always new again—how that the venerable servant of God, Mr. Wesley, being benighted on one of his journeys, obtained lodgings at a lone house, and on retiring to his chamber was followed by a huge black dog, which he knew to be an unhappy spirit, to whom, with a feeling of compassion, he flung his gown as a bed for it to lie upon, which it did, and he then making fast the door, went to sleep and had a good night's rest, and on awaking in the morning the dog was gone, though the door remained fastened, and no one belonging to the place knew of such a dog, or had seen such an one about the premises. At other times she would narrate the strange stories of Elizabeth Hobson, who could not walk abroad by night or day without seeing the spirits of departed persons; who being affianced to a young suitor, saw his spirit pass her in the street, and walk apparently through the wall of a house, and thereby she knew that he was dead, an account of which soon after came to hand; who made an appointment to meet a spirit at midnight on a lonesome hill, whither she was accompanied part of the way by devout persons, from whom, after earnest prayer, she departed, and by whom she was seen ascending the hill after being joined by others, whom, from her warnings, they knew to be spirits; who, after being on the hill a long time, during which her friends were praying for her, returned and gave an account of many things which she had seen; of the spirits of deceased neighbours and friends she had conversed with whilst on the hill, but refused to divulge certain matters which she stated she was immutably pledged not to disclose, and the awful secrets of which she never could be prevailed upon to utter.

In one of my aunt's communicative moods she told how her grandfather Bamford, being in a delirium, attempted to destroy himself, and was tied down in bed, where religious people came to pray for him, when in order to convince them that all their precautions were vain, and that the Evil One, to whom he was given up, would let him have his will, he drew his hand from the noose, as if he had been merely moving it in an ordinary way, and pointing to a corner of the room told them—to their great terror—that at that precise spot, and at that moment, the dark spirit was waiting to do his slightest bidding. That on learning this horrid fact—of which they had not the least doubt—prayers were redoubled, and doctors were called in, and the latter having bled the patient and forced medicine upon him, he, through God's mercy and "the efficacy of prayer," was restored and afterwards became a devout man. Or she would tell how her sister Mary—a beauty in person, and an angel in mind—died, in the bloom of her days, praising God and blessing all around her; or how her brother Abraham—the pride of the family—having taken a mixture given him by a quack doctor, died shrieking in torment. How James gradually wore away, and Samuel died of fever, and William of consumption.

On another occasion, I and she being alone in the house, she gave me an account which made my heart to thrill and the tears to gush from my eyes. She said no bereavement out of her own family had troubled her more than the death of my mother. "I was at home," she said, "here in Middleton, and was sadly grieved that I had not seen her before she died; both Sally Owen and I were troubled in our minds on that account; but it was no slight matter for the mother of a family to leave them all well here, and to walk into a great fever hospital which the workhouse was at that time. So we judged it best not to go, but to offer up our prayers on her behalf, and on behalf of thee and thy father, and all who were sick. We always remembered you in our prayers, and daily besought God on our bended knees that He would spare you yet a little while, and two out of the four were spared. Well, but Sally an' me cried many a time about thy mother—we never met but we cried about her, and sometimes we blamed ourselves for not goin' a seein' her, and sometimes we were comforted by thinkin' we had done our duty. What troubled us most was the uncertainty about the state of her soul. We were hardly satisfied about that, and we next prayed that if she was happy a token might be vouchsafed whereby we might know that she was so. Still nothing happened, we kept watchin' for tokens but none came, and months and months passed away. At last, Sally was taken in labour, and I went down from these club-houses here to th' Back-o'th'-Brow, and a good time and a safe delivery she had — thank God; an' tow'rd eleven o'clock thy uncle William came to fetch me home, an' we tarried till near midnight, an' as he sat smokin' his pipe, I donn'd my cloak an' bonnet, and said I would be going slowly up th' Bonk, and he would o'ertak' me before I had gotten far on the way, for theaw sees I was rather slow at walkin' i' consequence of my cough an' shortness o' breath. Well, I kept comin' slowly up an' slowly up, an' turning' to see if he were comin', an' I kept creepin' end way till I'd gotten to the bottom o' th' church steps. It was as fine a moonleet neet as ever shone eawt o' th' moon, as cleer very nee as th' noon-day; I could ha' seen to ha' gathert a pin off th' greawnd. Well, I stoode an' lookt back to see if he wur comin', an' I seed him just meawntin' onto th' bonk, when I yerd th' gate oppen behind me, and lookin' that way, I seed a very fine, tall woman dresst o' i' sparklin' white, come through th' gate an' walk deawn th' steps past me, and go straight under th' trees tow'rd Summer Heawse. The moment I seed her put her foot eawt to come deawn th' steps, that moment I knew her to be thy mother."

"My mother?"

"Aye, thy very mother, or at th' least her spirit."

"I' th' name o' Goodness, aint, whot aryo tellin' me."

"I'm tellin' the' God's own truth, lad; I seed her as plain as I see thee this very minnit. The mother had a foote an' ancle incomparable; I could ha' known her ony time by seeing her step eawt."

"And did you not see her face, then?"

"Nawe, I didno'. I felt a kynd of awe, an' ere I could look up, hoo wur past me."

"And whot then?"

"Oh! hoo walkt streight forrud as if hoor gooin' tow'rd th' Market-place, an' I turn'd me an' watcht her as lung as I cou'd see her, under th' trees, an' through th' moonleet, and through th' shadows, as fair as if it had been noonday. 'Blessed be God,' I said; 'yon's Han-nah; hoo's happy, an' I am satisfied.'"

"An' did you tell my uncle?"

"Nawe; the uncle towd me. He coom op to me in a minnit after, an' he said,

'Lisabeth, hooas yon fine woman at's just gone past the'?'

" 'Why, did theaw see her, then?' I asked.

" 'Aye,' he said, 'I seed her plain enoof; hoo'r not so very far off me, as hoo went deawn heer tow'rd th' Lodge.'

" 'Theaw'rt rnista'en, lad; hoo went o' this reet side o' th' Beawling Green, an' under th' trees.'

" 'Nay,' he said, 'theaw munno say so, lass, hoo went o' this lift side o' th' Green; heaw cud I ha' seen her gooin' tow'rd th' Lodge, if hoo'd gone under th' trees.'

" 'Well,' I said, 'that convinces me moor an' moor.'

" 'Convinces the' o' whot?'

" ' 'At ween both seen a spirit.'

" 'Nonsense, wench!' he said; ' ' it wur nobbut a very fine lady, o i' white. I seed her as plain as I see thee. Hoo walkt heer deawn tow'rd th' Lodge quite natural. Some body happen at had been a visitin'.'

" 'Visitin'! whot, at this time o' neet, or reyther mornin'! Beside, wheer cou'd hoo ha' come fro', an' wheer cou'd hoo begooin' to? There's no sitch fine foke heerabeawt.'

" 'True, lass, there isno', unless it's sumbody 'at's been at th' Clockyakers.'

" 'Th' Clockmakers! yon's no company for th' Clockmakers, as great foke as they ar. Yon's eawer Daniel wife spirit as sure as I ston heer. I knew her the moment I set my een on her. Thanks be to God 'at I seen her. Hoos comn fro' heaven, an' hoo's gooin' back theer. "The Lord gave, and the Lord hath taken away: blessed be the name of the Lord." 'An' so we turn'd an' coom through th' churchyard whom, an' the uncle wur afterwards convinc'd 'at th' appearance must ha' bin a sperit. An' when I towd Sally Owin, after hoo'd gett'n better, we both went deawn on eawr knees and returnt thanks for eawr onsur to prayer."

"Well," I said, "I'm glad you have told me of this, aunt. I never had a doubt about my mother's happiness. I always considered her as too good to go anywhere save to heaven. What you have said has, however, made me still happier, since you and Sally Owen, when she was living, and your most intimate connections, would all be satisfied with respect to my mother's spiritual state."

"Oh! quite so, quite satisfied. Would to God 'at I wur as sure o' my own salvation."

"Is it not strange, aunt, that I have often thought that walk, under the trees and towards the summer-house, was a very solemn place."

"Hasto ever thought so, then?"

"Aye, I've always felt strangely attached to the spot, and have taken many a ramble there instead of going with the others to play. Can it be that my mother's spirit haunts that place, think you? And that it would be fain to meet me there?"

"Oh, no, chylt! the mother's happy i' heaven, an' if theaw expects to meet her, theaw mun prepare to goo theer."

"Well, I cannot tell how it happens, aunt, but I always feel so calm and soothed when at dusk I walk alone round the green, or sit on the bright grass under the trees. It seems as if I had all the company I desire: I can converse better with myself, as it were — can commune more deeply with my own feelings and thoughts in that lone spot than in any other, Middleton Wood excepted, and probably some of the lone dells of Hopwood. I shall go there oftener."

" 'There's a deal o' sin committed thereabeawts; pitchin', an' tossin', an' drinkin', an' beawlin', i' summer time."

"Yes, but I go when the rabble are away — when nothing is heard save the distant murmurs from the surrounding habitations. There is something so quaintly hoary in the old summer house, and the tall trees waving in the mysterious twilight just before dark, that I feel as if I were almost in a new existence. I shall go there oftener. My mother has come there once, and she will come again if I wait for her."

"Tempt not God," said my aunt; "the spirit may come again if it is so willed."

CHAPTER XVII.
LOVE DAWNINGS.

I CAN scarcely recollect a period of my life when the society of females was not very agreeable to me. I was now, however, approaching that age when this general partiality was to become more individualising, and when amongst the mass which I always contemplated with tender regard, some would be found from whom I could not withhold a still warmer sentiment. Thus were the young germs of love beginning to quicken in my heart; and instead of repressing or controlling them, as I should perhaps have done, or have attempted to do, had I had a wise adviser to counsel me, I abandoned myself to delicious heart-gushings of romantic feeling, bowed in silent but earnest regard to female loveliness, and became soul and heart-bound—profoundly mute, however, except by sighs and looks—to more than one, in succession, of the young beauties of my acquaintance. Thus from an admirer of the sex generally, I became the worshipper of its most lovely forms in particular, and amongst those I was not slow to discover some who to me seemed to surpass all other mortals in beauty and modest worth. Such was the collier's darkeyed daughter who came every Sunday to school from Siddal Moor: such the tall fair girl who, all blush-coloured, and wild as a young roe, came from the meadow-top at Alkrington: such the pale vocalist from my native suburb, whose sable hair streamed like night-clouds around a statue of snow. Such, also, were others, but why should I dwell on these reminiscences, seeing that I cannot look back and reopen my heart and find it as it once was; seeing that death has swept some away; that Time has bowed those who remain; that age has subdued love, and that beauty is in ruins.

My cousin Hannah I could have admired because she was pretty, but she understood not my boyish endeavours to please, and repaid them with rudeness, so there was soon an end of romance in that quarter. Little Mima daily grew in my esteem, as well as in beauty, and I felt that I was likely to love her when she was more of a woman, but not as yet.

It would have been a fact entirely at variance with the well known penetration of females in matters in which the heart is concerned, if some of my fair Cynosures had not penetrated the secret of my feelings. The quick eyes and the virgin sensibilities of several of my young friends detected, as they were sure to do, the state of my feelings, and then whenever our eyes met we were covered with blushes, mutual acknowledgments of a sentiment too delicate for oral expression. And thus we kept meeting and blushing, and sighing at times, and looking with tender regard, whilst with rare exceptions the word love never escaped from our lips. My heart, though I knew it not, was yearning for the accomplishment of its dearest wish, and that was to be beloved by one worthy of my esteem, as well as of my devotion. And thus had many a young love-dream come and tormented me, and had passed like the rest, when the long nights of winter having come, I won a few kisses in playing at forfeits, or I was emboldened to a word or two in playing at Hide-and-seek, or at Blindman's Buff. Then winter was over, days lengthened, and spring approached, when, one evening in February, we were all sitting round the fire at my uncle's, having our bagging, and a girl who lived at the next house, trying to open the door to go home, found it jammed fast by something which stuck at the bottom. She pulled it out and gave it to my aunt, and on its being opened before us all, great was our astonishment at beholding a valentine displayed. There were Cupids, and darts, and bars of love, and birds and chains, and bleeding hearts, all cut out, and coloured, and set forth in most approved form. There were also lines of writing all around, and several verses and couplets in the middle. After a few minutes spent in admiration of the pretty missive, there was a general request to have it read, and I must own that I felt a mischievous glee in the idea that it would be found to be meant either for my bashful cousin Thomas or his sister Hannah, at whose expense, in particular, I was wishful to have a laugh. At length, after my uncle and aunt had examined the ornaments, it was handed over to Thomas to read, who began by reading the direction, which was, "To Mr. Samuel Taylor, at Mr. W. Taylor's," whereupon there was a general laugh at me, which I met by observing that the letter could not be meant for me, since my name was not Taylor but Bamford, and it was evidently intended for some person of the name of Taylor, and that Thomas was most likely to be that person. But when Thomas began to read the document itself — which he did with evidently mischievous glee — I was covered with confusion, and knew not where or how to look. "Read it; read it," was the general cry; and so he read a number of rhymes, and verses, and complimentary scraps, which removed every doubt as to the valentine being intended for myself and no one else. In the commencement I was addressed "My dear Samuel," then I was described as "tall and straight as a poplar-tree," next informed that

>"The rose is red, the violet blue,
>The pink is sweet, love, so are you,"

and that—

>"As sure as grapes grow on the vine,
>I'm your true love and Valentine,"

each sentence or couplet being followed by a laugh from the youngsters. My uncle enjoyed the scene in his own quiet placid way, whilst my aunt affected to view the affair in a very grave light. The paper was handed from one to another, in order that they might identify the writing, and they all mentioned some person whose writing it was like; at length, after much hesitation, I was allowed to examine the missive, and as soon as my eye rested on the heading, I was almost satisfied with respect to the person who had written it, but I kept my opinion to myself.

"Well," said my aunt, taking an extra pinch of snuff, "it's come to summut, at ony rate, 'at one conno' sit deawn to one's meat i' one's own heawse, but we munbi haunted wi' yung snickits comin' after thee, an' stickin' ther letters under th' dur. But I'll get to know hooas writ'n it, gentlemen. Thy feyther shall see this; heest know heaw theawrt carryin' on; he shanna be kept i' th' dark; it's none reet 'at he shudbe."

I protested that I knew nothing whatever of its coming. I could not prevent its being put under the door, and as for the writing none of them knew whose it was.

"But we win know," replied my aunt, still bent on tormenting me, though she could scarcely conceal the amusement she derived from my embarrassment, "we win know. This papper shall be sent deawn to th' skoo, an' laid afoie th' mesters, an' th' writin' shall be compar't wi' some o' th' copy books, an' th' writer will then be fund eawt, an' yo' shan bwoth be browt an' set ov a form, one aside o' th' tother."

The very idea made my heart sink within me, for I was sure if the writing was produced at school, and the copy books examined, the writer would be detected, and I was more concerned by the thought of the writer being exposed than I was by any care for myself. Instead, therefore, of being gratified and elevated by the compliment which had been given to me, I was both humiliated and unhappy, and I passed many hours in no enviable frame of mind. The day following I asked my aunt to give the valentine up to me, but she refused, and persisted in saying my father should see it, and it should be produced at the Sunday school. I therefore determined to gain possession of it by any means I could devise, and accordingly I stole up to her chamber one forenoon, and found it in a pocket-book under her pillow, and after having minutely conned it over, I destroyed it, and thus put an end to all talk—whether feigned or in earnest—about its exposure in other places. My aunt was now really displeased; and threatened me with my father's severest reprehension; but I was never better satisfied with anything I had done, inasmuch as I had secured the writer — whoever she might be — from the possibility of any annoyance in future, on that account. In a short time I expressed an intimation to Mima that I deemed her to be the writer, but she denied it with seeming displeasure, and I knew not then what to think about the authorship; and thus the occurrence was no more spoken about.

Let no one despise simple incidents like these. They are the rufflings which mark human existence — the joys and anxieties — the lights and shadows — of which humble life is composed.

In consequence of the great dearth of corn which marked the year 1800,[12] my uncle's family had to suffer in manner and degree with the rest of their poor neighbours. We dealt with one of the best provision shops in Middleton, but the meal which we got for our porridge was very often not fit for food, whilst flour for dumplings or pies was out of all question. Our bread was generally made from barley, and tough, hard, dark-coloured stuff it was. Instead of wheaten flour, we had

---

[12] The average price of wheat in 1800 was 110s. 5d. per quarter. It rose to 115s. 11d. in 1801, and fell to 67s. 9d, in 1502.

a kind of mixture which was nicknamed "ran-dan," or "brown George," and sad rubbish George proved to be; but all was welcome, nothing was refused by us hungry lads, whose only care was to get enough. Oaten cake, though made from meal which was enormously adulterated, was so much a dainty that we often took an opportunity for putting a piece of it out of sight, as a delectable snack to be eaten at leisure.

The pinching "barley-times" were over, and flour was selling at sixpence the pound, meal at fourpence, and potatoes at a guinea a load. Yet such was the profusion of work and the price of labour during the short peace of 1802,[13] that plenty was in every man's buttery. Common seven-eights calico, twenty-eight yards in length, was woven at ten shillings and sixpence the cut. A young soldier who came over on a two months' furlough, immediately set to the loom, and worked with extraordinary quickness and perseverance: when his furlough expired, he got it renewed, and again set to work, and when he returned to the regiment he took money with him which bought his discharge. But this prosperity was of short duration; wages receded as fast as they had advanced, and work became very scarce. War again raged fiercely, the nation was to be invaded by a French army from Boulogne, and the whole kingdom was bristling with volunteer bayonets, when one afternoon I was rather surprised by an intimation that my uncle and a neighbour were going to look at the canal at Slattocks, and that myself and cousin Thomas might go with them if we chose. We went, pleased enough of course, but I soon lost my company, and returning home, found the town people all out of doors with fife and drum, and the constables parading for volunteers. I immediately offered myself, and was rejected on account of my stature. But Long Tom, an old campaigner, insisted on having me; he said I was a straight thriving lad, and would make a fine soldier, and so at last I was accepted, though the lowest of any in the ranks, and I got a shilling bounty, a billet whereat to spend my shilling, and a black and red cockade. On being dismissed for the night I went home, and had to encounter another lecture from my aunt, who said it was the first time a cockade had ever been worn by one of their family, and that I was in the way to perdition. I bore her reflections very philosophically, consoling myself with the assurance that I had only performed a duty to my country, and as the corps were never called on—not even to parade—I got through that great "act of sin," as my aunt was pleased to designate my volunteering.

Meanwhile, on fine moonlight nights we enjoyed our wild and mirthful games out of doors, laughing until the echoes came back with laugh as gleesome as our own. Latterly we had also been sometimes joined at our play by one or two of our maiden acquaintance, who lived at a distance, and whom, as a matter of decent attention, I felt obliged to accompany part of the way home, taking many pleasant walks

"By heather brown and meadow green,"

---

[13] The peace of Amiens, March, 1802. War was declared again in May, 1803.

which I was rather pleased to perceive was not at all agreeable to others who, until now, I had deemed almost indifferent to anything which concerned me. I certainly had many compunctions of conscience; I thought, as my aunt said, that I was getting on very fast in sin, and that if I did not turn over another leaf of life, I should become quite abandoned.

But deeper involvements soon followed from a persuasion which about this time took possession of me, and that was, that I was far from being indifferent in the estimation of my fair friend Mima. I remarked that whenever I went into a place where she was one of the company, she was the first to make room for me and offer me a seat; that she always contrived to be near to me, and to be my partner in play; that she always seemed pleased whenever I made my appearance; pleased when I won at marbles or at any other game; and latterly I had to thank her in my heart for a very agreeable instance of her regard and solicitude when almost unheeded by others as I sat ill in the nook. The kind inquiries, the concern for my pain, the tender expression of her countenance beaming at once with pity and beauty, more beautiful from its goodness, could not fail to make an impression in which love was born of gratitude, an impression which I neither strove to conceal from myself nor to resist, since I now found that besides her rare personal charms, she had, what was in my estimation a still brighter charm, in the tenderness of her innocent and devoted heart.

A young lad, a companion of mine, being deeply enamoured of a coy lass who lived at Throstle Nest, he took the expedient of inditing love epistles, in order to interest her indifferent feelings towards his suit. In these occupations I frequently assisted, and gave my advice, as well as accompanied him in his night excursions, when he went to peep at her window, or to deposit his love billets. I also confided to him the secret of my attachment, and, when the season came round, we frequently sat down at his parents' house, after working hours, and penned letters and valentines to our several fair ones, and sometimes also, by way of joke, to others of our female acquaintance. He was a neat writer, and an ingenious framer of such things, and under his tuition I soon became as good a proficient as himself. I now set my ingenuity to task, and prepared a valentine the equal to which for painting, and gilding, and writing, and scissors work, had never probably been seen in Middleton, and this I gave with my own hand to Mima, when she came to play at my loom at night. I had seen too much of the chances of such things getting astray to entrust this precious offering to other conveyance than my own, I accordingly showed it to her first, and asked her opinion as to its merits, when, with admiration not unalloyed by a painful doubt, she inquired for what happy lass the beautiful thing could be intended? and I in a whisper said, "For you, if you can find in your heart to accept it for my sake, and as a sincere expression of my feelings." With joy in her look, and blushes lovelier than those of the queen flower of June, she said, "I do! I do!" and with a smile all modestly radiant, she placed it in her bosom, and went away.

So now we knew each other; we were united in heart, she was mine, and I was her own, but not one word of love escaped from our lips. Days and weeks and months passed, both of us happy in the assurance of mutual affection. I had no companionship with any of the other members of her uncle's family, and consequently I never went there except on an errand to the shop. She, however, being the confidante of my cousin Hannah, had a recognised privilege to come and go at our house without notice, and whenever she chose to do so, and seldom, indeed, a day passed, on which we were not favoured by a visit from the little Hebe, who would have a word of news for my old aunt, or a question to put to my uncle, or something to mention to Hannah, but who never went away until she had stood beside my loom, or tried to weave for me, or fetched me bobbins, or moved my rods, or spoken a word, or bestowed a modest glance, which said more than words could do. And thus we continued, thinking and looking unuttered things — heart united, soul blended, but never speaking of love, never daring to let that fearfully expressive word escape from our lips, never daring even to meet alone, when one day my aunt surprised and almost distressed me by the information that I was by my father's direction to depart that week and take up my abode in Manchester.

And as I am now about to quit this humble roof, and to launch on themes and scenes of a quite different description, it may not be out of place if I here introduce notices of a few scarce and original characters who were acquaintances of and visitors at my uncle's house, during my sojourn in his family.

One of the most singular of these was Richard Hall, a leader amongst the Kilhamite Methodists. Richard in his youth had been a most reckless fighter and drinker, the master and bully of the whole country side about Heywood, but having attended a preaching and a meeting or two of the Old Methodists, he was struck with remorse, became an altered man, and joined the society; and when the schism betwixt Mr. Kilham[14] and the Conference took place, Richard went with the former, and ever afterwards adhered to that party. At the time I first knew him, he was a grave and venerable looking man, gracefully stooping, with thin dark locks, a very dark complexion, a temper surpassingly dogged and immovable, and withal a manner as humble, and a speech as mild as might have become the veriest lamb. Old Richard, however, I believe was as sincere a Christian as many who make more pretensions, but his modicum of grace had to act on a bodily temperament of no common order, and amongst other besetments thrown in his way by the "Evil One," no doubt, was an enormous liking of savoury viands, at whatever time of day, or in whatever manner he became cognisant of their proximity. Richard, however, was not selfish; he was generous of his humble store, and was at all times hospitable towards preachers or poor brethren who came about dispensing the Word in the neighbourhood. On one occasion he invited a preacher to partake his Sunday dinner, and the invitation was accepted with thanks. Meanwhile, the preacher was to preach, and Richard as his host accompanied him to the chapel, where a goodly

---

[14] Founder (1797) of the Methodist New Connexion.

array of hearers awaited them. Well, the prayer was made, the hymn was sung, the text was taken, and the preacher expounded to the great edification of those present. Richard, however, was thinking of other things; the old "Father of Sin," knowing his weakness, kept presenting to his imagination the nice stuffed duck which was roasting for dinner; and such was Richard's anxiety to have it quite ready the moment the preacher returned, that he slipped out of the chapel and hastened home in order to make sure that no time should be lost. His wife, however, who was a little, expert, tidy woman, had the duck already cooked and the dinner waiting, and Richard, snuffing the delicious odour, thought there could be no great harm if he cut a slice and ate it, just to ascertain whether or not there was sage enough in the stuffing. So he took a little of the duck and most excellent it was; then a little more, with some stuffing and apple sauce, and that was delicious. Then he thought that as the duck was ready, he might as well e'en make his dinner at once, and there would be enough left for the preacher when he came. So Richard kept cutting and eating, and cutting and eating, until, when the preacher returned, there was only the pickings of the bones left for him. Richard, now conscience struck, made the best apology he could, which, I believe, amounted partly to a confession of his besetting temptation, and partly to an opinion that his friend had gone to dinner with some other of the congregation. The preacher took all in good part, forgave his brother, advised him as to the future, and concluded with a word of prayer. Richard was greatly humbled, and more guarded for a time, but to the last years of his life, nothing gave him so great bodily satisfaction as "a nice savoury chop," or a "bit of a frizzle."

He was blessed with two daughters, as dutiful and affectionate children they were as ever ate bread from a parent's hand. They worked for and supported their old father and mother when they were unable to support themselves: they tended them in their age and their sickness, nursed them whilst they lived, and buried them with decency. One is still, I believe, toiling with the world only to keep sinking deeper in poverty; the other met a sudden and dreadful fate. After having received such attentions as led her to expect marriage by a religious person, and having been abandoned by him, chiefly in consequence of the envious interference of other religious persons, she seemed to forget herself; became less careful in her attire, less guarded in her conversation, less cleanly in her habits, began to smoke tobacco, then to take liquors in small quantity, and at length, after a course of years, during which she abandoned every propriety save that of modesty, she was found one morning drowned in the mill-pond. If ever a young woman began life with a deservedness to be happy, this was the one; but worth was rendered worthless, a body was ruined— degraded—a soul all but lost. Let humanity shed a tear for the fate of this poor unfortunate:

Once or twice a year, generally when days became short, and cloudy, and stormy, and we had long nights to sit by the fire; at such a time of the year, and oftenest at the close of day, would the door of my uncle's house slowly open, and an old woman leaning on a stick, with her face half muffled, and her person concealed in an old brown cloak, and with sundry rags, bags, and pockets swaggering under her clothes, would enter. Instantly we knew her voice and made room for her to sit down, for "Old Ailse o' Bharla " was always a favourite at my uncle's fireside. She had plenty of tales, chiefly of an admonitory and religious turn; she had "a remarkable gift of prayer," had also been "unfortunate in the disposal of her affection," was "rather out of her mind" as they said, and spent her time in wandering about from place to place, seeking rest, but finding none. Her father was a farmer of some property, residing in Birkle at about the year 1745, and Ailse used to take the week's butter to Bury every Saturday. At that time she was a smart, handsome, young woman, and happened to attract the attention of a young dragoon quartered at Bury, who was himself of respectable parentage, and bore a good character in the regiment. The soldier became deeply enamoured of the Birkle beauty; and lost not much time in making known to her the state of his heart. The very idea of being beloved by a common soldier, Alice looked upon as an insult, and she consequently treated his advances with contempt. The young man tried all means to induce her to lend a patient hearing to his supplication, but the high-notioned maid could not be prevailed on to listen. The lover was respected by many of the townspeople as well as by his comrades, and he engaged several of the former to interest themselves in the promotion of his suit, but all was in vain — the proud beauty would not listen. The youth remained hopeless, and in that forlorn state he marched with the regiment from Bury to Scotland. From thence he wrote several letters to friends in Bury, which described in touching language the strength of his hopeless love and the deplorable state of his mind, and probably some passages at least of these letters would find their way to the damsel's ear. Whether, however, it was from something which she heard at Bury, or from some reproaches of conscience, or from "some dream or vision," or some "apparition," or "love spell" — for she seldom would converse on the subject even with her most confident friends — she suddenly became violently desirous to see the young soldier, and to make amends for the slight and neglect she had practised towards him. She procured a horse and money, and travelled to Scotland, to the town in which she knew he was quartered. She entered the place, and as she and her steed, all weary and travel-worn, went slowly up the street, the sound of a trumpet playing a mournful air attracted her notice, and soon after she met a soldier's funeral procession. She stopped her horse to allow a free passage; several of the troopers gazed on her intensely and began to converse; at length she noticed one whom she remembered having seen at Bury, and him she took the liberty of asking where she should find her lover, when the man, pointing to the bier, said that was his quarters, and the only place where he was then to be found. She fainted, and would have fallen from her horse; the procession halted; the soldiers collected around her; they knew her; they pronounced her name. She was taken care of whilst the funeral was completed. After some time she returned home — an altered woman — a faded rose, — lost in heart — lost in mind — a dream interpreter — a spell solver — a religious monomaniac — an object of pity and in some degree of dread to all who knew her. Such was the tale of "Old Ailse o' Bharla."

CHAPTER XVIII.
HOPE STILL DEFERRED—
NEW EMPLOYMENTS—NEW BOOKS.

ON leaving Middleton I went to live with my sister in Greengate, Salford, and attended once more the school of my father's old Methodist friend, John Holt, of Oldham Street, with a view to my improvement in writing and arithmetic, but my day for learning was gone by, and I took quite as much notice of certain pretty figures which sat in the girl's room opposite to me as I did of those in my book, and so I got not much improvement this time. Mima, however, was not forgotten. I had written to my cousin Thomas informing him of my situation, and in a postscript desiring him to remember me kindly to J. S., but the letter fell into my aunt's hands, and our secret was discovered. To add to my chagrin also, when I went to Middleton Mima was nowhere to be seen, having gone on a visit to Liverpool, so that instead of some faint chance of an interview which I had ventured to hope for, I got nothing save sly jokes and inuendoes about my love for J. S., and I returned home sadly disappointed.

But the time for confirmation arrived, and I, with many thousands of other young folks belonging to Manchester, received the bishop's blessing in the old church. It was with us a matter of some anxiety whether the right hand or the left of the venerable prelate should be placed on our heads, and it was my good fortune to receive the pressure of his right hand, which was considered a propitious omen. The day following the youth from the country districts were to be similarly admitted to Christian communion, and as I knew that Mima would be with the Middleton party, I was in the churchyard at an early hour, waiting with an anxiety which made me indifferent to every other object. First one group appeared, then another came up the Mill Gate, and many of my old schoolfellows and playmates were amongst them; but the right one—the little cherry-blushing maid, with her light auburn hair, and bright looks, and pale-blue frock, and straw bonnet—was nowhere to be seen, and it was not until I had waited and looked, and gazed down the narrow, crooked street, and scrutinised each party as they approached—my sight becoming weary and my heart almost sick—that I at length caught a glimpse of one amid a group of maidens who I thought must be she whose coming I had so anxiously sought for. Another glance, less rapid than the omen of my own heart, told me that I was not mistaken, and the next moment our hands met, and heart-throbbing, agitated, and happy, our only words were mutual inquiries, confused and almost incoherent. My cousin Hannah, I found, was her companion, and though I was always rather partial towards Hannah, in good truth, I would she had at that time been in any other place. She was, however, there, and I could not do less than behave respectfully towards her; it would have been unkind not to have done so; a proceeding which, when a female was in the case, was not to be thought of by me, was not in my nature. And so, after the communion was over, we three formed one company, and, after taking refreshment, spent some time in looking through the wondrous old College, and in viewing the shops in the square, and the toy-stalls in the Smithy Door, where I made each of them a present of a breast-pin with an initial, not all gold of a certainty, but as highly prized as if it had been so, and had come from other hands. When the time of departure arrived, I accompanied them a good distance on the way home, in the hope that some accident would occur which might detach my cousin and give me an opportunity of uttering but one word to my enslaver, and of receiving her assurance of affection in return, for of that I felt not the least doubt; but our attendant never left us for an instant, and I, though again sorely disappointed, made up my mind to remain as contented as I could, with the expression of kind looks, and one tender pressure of her dear hand only. And so, "hoping soon to meet again," we parted, that hope being destined not to be entirely realised.

I was shortly afterwards placed in the warehouse of Mr. Spencer, counterpane and bed-quilt manufacturer, whose rooms were at the bottom of Cannon Street. I was Mr. Spencer's only warehouseman, and my duties were to sweep the rooms, to light the fire, to dust the counters, and to fodder my master's horse, which was housed in a small stable in the yard. I also gave out goods, and took them in from the bleachers when my employer was absent, and on like occasions when a buyer came round it was my duty to show the goods and to sell them if I could. I was thus become a person of some responsibility all at once, and the estimation which I attached to my situation was not of the most humble degree. My wages were certainly rather of the lowest, being — if I recollect aright — about six shillings a week, but as my work was light and I was learning, as it were, the warehouse business, my wages were considered reasonable for the time being. My hours of attendance were from eight in the morning to six in the afternoon in summer, and to five in winter, with an hour at noon for dinner. My master resided somewhere near Levenshulme; he was punctual in his attendance in the morning and his departure in the afternoon. He was an exact and economical man, though not a severe master; he liked to have things done at a proper time, and to find every piece, and book, and paper, and wrapper, and string in its proper place; and as I was active and obliging and also took some pride in having the rooms neat, and the stock in order, I did not often incur his censure. His temperate and economical habits led him, as I understood, generally to dine on his return home; sometimes he would lunch in town, and occasionally he would send me to the Cockpit Hill for a fourpenny veal pie, which he took in the warehouse as a lunch. I liked my master very well, notwithstanding his careful habits and his rather distant manners; I liked his horse, however, better, when he and I had become acquainted. He was one of that useful sort which can work either in a cart or trot under a saddle, and was very docile — only, if there had been more riding for me and less rubbing, I should have liked our acquaintance still better.

After being in the employ of Mr. Spencer some considerable time, I got a situation, at the advanced wages of eight shillings a week, in the warehouse of Mr. Thomas Robinson, of Hodson's Square, whose residence was at Walshaw Lane, near Bury, and who carried on a manufactory there of dimities and quiltings. He also had an agent who made calicoes for him at New Church, in Pendle Forest; Mr. Robinson's town agent or salesman in Hodson's Square was a young man named W., who had lately entered into Mr. Robinson's employment from that of his uncle, a draper, of Melton Mowbray. My warehouse duties here were much the same as at my former place, only I had not a horse to attend upon, as Mr. Robinson, when he came to town on Tuesdays and Saturdays, put up at The Dangerous Corner Inn, and left his nag there to be hostled. My work was, however, much more laborious than at Mr. Spencer's, and consisted chiefly in carrying goods up and down the stairs, in taking rather heavy parcels out to buyers in the town, and in packing up for country delivery.

I cared little, however, about the weight of the work which I was called on to perform, for being an active, clear-winded lad, I was seldom really tired; but one piece of drudgery which Mr. W. set me to do galled my feelings very much, and more so because I neither deemed the manner in which I was made to perform it necessary, nor the performance itself at all within the intention of my contract with my employer. Mr. W., as was quite excusable in a young man of his condition, affected great smartness in his dress, and had his mind been as well cultivated as his person was draped, he would have been a very intelligent gentleman indeed; but his manners, pronunciation, and in fact every action and tone, betrayed the rustic provincialist just come to the great mart of trade with but one wish, one idea, that of gain, gain, gain. I, young and inexperienced, and ignorant of the world as I was, could not fail to draw comparisons betwixt my employer, the plain, unaffected, but perfectly well-bred, well-informed man, and the young country buck whom he had selected to do his business. Both of them wore top-boots, and as Mr. W. would have his perfectly clean, he initiated me into the mysteries of making excellent blacking and boot-top liquid, and then installed me in the honourable office of shoeblack and boot-cleaner to himself. I felt this to be an encroachment on my condition of service, but as I never imagined that Mr. W. would do less than make me a handsome present when I became expert at the job, I did my best to please him. Weeks and months, however, passed, Mr. W. having the distinction of sporting the cleanest and best polished boots in the town; but not one word did he ever utter having the remotest allusion to remuneration. Sometimes when he put them on and turned round his foot to see how smart they looked, he would, in one of his pleasantest moods, say, "Sam, thaw has done these very well," or, "Sam, thaw has made these tops very nyst; they almost look as well as new;" but never did my observant eye detect his hand gliding into his pocket for a sixpence or a shilling to give me for my trouble. And so when one morning he ordered me to carry a slop-basin full of milk—for top-liquid—from his lodgings in Salford to the warehouse, I refused, and told him, once for all, I would neither clean tops nor black bottoms any more. He looked a moment at me aghast and horrified by my audacious rebellion, but finding me neither abashed nor tractable, he only intimated that Mr. Robinson would have to be informed of my insubordination. I, however, never heard anything further respecting the matter, and probably Mr. Robinson was never made aware of the extra drudgery I had performed.

About this time I was delighted by the acquisition of two books, the existence of which, until then, had been unknown to me. One was the second volume of Homer's Iliad, translated by Alexander Pope, with notes by Madame Dacier, and the other was a small volume of Miscellaneous Poems, by John Milton. Homer I read with an absorbed attention which soon enabled me to commit nearly every line to memory. The perusal created in me a profound admiration of the old heathen heroes, and a strong desire to explore the whole of "The tale of Troy divine." To the deep melancholy of the concluding lines I fully responded.

> "Be this the song, slow moving tow'rd the shore,
> Hector is dead, and Ilion is no more."

With Milton I was both saddened and delighted. His "L'Allegro" and "Il Penseroso" were but the expressions of thoughts and feelings which my romantic imagination had not unfrequently led me to indulge, but which, until now, I had deemed beyond all human utterance.

> "Some time walking not unseen
> By hedgerow elms, on hillocks green,
> Right against the eastern gate,
> Where the great Sun begins his state,
> Rob'd in flames, and amber light,
> The clouds in thousand liveries dight.
>   *   *   *   *
> Meadows trim with daisies pied,
> Shallow brooks and rivers wide:
> Towers and battlements it sees
> Bosom'd high in tufted trees,
> Where perhaps some beauty lies,
> The Cynosure of neighb'ring eyes,"

were the very whisperings of the spirit ever present in my day musings, and which brooded over my night dreams. Then again in "Penseroso" the line—

> "Call up him who left half told,"

set my imaginative curiosity to work. What him? who was "him?" when did he live? where did he reside? and how happened it that he

> "left half told
> The story of Cambuscan bold?"

What a strangely interesting subject for thoughtful conjecture was his "story half told," with its Cambuscan, and Algarsife, and Canace, who, whether or not she was ever wived at all, was a mystery impenetrable to me. "Samson Agonistes" and "Paradise Regained" were less attractive than were others of the great bard's miscellaneous productions. His night witchery of "Comus" was the very revel of poetry,

> "The star that bids the shepherd fold,
> Now the top of Heaven doth hold,"

for instance, and

> "Braid your locks with rosy twine,
> Dropping odours, dropping wine,"

conveyed to my heart and my imagination ideas almost as fascinating and dangerous as the spell which bound the fair lady in her "marble venom'd seat," while the concluding lines of the mournfully quaint "Lycidas " inspired me with those pleasing anticipations which are always awaiting the behest of healthful, active youth.

> "Thus sang the uncouth swain to th' oaks and rills,
> While the still morn went out with sandals gray,
> He touch'd the tender stops of various quills,
> With eager thought warbling his Doric lay:
> And now the sun had stretch'd out all the hills,
> And now was dropt into the western bay;
> At last he rose, and twitch'd his mantle blue:
> To-morrow to fresh woods and pastures new."

Oh! John Milton! John Milton! of all the poetry ever read or ever heard recited by me, none has so fully spoken out the whole feelings of my heart—the whole scope of my imaginings—as have certain passages of thy divine minstrelsy.

CHAPTER XIX.
THE WOODLANDS - LIMPIN' BILLY - CATHERINE

"Why should unavailing love
Be kept like hidden gold?"

NEVER, probably, were the reveries of love and poetry more deeply indulged in than they were by me in these my young days of visionary romance. My warehouse work was certainly a laborious reality, but what then? I was more than equal to any fatigue which I had to encounter. I performed all I had to do cheerfully, readily, and thoroughly, and the hours flew swiftly, if not altogether pleasantly, whilst my deepest thoughts were engaged in far other scenes, and the objects constantly occurring to my mental perception were of a quite different nature. Very often, whilst bending beneath a load of piece goods, as I carried them through the crowded streets, or wiping the sweat from my brow as I rested in the noon sun, would I be unconsciously wandering in imagination in the free forest glades with Robin Hood, or

"Over some wide water'd shore,"

with Milton. Then, in such a place as Manchester, where beauty adorned by graceful art appeared at each step, I frequently encountered objects which led my thoughts far astray; and not only was the hardship of my situation forgotten, but, the present overcoming the distant, she to whom I had silently vowed my true and loyal troth, was too often absent from my meditations.

My chief companions at this time were a lad of about my own age named Booth, who was serving an apprenticeship to the business of a letter-press printer, and a young warehouseman named Fielding. After working hours we used frequently in summer time to take our rambles in Broughton, and one of our favourite spots was a piece of rough-broken ground lying on the left of the first ascent of Stony Knows, and known by the name of The Woodlands. Here were various out-of-the-way footpaths, round green hillocks, and through winding dells and hollows, with natural arbours of hazel and wild-rose, and quaint cell-looking little nooks to sit in, where either in the warm sun or in the shade, we could choose our seat; either in the breeze or under the wind that ruffled the gnarled oak, and brushed the grey birch, and swept through the boughs of the red-berried rowan, for such were the only woods remaining, could we lie down, or sit up, or read poetry or romance, or sing, or laugh, or talk over our own little love affairs or those of others. Pleasant Sunday rambles were these, on cool dewy mornings, or on fine sunny afternoons, and vastly did we young joking, laughter-loving frolickers enjoy whatever was enjoyable in our own simple, humble way--from a scramble which should pluck a dog-rose, to a race which should first win the smile of a milkmaid and purchase the warm cream from her can.

On one of these occasions, I and a companion were taking this very pleasant round, and wishing that some beautiful apples, which hung on the other side of the hedge, were ours, when thump went a fine one on my companion's back, and in a moment after I was very near being hit by another. We gathered the fruit and laughed heartily, being greatly pleased with the joke, but were puzzled in what terms to thank the donor, whose person remained beyond our ken. "Who's thrown 'em?" asked one. "What's thrown 'em?" asked the other. "Well, but mine's a good un," said the first taster; "An' mine's as good," said the second. Thank the thrower, whoever threw 'em," said the first speaker; "Aye, an' twenty times o'er were the thrower but a bonny lass," said the second. "If she be a bonny lass, and she's as good as she's bonny, she'll perhaps throw another," said the first speaker; "I shouldn't wonder," said the second. And with that two more apples were thrown, and we heard a laugh and just caught a glimpse of a fair young maiden hastening from the orchard and crouching beneath the apple trees. Quick, however, as was her disappearance, it was not so quick but I knew her to be the sister of one whom I had seen in the town, and who had recently come in for a very considerable share of my deepest considerations. She whom we had seen was indeed a bonny lass, as fair as alabaster, and with locks as dark as those of an "Ethiope queen," whilst the one who had disturbed my equanimity was older, taller, and bore in her manner and her features an expression of sedate and comely beauty, the impression of which I in vain tried to efface. To my poetic fancy she seemed a near personification of Milton's "Nun"--

> "devout and pure,
> Sober, steadfast, and demure;
> With sable stole of Cyprus lawn,
> Over her decent shoulders drawn;"

whilst the sable stole which she wore, being in mourning, was truly befitting her grave and modest demeanour.

After I had been in Mr. Robinson's employ a considerable time, he removed from Walshaw to Bent House, in Prestwich. Here he had a small farm attached to his holding, and when they were busy in the hay, at his request, I willingly went over to help them during a week. In some time after he disagreed with his farming man, and he then wished me to go to Bent House and undertake the man's work. I hardly relished this; I was not satisfied of my ability to do the work as it should be done. I liked my master, however, very well, and his lady, and their little daughter "Mittey," as we used to call her, when I carried her in my arms during the hay season; and as it was a pleasure for me to do anything which pleased my master, considering also that it was my duty to do so in every lawful thing, I consented, for a time, to resign Manchester and its attractions, and so take up my abode at Prestwich. I set about doing my work in the best manner I could, and as "where there is a will, there is a way," I was not long in becoming tolerably handy about my business. I had some notion how to clean a horse before, and I soon learned how to bed my master's neat tit down, and to rub the bits and stirrups, and sponge the saddle, and bridle, and girths. In the shippon I was equally active, except at milking, which was done by one of the women. Knife cleaning I had to learn, but that was easily done, whilst in the business of boot-and-shoe polishing, the instructions which Mr. W. had conferred on me came just to hand, as if this predicament had been foreseen. Martha, the cook, a woman of mature age, was very kind to me, for I was generally cheerful and in good temper, and whenever she had to go anywhere after darkness set in, being afraid of "spirits," I had to go with her. The other cook, who came after Martha left, was kind also; so that I thought cooks were the best creatures in the world. Nancy, the nurse, got blamed, poor girl, for coming about the stable; whilst Sarah, the housemaid, a plain-looking, careful Yorkshire lass, soon left, and her place was supplied by Mary H., the daughter of a cottager residing close by, as thoroughly innocent and sweet-looking a damsel was Mary as ever stepped in England. My mistress got me to clean the plate, and next she wanted me to wait at the table; but that was a thing I could never take up. I was thinking of far other things, and always making some blunder, and at last Mary had to do it instead of me. I had soon plenty of acquaintance in this new place; there was Robert B., who courted Mary, and young Tummus C., who trailed the wing after Nancy. Then there were milk customers from Rooden Lane, and last, though not least to be thought upon, Old Wilde the farmer, whose daughter Mary always welcomed me to a seat by the fire. My mistress, though I could not please her in all things, was a very kind and considerate lady towards me. When I was attacked by a severe quinsy she attended me herself, blistered my throat, dressed the blister, prepared a gargle, and saw that I used it; in short, she did for me what none of my fellow servants could or would do, and she had the satisfaction of receiving my grateful thanks after a short but severe crisis. My master and mistress were both young people, and a handsome couple they made, and with their two little ones, they presented a group the like of which is but seldom found in this world's scene. My mistress was very orderly in her family arrangements, whilst my master was a steady man of business, though not always fortunate. He made no parade of religion, but read prayers before the whole family every Sunday night.

On one occasion my master and mistress went on a visit, during a week or so, leaving myself, the cook, and the housemaid at home. One night the subject of fortunetelling was talked about as we sat on the hearth, and it was agreed that on the very next night I should accompany the women to a famous seer of that description, known by the name of "Limping Billy," who lived at Radcliffe Bridge. The thing was to be quite secret, and so we got Mary Wilde and another woman to keep house whilst we were away, telling them, what indeed was true, that we were going over to Besses-o'th'-Barn, and would soon return. So away we went on foot, and through

Besses-o'th'-Barn, and over the top of Pilkington to Radcliffe, where we found the old conjurer domiciled up some steps in a back yard. According to arrangement, the women entered the place at once, whilst I retired to get a cup of ale at a public house. So I waited here some time, and when I supposed the secrets of futurity had been unveiled, I mounted the steps, and without much ceremony opened the door and entered the room. If my recollection deceive me not, the apartment was a dimly lighted, roomy place, with a close musty smell. Opposite the door stood a plain uncurtained bedstead, containing what appeared to be a bed, the colour of dirty sacking. A table with some spoons and basins stood propped against the further wall, an old oaken chair occupied a dark corner, a miserable-looking fire glimmered in the grate, beside which, with his knees almost up to his chin, seated behind a dirty, sloppy table, with a single candle burning, or rather flickering, appeared the wizard. My two companions sat with their backs towards me, and he with his bony fingers, taloned with long black nails, kept turning round and peering into a tea-cup, mumbling all the time words the meaning of which I could not comprehend.

"Hooas theer?" said he, suddenly looking up and gazing full at me with a malicious and angry grin.

"It's only me," I replied.

"Hooa arto," shouted the conjurer, "an' wot dusto want?"

"I'm waitin' o' these two young women," I replied.

"Then goo an' wait sumweer elze," he said, in a still angry tone, "an' when they want'n the, they'n know wheer to find the."

"Oh, it's only the lad 'at's comn wi' us," said one of the young women.

"He may as weel wawk off at once," said the seer, "I'll do no bizniz while he's i'th' place."

"Hee'l happen hav' his fortin towd," said the other girl.

"Hee'l ha' no fortin towd heer to-neet," said the conjurer.

"An' if it comes to that, I care no great deal either for you or your fortin," I said, pretty well satisfied with what I had observed, and coming out of the place.

More mortified than disappointed, I awaited the arrival of the women in the street, when we adjourned to the public house, and whilst there partaking a glass of warm liquor, they told me that old Billy had caught me laughing, and was very angry at my daring to laugh in his presence. I admitted that I certainly had been betrayed into a not very reverential feeling when I saw them listening so demurely whilst the old impostor peered into his dirty cup and mumbled his prognostics. Nor, as I learned from various hints, was the result of their inquiry such as they had hoped it would be. One of them could not hear anything whatever respecting a particular "old sweetheart," whose coming she had awaited during years, but who never came; whilst the other, whose cheeks were burning, and ears almost cracking, to be assigned to a certain "young man of a fresh complexion and light hair," was inexorably awarded, so said the cup, to one rather aged, stooping, and dark haired. Neither of them, I found, was satisfied, and in order to dispel their evil bodings, I ridiculed old Bill and his trade until they joined me in laughing at their adventure as well as my own, and so in this lively mood we set off towards home, and arrived there better pleased with ourselves and our journey than we had at one time expected to be. I may mention, that in the end, the one got married to her "old sweetheart," and the other to her "fresh complexioned" young fellow. Whilst I was very near being a prophet, old Billy proved an impostor, and the mirth of our home walk was the wisest part of the whole affair.

One day when returning from Manchester, I was overtaken in going up the Red Bank, by a heavy storm of wind and rain, and seeing before me an old woman muffled in her cloak, well, thought I, the old creature shall, at any rate, have a share of my umbrella, if she will. So I walked up beside her and said, "Good mother, come and take shelter under this covering of mine," and I stepped short that she might come under, when at that moment looking up, she displayed a countenance the very type of angelic loveliness, so youthful, so abashed, so gentle, so innocent, and withal so serious, that I blamed myself for having accosted her in that abrupt manner, though with the best of intentions.

"Lord, save us!" at length said I, "that I should have taken such an one as thee for an old woman!" For as a country lad, I was in the habit of theeing and thouing my equals in years and condition.

"You shouldn't try your jokes on strangers," she replied, with a look of reproof, and pausing in her gait that I might pass on.

"If there be truth in human words," I said seriously, "I could not attempt to jest with thee."

"Why not?" she inquired, "you seem rather apt at the thing."

"Indeed I do often jest, like others of my condition, but if thou will believe me, I could not do so whilst looking on a face like thine."

"How then could you pretend to have taken me for an old woman?"

"I had not then marked thy bonny look, and the wind and the rain had caused thy cloak to be so muffled, hood over bonnet, that thou wert in a close guise. Besides, speaking truly, I did think thou walked somewhat wearily up this hill; and I felt moved, for my own mother has travelled this road in many a storm; and I thought this is also somebody's mother, sure enough." And then, when the fair being saw that I was moved, she gave a pardoning look, and said:

"Well! since you do not intend to banter me, I will confess I did walk slowly, for I have a pain here," pressing her hand on her left side.

"If, then, when thinking thou wert aged, I hastened to show thee kindness, surely now I find thee to be young, and passing fair also, I may be allowed to show thee respect. See how the rain again pours, and how the wind blows, and how the leaves are swept from the hedges. Trust me, lass, and walk on this quiet side, and I'll break the storm, never fear."

And so I kept my stout umbrella to the wind, and she walked by my side, her golden hair scarcely ruffled by the wind. And when there came a flash and an astounding roar of thunder, she stopped, trembled, and looked imploringly, and I drew her arm over mine, saying, "Trust God, and fear not. He who hurls the bolt can avert the blow."

Such was my first meeting, and such nearly the terms of my first conversation, with my beautiful Catherine--the daughter of a widow who kept a small farm in Crumpsall.

The thunder soon rolled at a distance, the rain began to abate, the wind almost ceased, still, arm in arm, we proceeded until we arrived at the top of Smedley Lane, where there were stumps leading to a footpath across the meadows, and here we parted, but not before an appointment had been made for a second meeting.

Oft we met again, and took lonely walks in those pleasant undulating pastures, and when her mother came to know about our meetings, she said no one should marry her daughter who could not fetch her away on his own horse. And thereat I felt abashed, I thought I was sure enough presumptuous, and that I had not any right to stand in the way of the old mother's expectations on behalf of her daughter; and so I said at one of our stolen interviews, "How shall this be, dear Catherine?" and she advised that for the present our meetings should be discontinued. "My mother will become more reconciled," she said, "and we shall become older, and better settled in the world; meanwhile, let us not forget each other, but exchange tokens of affection, to be looked upon with kind remembrance when we are distant." And we exchanged love tokens; and after a long interview, and many last words and turnings again, we parted, and I went to Prestwich very downcast, and wishing I had a farm and a horse of my own, that I could make a home for my dear Catherine.

CHAPTER XX.
OTHER SCENES.

SOON after this my master gave up his manufacturing concern and removed to Manchester, and after a short stay there, he commenced business as a shipbroker at Liverpool, where I believe he died. On his leaving the Manchester trade, our late bookkeeper and salesman, Mr. W., began business himself, and I went with him as porter and warehouseman the same as before. Our establishment was removed to High Street, and we did much business in prints and calicoes, both grey and white: a cheap bargain of any kind had always a good chance of being taken up by my employer. Trade was now going very well, and vast sums of money were speedily realised by shrewd, active, and enterprising tradesmen, and of this class my employer was certainly one of the most remarkable. I continued my poetic readings at all leisure moments. I procured and read speedily a complete Iliad in English. Some of Shakespeare's works having fallen in my way, I read them with avidity, as I did almost every other book, and though deeply interested by his historical characters and passages, I never either then or since relished his blank verse, or that of any other poet. I never, as it were, could get the knack of it; and as compared with rhymed poetry, it has always seemed to me, indeed,

"Like the forc'd gait of a shuffling nag."

If any one wishes to see a play performed he has only to walk the streets of Manchester, or any other of our large towns, and he may behold the perfection of either tragedy or comedy enacted by performers who need neither prompter, call-boy, nor rehearsal; but all coming and going as regularly as if the piece were a play "got up" and "put on the stage, as the phrase is, "put on ready for representation." The scenes are admirably painted--the machinery perfect in its operations, of wonderful construction, and sometimes of most awful effect. The actors might have been made for the performance of their several parts, so aptly do they go through them; whilst the dresses, decorations, and all the accessories of the piece, are sure to be wonderfully befitting. And with such a stage as this, with its ever-varying reality before our eyes, who can require sham repetition as an after-part? Not I at any rate.

Milton's miscellaneous works were still my favourites. I copied many of his poems into a writing book, and this I did, not only on account of the pleasure which I felt in their repetition, and in the appropriation, so to speak, of the ideas, but also as a means for the improvement of my handwriting, which had continued to be very indifferent. The Odyssey and Æneid, which I also procured and read about this time, seemed tame and languid, whilst the stirring call of the old Iliadic battle trumpet was ringing in my ears, and vibrating within my heart. In short, I read or attentively conned over, every book I could buy or borrow, and as I retained a pretty clear idea of what I read, I became rather more than commonly proficient in book knowledge, considering that I was only a better sort of porter in a warehouse.

I was now a strong, active young fellow, fast rising into a man, with somewhat of a will and away of my own; and with a coolness of thought, and a steadfastness of purpose, increasing with my years, and strengthening with my strength. I had not yet become a beer drinker, but I could take my half pot of porter whilst at work on a hot day without feeling the effects of the liquor, and though I was not in the least quarrelsome, but on the contrary was given to good-humoured jocularity, I would as lief almost have had a battle on my hands, in a right cause, as have been without one; and so in this line I not unfrequently met with some rough amusement. I kept still, however, adhering to my simple habits and diet, working my work promptly, and perhaps zealously, and giving the remainder of my time to the reading of my favourite authors, to country strolls at eventide, or on Sundays, or to a good swim or two in season at Sandy Well or Broughton Ford, with my acquaintance. Seldom did my inclination or my connections lead me to the theatre. That sort of thing did not please me; there was too much of tinsel and clap-trap, too little of reality, of thorough natural freshness for my taste. And when I did go, I never came away without an impression which spoiled all the rest, that I had been witnessing a delusion. Neither my spare hours, therefore, nor my loose change were often spent at the play-house; my home-goings were consequently more early and regular than they other wise might probably have been. I went to rest betime, and rose clear-headed, and with a strength and buoyancy of limb that mocked toil and weariness. My breakfast was generally a basin of milk, with a good thick slice round a loaf toasted and soaked in. My dinner I either took at the cook's shop at the corner of Brown Street, where the Commercial Hotel now is, or at the pie-house in Cockpit Hill, where in repay for my free and cheerful discourse with the old lady, and my gentle deference to the daughter, I was frequently offered the use of a plate and knife and fork, and those were favours not accorded to many. My supper would be bread and milk again. My bed was a very humble but cleanly one, in the upper room of a tall sombre-looking tenement occupied by one widow Pick-Lip and her daughter--a little pale, prim, automatic, fastidious body, whose only solace now was in the artless prattle of her young unfathered child. The house was situated in a strangely isolated yard, bounded on all sides by a high wall, or by the back walls of other houses, and approachable only by a narrow covered passage closed by a door, and leading out of another long alley called Ditchfield Court, which latter place was accessible only by steps from that end of that quaint and antique old street called Long Mill Gate, which emerges in the open space, formerly known as The Apple Market, close to the Old Church.

From this part of the town, Strangeways, Broughton, and the Cheetham Hill road being the most ready outlets into the country, it not unfrequently happened that my steps almost involuntarily took the direction of the latter quarter, and that on many occasions when I merely purposed to stroll as far as Smedley or Cheetwood, I found myself lingering upon and retracing the footpaths on which Catherine and I had so often strayed. A feeling of profound but benignly soothing melancholy was at these times ever present, humbling my heart and straightway reassuring it

> "Wounding as it were to cure,
> Strength'ning only to endure."

On one of these occasions, when these sadly solacing communings, protracted until night, found me wandering like something lost, I was recalled to consciousness by the barking of a dog, and the flashing of a light, and the clapping to of a gate, through which I saw Catherine pass swiftly towards a dwelling at a short distance from the one she had left, which was her mother's. I took my station under a hedge and awaited her return, and when she approached, I gave the same low whistle which she had often heard before, and she stopped, holding up the lanthorn, and exclaiming, "Bless us, lad! can that be you?" I came from my covert and convinced her it was myself, come I scarcely knew how or why, as I said, but hoping against despair that I might once more catch a glimpse of her dear form through the window, or hear her voice, or at least see some one of the family who I knew had seen her, and then I could return contented. "Indeed," she said, taking the hand which I extended, "you are very kind; but how cold you are--you have been out in the dew until you are wet and starved: wait a few minutes, and I will make an excuse to come out again; I have something to tell you." And with that she disappeared through the gate, and went into the house. She was as good as her word. In a short time I heard her well-known step, and went to meet her, and as I modestly embraced her, and expressed a thousand thanks for this token of her kindness and confidence, she bade me hush, and leading me beneath some trees, said she believed me to be worthy of her confidence, even of her affection, or she should not have met me again, but that her stay must be short, and that this meeting would perhaps be our last as lovers.

It would be of little use were I to attempt to narrate the particulars of all that was said on that mournful occasion. The conversation of lovers is seldom interesting to any save themselves. I urged, I pleaded, I besought, I even reproached and again pleaded, with every persuasive which my unpractised but heart-bursting emotion could pour forth, in order to induce her to say that we should once more live for each other, but in vain. All she would promise was that this should not be our final parting, but that, whatever might be the consequence, she would meet me once more.

The simple-minded but tenacious girl made known to me, however, in the most kindly and confiding manner, the circumstances which had induced her thus unexpectedly to sacrifice our mutual happiness. She, like the girls at Prestwich, had been trying to look into futurity, and had given ear to the prophecies of an old fortune-telling woman, who said "it was not our fate to be united," "that if the connection was not broken off one of us would die," "that an evil star was in the table of our destiny," "that, in fact, if the acquaintance was continued, I should prove false in the end." "And so," added the distressed and almost terrified girl, "what must be, must be." "It is of no use striving against the decrees of Providence." "It is a great misfortune, but it might have been worse; we can still esteem each other, nay, love each other as dear friends, even meet each other as friends in passing through the world, and surely that will be enough. If we can each be certain of one true 'friend in need and indeed,' we shall be fortunate after all."

When I tried to reason her out of her delusion, she informed me that the old woman was "infallible," and that before she gave a final decision she always had access to the body of a lady which lay embalmed in one of the rooms of a certain great house which stood on the roadside leading to Manchester, and that whatever she in consequence foretold, it was useless to attempt to evade.

And so, with one fond embrace, and mutual prayers that God would protect and bless us through life, we again parted, and I, with my heart somewhat consoled by the assurance of meeting her once more, returned to my quiet and solitary old domicile.

I now became moody and melancholy, brooding over my ill success in courtship, and wondering how it happened that love like mine should go unrequited. I felt piqued also, and my pride was wounded, that the fiat of an old woman should have had more influence than all my entreaties. In my intercourse with the fair sex, the emotions of the heart had hitherto been my only offering, and now the unworthy surmise first occurred that the offering had been too pure, that the heart and the imagination alone of man could not suffice for womankind, that the beings I had adored were not so entirely divine as my poetry had painted them, and that, if I would be really loved with a womanly love, mine must be of a less ethereal nature than it had hitherto been. This notion I found to be the confirmed opinion of some of my more experienced acquaintance, who laughed at my simplicity, and with this dangerous and debasing impression on my mind, I began to think there would be but little sin in my acting differently from what I had done. That persuasion had an immediate and injurious effect on my conduct, and the consequences soon followed.

I first set about ridding myself of the influence which every female, in whatsoever degree, had upon my feelings. I resolved to love them all alike, and never more to give to woman the power of inflicting pain such as I had endured. With the aid of pride, which I summoned to my assistance, and a strong resolve to be free, I flattered myself that I had accomplished this feat pretty soon, and I began to breathe with greater confidence. From all the female sex I had taken a distance, one was as near to me as another, and none were near enough to wound. I could gaze on beauteous woman without emotion; I could converse with her in terms of the coolest civility, whereas my heart-movings would in past times have embarrassed my utterance. I was no longer her slave; and the only duty I thenceforward acknowledged as owing to her was to protect and please her, and in return, when so disposed, to accept of her endeavours to please. But never again was she to have my happiness at her disposal. So I became, as I thought, a free-and-easy young fellow, with few things to care about save the performance of my labour, the receipt of my wages, and the partaking of such amusements as my humble means afforded. A dangerous position was this for youth of my present turn of mind to occupy. My father, whom I frequently called to see, never failed to give me the best of advice, and I deferred to it for the moment, but seldom did its influence long remain after I had quitted his presence. To three points of his advice, however, I have, I hope, adhered through life, namely, to stand up for the right and fear not, to be inflexibly honest, to avoid all approach towards presumptuous assurance, and rather endeavour to be marked for solid worth.

Hitherto "fond and sinless love" had been my protection against many temptations, but now that was gone I found myself beset with inducements to vice which I had previously deemed not worth a thought. There was a void in my existence, and it required to be filled up by some means. Small tipples of ale became not unfrequent; my company keeping was more promiscuous; my conversation less modest; and my deportment less reserved. Irreverent thoughts would obtrude whether at church or chapel, and those places became mere rendezvous, where this one might be seen, or that one might be found, or where an hour or two might be spent as at a theatre, in the show of fine clothes, and hearing the drone of tranquillising music. In short, I was fast ripening into a graceless young ruffian, loving no one as I could once have loved; beloved by no one as I would have been beloved; and preserving only so much of self-respect as guaranteed my integrity, and the performance of my duties to my employer.

But a new allurement now crossed my path, and had it not been that the instrument for trial was just the one it was, my demoralisation might have taken a decided and fearful course.

One night, as I was proceeding home, a woman of the town took hold of my arm, and desired me to go with her. I had never been so accosted before, and as she walked on with me the thoughts of being seen with such an one at my side covered my cheeks with burning shame. Confiding, however, in my own self-control, I took the dangerous resolve of hearing what she had to say, and of observing what she would do. I therefore suffered her to continue her conversation, and she led me into less frequented streets, and by back corners, where under the shroud of darkness her blandishments had well-nigh shaken my virtuous resolves. Something she said about "the sweet air of the country," when I asked her if she came from the country? and on her replying that she did, I questioned her as to where she came from, and did not my ears tingle, and my heart leap, when she said "from Middleton." "Ah!" I said, "I come from Middleton." "Did I?" what was my name then? I told her, when, uttering an exclamation of joyful surprise, she would have smothered me with caresses. I next questioned her as to her name, and seemingly incredulous, she asked me if I really did not know her? I assured her I did not, and she wept to think, as she said, that she should have carried me in her arms when I was an infant, and now that we should meet here and I did not know her. Who could she be? I again asked, and she mentioned a name at the hearing of which I almost sank to the earth.

She had been born and brought up at the house next door to that of my parents; she was the beloved child of their early friends and associates; she married when I was but an infant, and her husband, when I could run about, used to make whip-cord, and kites, and banding to fly them with for me. I knew the man well at that time; he was still living, and it not unfrequently happened that I was in his company when I went over to Middleton. I was disgusted with myself and her. I shuddered at the sin which I had well-nigh committed, though she would have continued her blandishments, and even pressed me for an assignation at another time. But my soul revolted, and I got rid of her by paying for a glass of hot liquor at "The Dangerous Corner" public house. Dangerous indeed.

CHAPTER XXI.
OLD FEELINGS AWAKENED -
A VISIT, AND OTHER MATTERS.

FORTUNATELY, however, for me, I was for the present somewhat recalled from this unsettled course of life by an incident which, though trifling in itself, gave a startling impulse to my dormant feelings. A young woman, an acquaintance of, and near neighbour to, Mima, my young Middleton favourite; accosted me one day in the streets of Manchester, and reproached me for having, as she said, forgotten the little maiden, who, she gave me to understand, still retained a tender remembrance of former days. Was that true? was it possible that she could cherish a kind recollection of one who had been so long absent? I asked. She said it was even as she had stated. This moved the old pulses of my heart, and awoke that tender feeling of regard which had been too long dormant. I entrusted the young woman with a kind message to Mima, confirming it with a small token which I thought would be acceptable, and I did not forget to make a present of a gay ribbon to the bearer of this unhoped-for but welcome information. I now resolved to see my fair agitator, at all events, and to learn from herself, frankly and promptly if possible, whether or not our former friendship was to be renewed, or abandoned at once and for ever. I therefore went to Middleton the Sunday following, and as Fortune I suppose was just at that time not in a humour for throwing impediments in my way, I obtained an interview with the object of my solicitude, and besides finding her as modest and bewitching as ever, the very model of a little head-bowed, health-flushed Hebe, a lily rose-tinted, I had the ineffable pleasure of receiving in her own words, with every grace of maidenly shame, an acknowledgment that I had long been, and still was, regarded with a more than friendly interest by her. This was enough for the present, and after making arrangements whereby we might correspond by letter, I bade adieu to the dear little girl, and walked back to Manchester in a state of mind to which I had long been a stranger. I felt that in this transaction I had, in fact, only performed a duty: that my early love had after all the most rightful claim to my affection; that she was in every respect worthy of it; and that, in this instance as in many others, the performance of duty had been my guide to happiness. I was again as deeply in love as ever, only this time I was serenely contented; my confidence was greater, the void in my heart was filled, and I was happy.

I had been of opinion for some time, that my services to Mr. W. were worthy of an increased remuneration, and I mentioned the matter, but my employer could not be prevailed upon to adopt my views, and so after the expiration of a month's notice I left his service.

It was about this time that on going home one evening, I saw a young fellow beating a girl in the street.

"Hallo, you fellow," I said, "what are you abusing that girl for?"

"What's that to you?" said the blackguard.

"I'll let you see what it is to me if you lay a finger on her again."

"Oh, you will, will you," said he; "come on then."

So we set to, and in five minutes I beat him till he was dizzy and had enough. I then led the girl from the crowd, and as we were going she told me he had beaten her because she could not supply him with money for his night's revel. Was he her husband then? I asked. She said he was not, and gave me to understand that she was an unfortunate girl, and that he had latterly been supported from the wages of her prostitution. "He wanted some to-day," she said, "whereas I have not tasted meat since yesterday morning."

"Not tasted meat?"

"Not one crumb," said the girl, wiping her bleeding mouth and tear-wet cheeks; "not one single crumb has passed my lips."

"If that be the case," I said, "thou hadst best come this way;" and so I led her to a cook's shop, where according to her choice, she had a plate of hot pie, which I paid for and left her eating it.

"Did I not promise that I would meet you once more," said a gentle voice, as I stepped into the street.

"Good heavens! Catherine!" I said, "is that you."

"It is even me, and I have now redeemed my promise." "Did you see me go in here?" I said.

"I saw both you and your companion go in," she said; "I marked you coming down the street."

"Dear Catherine, you seem unwell--you are agitated; let us seek a more suitable place."

"This place is very suitable, for all I now have to say is--to bid you good-bye."

"Shall I not go with you?" I asked.

"No, I have company here," she replied, pointing to an elderly woman who stood at a short distance. "Farewell," she added, "Old Lissy might have been further mistaken;" and with that she stepped over to the old woman, and they both went down the Mill-Gate--one of them looking back, as I perceived, ere they finally disappeared.

Poor Catherine! Three months previously I could not have believed that a meeting and parting of ours could have taken place with so little emotion on my side.

It was now the season when Middleton wakes was approaching, and as Mima would have to come to Manchester to buy a new gown, we arranged in all the simplicity of our hearts, that she should call at my lodgings, when I would accompany her in shopping, and afterwards see her on the way towards home. I gave my landlady to understand that a young woman, "my cousin, from the country," would be there that day. Well, I waited all the morning, but Mima came not; all the noon, but there was no appearance of the expected one. Two, three, four o'clock were gone, and unable to rest I kept passing and repassing from my lodgings to the street and back again; still my "dove appeared not at the window;" and during a pang which was not to be borne, I rushed into the street, and paced, very probable like one deranged, two or three times across the Baron's yard. In a few minutes I controlled myself sufficiently to return, and was preparing to stride desperately the steps of the entry, when, looking up, who should be coming down, agitated and trembling, but the dear one who had caused all my uneasiness. "Eh, Mima!" "Eh, Samhul!" were our only exclamations, as we stood gazing on each other, unable for a moment to reciprocate any other token of pleasure. My old landlady and one or two old neighbour women stood at the upper end of the court, eyeing us and our motions with the knowing curiosity for which persons of their condition are remarkable. "She's Samhul's cousin from the country," said my landlady. "Nay," replied another, "yonder are no cousins." "If they are cousins," remarked a third, "they're cousins an' something else besides."

I wished Mima to stop and have tea, but she declined, not liking the scrutiny of the old women, who had been putting questions to her when she went up the court to inquire for me. Besides she had two young girls with her whom she had left waiting in the churchyard, so I went with her and we found the girls, and after shopping and looking through the town, we returned and rested at Tinker's Gardens, then a sweet bowery place, and still as solitude on that week-day afternoon. Here we took refreshment in one of the secluded arbours, and whilst our two young companions strolled round viewing the gardens, I and my fair one had a most agreeable opportunity for expressing all that our full hearts permitted us to say. As night approached, we left this pleasant place, and I escorted my company into the new high-road which was then in the course of formation betwixt Manchester and Middleton. We knew not how to part, and I kept going further and further until we arrived at Middleton, where having seen Mima and her companions within a few yards of home, I left them and returned to Manchester with as much happiness in my heart as a human being could experience and live.

The ensuing wakes at Middleton was probably celebrated with a greater degree of finery and a more plenteous hospitality than it had ever been before, or has been since: besides banners, groves of evergreen, garlands of flowers, and dancers numerous, not fewer than six bands of music paraded the town, and eleven rush-carts. But Mima and I left all the gaud, and the music, and the wonder-seeing crowd, to have our lone walks in the woods. To us the wakes and everything connected with it appeared as vanity unworthy of human thought. Mima took her milking cans and I went with her, but when we got to the woods the kine were not to be found, so we left the cans at the milking booth--a shed of wattles--and a most pleasant excursion we had in search of the cows, and after rambling long, often, indeed, forgetful of the beasts, we found them at last, in a shady hollow, licking the tender herbage that fringed a little rill. So we drove them to the booth and Mima milked them, and then with her cans, one in the other and gracefully balanced on her head, we returned to the crowded street and separated. That evening; however, we had another and a longer walk. Turning away from "vanity fair," we sought the lone bypaths and sweet meadows of Hopwood, where, whilst the jingle and hubbub sounded afar off, we

> "Wander'd by the greenwood-side,
> And heard the waters croon;
> And on the bank beside the path,
> For hours thegither sat,
> In the silentness of joy."

And many a time since that happy eve have the same twain been seated on that "Bank beside the path," in the muteness of sorrow, as well as "In the silentness of joy."

CHAPTER XXII.
SELF-DISPOSAL, BUT NOT SELF-CONTROL—FURTHER DEROGATION AND CONSEQUENT TROUBLE.

AT this time the trade was going remarkably well, and weaving was a very profitable employment. I went back to live at Middleton, and got a loom with board and lodgings at an old acquaintance of my father's. Being now master of my own time, I partook of country amusements with the other young fellows of the neighbourhood, and frequently went out a-hunting. After one of these gatherings when we had a very hard run, during which I had footed it pretty cleverly, one of the old hunters, Sam Stott by name, was so pleased with my performance, that when the hunt was over he insisted on treating me. We accordingly turned into the first public house we came to, and that happened to be the identical one at Trub Smithy, at the door of which "Tummus' Cawve " was unfortunately killed, which accident is so well described in Tim Bobbin's celebrated "Lancashire Dialect." The clay had been excessively wet, which had not, however, prevented a very large attendance at the hunt. The public house was consequently crowded, but Old Sam contrived to make a way into a corner, where he having ordered some "warm ale and ginger," the best thing in the world, he said, after a wet day, we sat drinking until our clothes were dry on our backs, that being the only natural and proper way, as he insisted, in which clothes ought to be dried, fires being intended for roasting and boiling meat only, and to warm old women, but never meant for the drying of hunters' clothes. So we made ourselves comfortable, and as may be supposed, by the time our clothes were dry, we were rather far beyond the line of sobriety. This was, I believe, my first decided offence of that nature, and well had it been had it been my last.

This breach, slight as it appeared to me at the time, was followed by grave consequences. It led to a new set of acquaintances, to a wider and wilder range of enjoyment; it wonderfully loosened my notions of propriety, already too much relaxed in one respect, and brought me to the conclusion that "as a young man was not answerable for the conduct of those whose company he kept, neither was he to be damaged by the associating with them," that there was no great harm in "doing as others did," and that "there were worse things after all, than a young fellow getting a drop too much, now and then." This was a pitiable state of mind for one of my age to be in; and though I did not, in consequence, become a reprobate and a habitual drunkard, I became more easy about the scandal and the sin of inebriety, and the path to other transgressions was thus temptingly laid open.

One day I was startled by the sound of the fife and the drum, and on going to learn the cause, I found the overseers and constables at one of the public houses, enlisting volunteers for the "army of reserve." I immediately offered myself, and was the first that was accepted. After that a number of young men joined; we got a shilling each and a cockade, with as much ale as we chose to drink, and the consequence was that, like the rest of my comrades, I went home in much the same condition as that in which I returned from the hunting bout. On the day following we had another meeting with the town's officers, and after parading round the neighbourhood with fife and drum, we enlisted as many as we wanted, and we separated in the same state as we were in the night before. After which we were never more mustered, or even called upon; and all the money expended, as far as the township of Middleton was concerned, was entirely thrown away. Constables and overseers had, in those days, a very straightforward way of doing business. On receiving an order, or even a direction less tangible, from a magistrate or magistrate's clerk, it was forthwith carried into effect. The magistrate was everything, the ratepayers and vestry nothing, and money was expended which was never inquired into afterwards. If the minister, or some one or two of the "gentleman ratepayers," put a question or so to the overseer when he met him, and the reply was, "Oh, Mr. A. or Mr. B. the magistrate ordered it," all would be right, and nothing further would be said about the matter. These sort of affairs are managed somewhat differently now in this year 1848, when I am writing these lines.

It was at this time, whilst I was a recruit with my cockade in my hat, that I first heard the song of "Jone o' Grinfilt," at Manchester. It was a sort of doggerel that took well, being just suited to current events and the taste of the loyally vociferous multitude. We have now been at peace during thirty years, and the multitude is still here, many-headed, loud-tongued, as of yore, but where is the loyalty? Here absolutely it is not. With no English multitude is it to be found. How, then, has it been banished, and whither is it gone? These are questions which I think are worthy of the deep consideration of our philosophers and statesmen, and to their elucidation I must leave them. One opinion, however, I, humble as I am, may venture to propound, and that is, there have been great faults somewhere, or all the ancient loyalty of our working population would not have disappeared and left, as it has done, in its stead, Irish felony in our towns, and riff-raff Chartism in our villages. Assuredly there has been enormous mismanagement somewhere, and our gracious Queen, when she meets her faithful Commons, would do well to put the question— What has become of the loyalty of that "bold peasantry," once their "country's pride"? Is it destroyed? Why has it been destroyed?—These would be found to be potent and puzzling questions, I think.

Having thus wended my downward course pretty rapidly, with now and then a pang of conscience which was soon quieted, and a flush of shame which was soon suppressed: having become a hunter with the wildest, a lover of company not the choicest, one no longer a stranger at the tavern, and a follower of the fife and drum, the reader will scarcely be surprised at learning that further humiliation awaited me; and that during one of my wild outbreaks, having obtained the company of a

Yorkshire lass, as thoughtless as myself, it was not long before I became amenable to the parish authorities, for certain expenses which were about to be incurred.

My old uncle and aunt, with whom I again lived, read me some very grave lessons when the news of this affair broke out. For my part, I was covered with confusion, and torn, by remorse, for I had early discovered that, had there been no other female in the way, I never could have made up my mind to become the husband of the one I had thus injured. I was somewhat relieved, however, by learning that she took the affair less to heart than many would have done, and that the obtainment of a handsome weekly allowance was with her as much a subject of consideration as any other. I say I was relieved, but I never hoped, never attempted to palliate the wrong I had done, or to evade the shame I had incurred.

One morning about Christmas, after being out spending the night, I returned home and flung myself on the bed with my clothes on. It was just breaking day when I heard the front door, which I had left unbolted, open, and a rough voice shout "Hallo!" I desired my cousin Hannah, who I had heard was awake, and who slept in the same chamber with her brother and myself, to ascertain who the person was, and she tried to do so, but could only make out that it was some strange person, and that he wanted her father. I being dressed, went downstairs at once, and found a tall, powerful, broad-set man standing with his back against the door-post, and holding the door catch with one hand. I knew him instantly to be Samuel Fielding, the constable, for the shutters being closed and the place quite dark, I could see him against the grey of the morning whilst he could not distinguish me. "Whot," I said, "aryo wantin' mi feyther, then?"

"Aye," he replied; " but dusno one Samhul Beamfort live heer?"

"Yoy he dus," I said ; "dunyo want him too?"

"Aye, I awnt him too," he replied, "thy name's Beamfort isno it?"

"Nowe," I said, "my name's Taylior, but Samhul's upstairs; I con coe on him deawn, as yo want'n him."

Meanwhile I had been getting my feet into my shoes, my hat being beyond my reach, and now standing at the bottom of the stairs, I shouted lustily, "Samhul! come deawn, theaw'rt wanted directly. Dusto yer, Samhul? come deawn." "Yod'n better step in an' sit yo' deawn;" I said to the constable, "Samhul will be heer in a minnit."

The cunning old fox, however, would neither come in nor sit down; so I loitered about, as it were, in the dark, humming a snatch of a tune, and shuffling to and fro, betwixt the house and the kitchen.

I could hear that some of the family were stirring upstairs — in fact, my very unaccountable summons had awakened them all.

"He'll be heer directly," I said; "he's comin':" and with that I shot the bolt of the back door, flung it open, and darted down the street, never stopping to look at another man who made a grasp at me, and the wind of whose fist, as I sprung past him, I felt on my ear.

Down the street I went, and this new foe at my heels. He was one of the best "sprint-runners" in Middleton, but he might as well have run after a hart-royal. I leaped the fence in the lane, crossed the broad meadow, and was safe in Middleton Wood by the time the disappointed official got back, puffing and blowing, to the bottom of my uncle's stairs. For it would seem the constables were not quite certain whether or not the delinquent had escaped. By that time my uncle was coming down, as was his wont, part dressed, when the officers eagerly inquired where Samhul was.

"Marry," he said (a common exclamation), "I reckon he went eawt at th' back dur, an' I conno tell where he is neaw." "Wur that really him, then?" asked the constables.

"Well, I believe it wur," said my uncle, laughing till his sides shook as the two worthies hurried into the street.

By that time, however, I was walking leisurely towards Prestwich, where I arrived at breakfast-time, just as Mary Wilde and her father were sitting down to their porridge. They were very glad to see me, though surprised that I came without hat. I, however, explained my circumstances as briefly as possible on account of Mary. I got a breakfast with them, good enough for a king; and the kind girl cleaned my shoes, and washed my stockings, which were covered with mud. She also borrowed me a hat, and after dinner, being again in travelling trim, I went to my father at Manchester, who, after a sound rating, made all things right with the overseers, and I returned to Middleton.

CHAPTER XXIII.
A LONG JOURNEY AND A NEW LIFE.

BUT I had become strangely unsettled, and it was time that a change of some sort should take place. I again left Middleton, and seeing bills up at Manchester that a number of young men were wanted for the coasting trade betwixt South Shields and London, I engaged with a person appointed to make contracts, and after parting from my father, who went down on his knees and prayed earnestly that God would recall me from sin, I went through Middleton, bade adieu to Mima, who was heartbroken; and mounting a coach at Oldham, I, with seven others—volunteers like myself—reached York that night, and stopped there. The morning following our conductor led us through that wonderful structure the Minster, after which we mounted coach again, and finished our second day's journey at a large inn at Sunderland, where we again stopped all night.

My companions were chiefly lads from factories and dye-houses: a rude and simple set they were, and, I believe, pretty honest also. I know not how it happened, but certainly the people of the house seemed to feel an interest in my welfare. They knew for what service we were destined, and I received more than one hint that I should repent of the step I was taking. The cook and the bustling old waiter both seemed to think that I was cut out for something else than a sailor, and they dropped privately certain ominous intimations about hardships, and dangers, and impressments. At last I was given to understand that if I would remain at the inn, and make myself useful in whatever I could do, my conductor should be satisfied, and I should be well treated, and be protected from the press-gang; but thanking the motherly-looking hostess for her kind offer, I declined it, and went forward with my party to South Shields.

Here we were quartered at a public house by the quay side, and at night slept on board a brig which lay alongside, my bed being made of sails spread on the floor of the half deck, with a coil of rope for my pillow. In the course of a few days we signed indentures to serve Nicholas Fairles, Esquire, during three years, in return for which we were to have £20 per annum, ship allowance, and protection from impressment, every man receiving at the time a document from the Admiralty which was to be his protection. Our ship was the brig Æneas, Matthew Peacock, master; and after having received our outfit of clothes and sea stock of groceries and other articles, we took on board a cargo of coal, and heaving our anchor, we sailed with the night tide, and were soon out of the harbour. Five of our Manchester party, with some old hands, formed the crew of this vessel; and after the anchor was secured, the spars lashed, and the sails set, the watch was called over, and I, being on the captain's watch, went below with the rest; the mate, William Peacock, the captain's son, a fine young seaman, remaining on deck with his portion of the crew. And thus was I, at last, a sailor on the North Sea.

From what appeared to me to have been a very short sleep, I was aroused by three thundering knocks and a hoarse shout down the hatchway, " Starboard watch, ahoy." I was on deck immediately, indeed I had not undressed, but had slept on my old bed of sail and rope. Our captain was standing near the companion, and after rubbing my eyes I saw the shore with its green hills and homesteads on our starboard, or right hand, whilst the open ocean lay glistening and heaving beneath the new light of the morning on our left. I was not long, however, in discerning that several ships seemed to be crossing towards the course we were steering, and from a sense of duty, pointing them out to the captain, I asked him whether they were not French? Though he was not much given to pleasantry, he pretended to be of opinion that they possibly might be "Frenchmen," and asked what I thought should be done in case they were? "Well," I said very simply, "I reckon we shan hato feyght 'em then." "I suppose we shall in that case," he said. "An' so, Captain," I continued, "hadno we better be gettin' th' cannons ready," alluding to two carronades on the quarter-deck, and two stern chasers. This answer so diverted him that he gave a hearty laugh, and afterwards I was rather a favourite with him.

When we were off Robin Hood's Bay, one of the stern guns was fired, and in a short time a fishing cobble came alongside, and the captain went ashore. His family lived there, and as it was probable we should go from London to Montreal for timber, he wished to bid them good-bye. In a short time he returned, bringing his wife with him; a clever, good-looking woman she was. She took leave of her son, and the captain saw her back on shore, and then coming on board, we set sail and again made for the open sea. We had scarcely got from under the rocks of the bay, when the wind began to blow against us, and we had a threatening sun-down, and a terrible night—at least, so it appeared to me. I was awoke at one time by three thundering knocks as before, followed by the summons—"All hands, ahoy," and on getting on deck the first circumstance that took my attention was that waves, having the appearance of streams of fire, were breaking over the bows of the vessel and sweeping the deck. In a moment I was up to the knees, and I actually jumped, thinking I should be burned, but I soon found out my mistake. The scene on deck was such as made us young seamen feel very grave. There was the vessel, climbing, as it were, up the huge billows, and next plunging headlong as if she were going to the bottom at once. Then the horrid tempest of waves uprushing, and of winds down-sweeping, filled space with their terrible howl. The hoary old deep moaned as it were rent into chasms, or sobbed as it closed weltering and rose into precipices. Then would be a momentary lull, and presently the tremendous strife would be renewed, as the heavens would at last rend the deep from its bottom, and the deep would bury the heavens in its abyss. Nothing else was heard save the thousand frightful tones of the wind amongst the rigging-tones more appalling, if possible, than the roar of the giant storm. When the captain's voice was at last distinguished, he was giving rapid orders to the men to secure the sails and haul taut the ropes. We young ones were not sent aloft, and we were but of little use on the deck, except in helping the seamen to pull such ropes as were pointed out to us. All that night the storm continued, the waves continually breaking over us, and all hands constantly on deck. We then began to compare our present situation with those we had left, and most of us would have made any sacrifice, short of life, to have regained our humble homes on shore. For my part, when daylight came, and I beheld Whitby Abbey, and next Scarborough Castle, rock-grafted on their stubborn heights, and steadfastly secure amid the drifting clouds, I should have deemed myself fortunate had I been cast even naked amid their dark and frowning ruins. I thought of my father and his earnest prayer — I thought of dear Mima, and was not left without hope. One consolatory reflection opportunely occurred, and that was — that I stood as good a chance of outliving the storm as did my shipmates — and that whilst there was a chance it was of no use to despair. And so, as the saying is, "setting a hard heart agen hard wark," I did my best towards bearing a hand wherever I could be of use. This our second day was almost as stormy as the night had been, and bitter cold. The shrouds were coated with ice, and the hands of us landsmen were blue and benumbed, notwithstanding which, when the men had to go aloft to handle the sails, I and a Welsh lad mounted with them, but the men sent us down, saying we could not be of any use, and if we went on the yard we should only go overboard. So we came on deck, and worked as well as we could there; but our willingness to share danger and hardship with the old seamen got us more favourably looked upon. The storm continued all this day and all night again. The captain began to serve out grog, the seamen muttered to each other, and exchanged cheerless glances. The pumps were set to work, as the vessel was said to have too much water; and we landsmen were useful at this labour, in doing which we also kept ourselves warm. On the third morning the wind began to lull; it also changed to the north, and after a pleasant run, we anchored in Yarmouth Roads.

The storm had done much damage all along the coast, and in sailing betwixt Yarmouth and Lowestoft, we counted no fewer than nineteen vessels, of various descriptions, which had been driven on shore. We now went smartly before the wind, and soon had the Essex coast on our right, and the Kentish one on our left, entering the mouth of the Thames. And now, after getting a little inland, such a paradise opened before us as I had never previously imagined could exist in England. Splendid villas amid groves, fairy-looking little bowers, sweet nestling places for happy families, peeping behind verdant shrubberies, or glimmering all white in shadowy vistas; the gently waving foliage was of a living, new-made green, whilst the shorn sward that came sloping to the water's edge was of an emerald brilliancy, and hung lipping the waves as if it would suck them for ever.

On the first Sunday after our arrival, we apprentices were indulged with a walk on shore. Being provided with Admiralty protections, and instructed how to act if we were molested by the press-gang, we first made our way to St. Paul's, where we stood beneath the wondrous dome, twice the height of our top-gallant mast, and with almost awful surprise, expressed our doubts of the strange things we heard about the whispering gallery; for we did not go up, the state of our finances would not allow that. Next we went to Tower Hill, and viewed the moat, and walls, and battlements of the tough old fortress, our finances, as before, preventing us from going inside. Westminster Abbey was the object which next attracted us, and here we stayed viewing the monuments, many of which were in commemoration of authors by whose works I had been delighted. Ah! and did I not stand, with long-looking and tear-wet eyes, before the tablets of my old Homeric Pope, and my divine Milton, my companions asking at last why the sleeve of my jacket was put so often in requisition, and I replying by telling them what wondrous books these two had written, a reason which soon satisfied my comrades, who, the Welsh lad excepted, neither knew nor cared anything about books. So having wandered about the city till we were tired, we got some refreshment at a public house, and then returned to our ship.

In due time our cargo was discharged, and we took in ballast, after which we weighed our anchor, and dropped down the river, and instead of taking our course for Montreal, as we had at one time expected we should, we steered back the same way as we had come, and, after a short and pleasant trip, again entered the Tyne and anchored at South Shields, where we again took in coal, and again returned to London.

The name of our vessel, as before mentioned, being the Æneas, I took an opportunity one day of leading our mate into a conversation on the subject, when he narrated the old tale of Æneas carrying his father on his shoulders out of the ruins of burning Troy, and said there was a book in the cabin which told all about it. Was there, I said, what was the name of the book? The name of the book, he said, was the Æneid. Ah! that was a famous book; once I had read it, and would now like to read it again. As for that, he said, he could not make me a promise, but sometime when his father was ashore, he would let me see the book. So accordingly one day, after we had put his father ashore, he beckoned me into the cabin, and there, lying on a table in a kind of state, as a family Bible does at the head of a cottage, he showed me a handsome, old-fashioned looking folio volume, which indeed I found to be the Æneid in English, with notes. I would have sacrificed anything almost for an opportunity to examine the interesting volume, but the mate seemed to think he had indulged me enough, and so I thanked him, and withdrew.

I was always the first of our party to go aloft, and I could soon mount to the top-gallant mast without going through "the lubber hole." I also became expert at furling and reefing, working with the other hands at whatever had to be done aloft. At handling the braces I was also pretty clever, and at the windlass, the capstan, or the pump, I was as good as any on board. I was also the bow oarsman of the jolly-boat, and generally attended the captain when he went on shore.

The perils attending a sailor's life are no doubt many, but those which have to be encountered on this coast are probably far greater than are presented on any other coast of our island. The perils, however, are almost as nothing when compared with the hardships which young sailors in this trade have to endure. Hence, mere danger is not so much thought of by them, and anything which interrupts the wear and tear which they daily undergo is felt to be a relief rather than a misfortune, and is accepted accordingly. Thus it is that our unconquerable sailors are made, and such is the rude and ruthless school in which they are nurtured and brought up. With them, a battle or a storm is little more than a divertisement, the increased labour for the occasion being forgotten in the excitement of action. The hardest workers will always be the hardest and best fighters;—hardest because assured and persevering, and best because, whatever situation they are placed in, mind is ever present directing to the best effect. None, save a working nation can, therefore, ever conquer England. And where are such workers as ours to be found? Let us then cherish our workers. Let them be anxiously cared for, they are the strength and the defence of the country, and of everything within it which is worth defending. Let them never have less than plenty of all comfortable requisites, whatever other class is stinted. Let them be accepted with respect, so long as that respect is merited. They are all fellow-men; the honest hard-handed ones are the noblest of men in God's High Court, and that is high enough for any ambition; and, take ours for all in all, with their faults and depreciations, the wide world has not, in this our day, such another race as that which guards the shores, and labours on the fields and in the manufactories of Old England.

In one of our voyages, or rather trips, as we used to call them, we passed through a fleet of ships of war, which lay at anchor in Yarmouth Roads. We expected being overhauled for hands, but were not, and we sailed forward without stopping. The sight of those huge floating masses, instead of inspiring me with chivalrous feelings, called forth those of a quite different description. I looked upon them as so many prisons where men were hopelessly confined, and punished according to the caprice of unreasonable and irresponsible taskmasters. The bit of smart discipline which we now and then had on board our own little craft gave me an idea of what these great fire-belching concerns must be. Our old sailors also had given us a few lessons respecting the manner in which order was maintained in those communities, and as I eyed them unseen—for our captain ordered us not to show ourselves—I almost shuddered at the idea of becoming one of their crew. The fleet, as a whole, was certainly a noble spectacle to behold. A demonstration of that sublimely audacious spirit by which Britain proclaimed to the world, "I reign!" and the world submitted. But its details I could not contemplate without a shudder, and I secretly wished that I was beyond the chance of having some day a closer acquaintanceship forced upon me. On our return trip the fleet was still there, but considerably augmented by transport ships having troops on board. A large number of coasting vessels were now returning to the north, and as they approached the fleet nearly every vessel was brought to and boarded, the best of the hands being transferred to the ships of war. From the vessel which immediately proceeded ours several bands were pressed, but it so happened that when ours came to pass, both the guard boats were full, and were taking their prizes to the ship appointed to receive them, whilst in the hurry of the moment we got clear through, and so escaped that very unpleasant visitation.

I had now perhaps made some half-dozen trips betwixt Shields and London, and having seen enough of a sailor's life to banish the romantic notions with which the popular songs of the day had invested it, wishful also to enjoy once more the sweets of liberty whilst yet its attainment was possible, I secretly determined on leaving the ship whenever an opportunity occurred for my doing so. On our next arrival at London, therefore, with a view to disguise my intention, and render my flight doubtful, a day or two before we were to proceed to sea again, I laid in a good stock of groceries, and whatever other matters it was our custom to procure. I washed my linen, mended my clothes, and placed everything in excellent order in my berth, so that when the captain and my shipmates went to examine it, as I calculated they would when I became absent, they might find a complete preparation for my going to sea with the vessel, and in consequence be impressed with the idea that I was not a voluntary absentee, but that I must have been crimped into some of the sponging houses, and smuggled on board a king's ship. This, I supposed, would cause an advertisement to be immediately put out, or a hue and cry to be issued after me, and inasmuch as the most probable course which the captain would take would be to make a day or two's inquiry in such places where he would suppose I was most likely to be found, I should thus, at any rate, have a decent start of my pursuers, if, indeed, after such a loss of time, they should deem it worth their trouble to follow at all. My plans being thus arranged, I one evening asked permission to go ashore for the purchase of one or two articles which I still wanted. The permission was readily granted, and the boat landed me opposite to Bell-wharf pier. I immediately proceeded to Ratcliffe Highway, and after purchasing a pair of stockings—my own having been left on board as a blind with my other things—I entered an eating-house, and there spent some time till dusk was pretty well set in. I thence went into the city, to St. Paul's, inquiring my way into Aldersgate Street, and when there I ventured to accost a respectable-looking person and requested him to be so kind as to direct me towards Islington, which, of course, he did, and I passed through that suburb without stopping or being questioned. An officer, in naval uniform, whom I met, certainly took more notice of me than was quite to my liking, but he passed on and did not speak. I next inquired the way to Highgate, knowing that if I got there I should be on the direct great northern road, and at Highgate, whilst stopping at a public house, I ascertained that the next place on my route would be Whetstone, and the next after that Barnet. I accordingly walked through Whetstone and through Barnet without stopping. I now considered myself fairly launched on my journey. I had been fortunate in getting clear of the vicinity of the shipping and of the city without being questioned, and was now ten miles from St. Paul's. I once more breathed the sweet country air; the smell of mown meadows sometimes came across my path. I had seven shillings in my pocket, and though as yet uncertain of my success, I was full of hope and delighted with the present enjoyment of freedom. I had not gone far, however, before I became somewhat embarrassed, the night was getting far advanced, the country less populous, and I was uncertain both as to the name of my next stage and the course I should keep. I had not gone far, however, before I met a man to whom I put the necessary questions, and who told me to keep on the broad highway, to the left, and that the next town of any note which I should arrive at would be St. Albans. I thanked the man for his information, when he said, "Stop; I know what you are, and what you are about."

"Do you?" said I, rather surprised, but in a good-humoured manner.

"Indeed I do," replied the man; "you are a sailor, and are running away from your ship."

"You might be a wizard," I said, "for what you say is perfect truth."

"Well, now," said he, "as you have been as candid as I was frank, I'll tell you something which may be of use to you."

I thanked him.

"At St. Albans," he continued, "a party of marines are stationed, who press every sailor that appears in the town. They even press them off the coaches, or other vehicles, if they get a sight of them. Through St. Albans, however, you must go, and you will be pressed if you appear in the streets; you must, therefore, get through the town without being seen, if possible. Fortunately it may be done. In a short time you will overtake a waggon which carries goods on this main road. You must get to ride inside of it, get, stowed amongst the packages, and never show your face until you are clearly on the other side of the town."

I thanked him most gratefully for his information, and begged that he would not mention to any one having seen such a person as myself on the road. He desired that I would make myself easy on that score, and so with expressions of thankfulness on my part, and of kindly wishes on his, we separated.

It was now about midnight, all was still and silent on the road. I was about eight miles from St. Albans, and by the time I had shortened the distance by three I overtook the waggon, the tail of which being full of soldiers' wives and their children, I could not get in there; the driver, however, offered me a snug place in the hay-sheet—a large and strong horse-hair cloth which fastened in front of the vehicle, and presented a resting-place as comfortable as a hammock, and quite large enough to conceal me. I, therefore, got into my hiding-place, and was almost instantly fast asleep. I must have ridden about four miles, though to me it seemed but a few minutes since I got in, when the driver awoke me and asked which road I was going when I got through the town?

"Why the main road, to be sure," I said.

"Yes, but which main road?" asked the man.

"The main road down into the north; into Lancashire," I said. "There is none other, is there?"

"Oh, yes," said the man, there is the main road to Bedford and those parts, and that's the road I'm a-going."

Instead of saying, "Well, drive me to Bedford then, or anywhere else, so you don't land me here in sight of the pressgang;"—instead of so considering in my own mind, I might have suddenly become demented, for I alighted from my covert, and shaking the hay-seeds from my clothes as well as I could, I gave the man some copper, and walked right into the broad street of St. Albans.

Had I been acquainted with the topography of the country, the road to Bedford was the very road I should have taken after being once at St. Albans. But as it happened, I was ignorant of these things, else the main road was the one I should have most avoided. After all, however, though the Old One himself seemed to be leading me, it was, perhaps, for the best.

It was a very fine summer's morning, and being Saturday, the market-place was occupied by numbers of country people setting out their standings of butter, eggs, poultry, and vegetables. Directly through the midst of these market people lay my way, and I stepped it with seeming equanimity, and as much of real indifference as I could muster, for, after all, as I reflected, if the very worst happened, I should only be disappointed in present hope, and be sent on board a ship of war as many hundreds had been before me. So I walked forward, the people almost lifting their eyes in wonder at seeing a tall, gaunt, weather-browned sailor traversing that perilous ground.

I had got clear of the market-place, and was proceeding down a flagged footpath leading to the outskirts of the town, and already breathing more freely, when the sound of a light slip-shod step approached behind me. I thought it was some servant girl going out for her morning's milk or hot-roll, and never turned my head. A slap on the shoulder, however, and the salutation, "Hollo, shipmate," caused me to face about, when what should stand before me but a marine, in his blue over-coat and girdled hat without feather.

At that moment I felt as little ruffled as if we had been old acquaintance, determined, however, not to be taken if either presence of mind or resistance could prevent it.

"Hollo, shipmate," said I.

"What are you?" asked the man.

"What am I? I'm a servant," I replied. A term not used in the Royal Navy, but by which persons under contract are distinguished in the trade of our Eastern Coast.

"A servant?—what's that?"

"Why, a servant—that's all," I replied.

By this time three other marines had joined us.

"Where's your pass, to pass you through the country?" asked the first man.

"I have no pass," I said; "I'm a free-born subject of this kingdom, and can travel this or any other high-road without carrying a pass at all."

The men looked at each other, and then at me. They could not comprehend the reason of my cool manner and unusual language. They had no idea of free-born subjects, nor of sailors travelling without passes.

"Then you have no papers?" said the first man, who seemed to be the superior of the party.

"Why, as for that," I said, "I daresay I can show a kind of a small matter which will, perhaps, satisfy you for the present." Saying which, I took my protection from an old black pocket-book which I carried in my hat.

"Oh, if you have any written papers to show," he said, "you must go with us to our captain, I can't read writing." So much the better, I thought, and straightway displayed the document at length, knowing if it could do me no good, neither could it do me any harm. "Do you see that?" I asked, pointing to the broad seal of the Admiralty, stamped with an anchor.

"Oh! be d—d," said the man; "you have been discharged from a man-of-war."

"Why, you lubber," I said, in a half-familiar way, "do you think if I hadn't I should have come here?"

"Ah! he won't do," said one or two of the party.

"You may go about your business," said the first man, turning to walk off with the others.

"Ahoy, there," I said, "are you going to stop a shipmate on shore this way, without standing so much as a glass of grog for him?"

"You be d—d," said the corporal, and hastened up the street to join his comrades.

Several decent-looking farmers, who had left their produce in the market, stood in the cart-road watching the whole proceeding, and when the marines had left, they said, "Well, young fellow, you are the first blue-jacket that has slipt through the fingers of yonder scoundrels this long time." I entered into friendly conversation with these men, and as they were going my way I had their company on the road as far as Redburn, where, after partaking with them a glass or two of ale, we parted.

I next passed through Hemel Hempstead, Market Street, and Dunstable, always concealing myself, as well as I could, when I heard a coach coming either way, until it passed. At Hockliffe I rested some time, and had a good sleep behind a hedge. I thence went through Woburn, and afterwards through Newport Pagnell, and when night came, and the glow-worms were shining in the hedges I found myself opposite to a small lone public house, near the village of Stoke Goldington, in Buckinghamshire, and about eleven miles from Northampton.

CHAPTER XXIV.
JOURNEY PURSUED—ADVENTURES—
DIFFICULTIES—HOME.

INTO this humble hostelry I entered and got some bread and cheese and ale for supper. The house appeared to be kept by an elderly couple, with a woman servant, and when I mentioned my wish to stop there for the night, they said they could not find me a bed in the house, but if I would put up with a good litter of straw in the stable, I should be welcome to rest there. I accepted their kind offer with pleasure, and lay down, thanking God that I could rest without the hated "Starboard watch, ahoy" breaking my slumbers; and save that once or twice I was awaked by rats tripping over me, and by the cackling of fowls and the quacking of ducks, a king never enjoyed sounder repose. In the morning, it being Sunday, I brushed my shoes, washed myself well at the pump, and turned my linen the cleaner side out, after which I got a basin of milk and bread for breakfast, and demanding my shot, the old folks told me I had nothing to pay, and so with truly grateful thanks for their kindness I bade them farewell, and continued my journey.

It was a lovely morning, and my way lay through a tract of country which at every bend and undulation of the road, presented some object, or group, or opening upon scenery, which was continually suggestive of the fact, that this was indeed a land where men and women knew how to live and be happy at their own homes. Here, on one hand, would be a substantial farmhouse, with its open door displaying much plenty within, its strong-limbed hinds feeding the horses or cleaning the stables, and its ruddy-brown damsels milking the kine, which stood sleepily lashing their tails on their backs or flapping their ears in the sun. The next habitation would probably be a little white cottage, with a low door, and small leaded windows shadowed by vinery, and the eaves of the thatch slouched down, as if to prevent the wind from up turning them. A whine and a grunt would be heard in the sty, and a broad garden, darkened at one end by fruit trees, would be abundant

"Of herbs and other country messes."

Next a clear tiny rill comes trickling by the road-side; soon we are under a tall young wood, with an old tree here and there matted with ivy or robed in hoar lichen. Soon we perceive a house of the higher order, with its palisades, its gravelled walk, its bright evergreens, its clean steps, and its stately and decent quietude; although if the white blinds were rolled up instead of being down, it would seem all the more frank, cheerful, and Christian like. Next, perhaps, we have a glimpse of a spire rising above tall trees, or the turret of a grey old-looking bell tower sends forth its summons to the villagers for their morning's devotion. Wending on our journey, hills and vales, with meads, pastures, and green crops spread all over their ridges and down to their brook margins, are laid out luxuriantly before the ever-pleased eye; whilst far off, in the opening of hoary old woods, are seen tower and battlement of some lordly hall. Such, O England! are the objects constantly presented to the eye of travellers amid thy rural scenes. Such are the cause and the results of thy true greatness. First labour and its reward, from which follow plenty, peace, reverence, obedience, order, security, opulence; and, as a consequence of these, encouragement to continued exertion. Cherish, then, these elements of giant power for the sake of their inestimable results, which are the guarantees of untold blessings for all. Promote honest labour. Honour it wherever or however found. Have respect to the horny hand and the dewy forehead, and oh! with kindliness endeavour to attach the heart which has the courage to encounter peril, hardship, and stringent toil day by day, without a murmur, and without a wish, save only that it may be duly rewarded. Yes; be just, noble England, to thy sons of labour. Then, so long as thy rock foundations endure shalt thou be happy: the conservator of thy own strength, the arbiter of thy own destiny.

Through such a country as this, and breathing an air sweeter than which none ever wafted over Paradise, had I walked some five or six miles, when the bark of a dog, and the appearance of sundry low tents, a horse, a mare and her foal, an ass or two, a heap of panniers, a lurcher and a couple of terriers, pans, pots, and a kettle on a fire, which a lad was blowing into red heat, made me aware that I was, for the first time, about to behold a family of gipsies, in their favourite state of encampment. The tribe consisted of three stout men and as many women, one of them very old and deformed, and one, a superb being, with majestic golden pendants, that touched the crimson hood on her shoulders; a coil of luxuriant hair lay across her knees, as thick as a mainshroud and as glossy as a skein of silk, whilst her magnificently black and darkly shadowed eyes were like two gems, light-emittent through midnight. Two of the men and one female were asleep in tents, some children were also at rest, a boy or two were engaged with the dogs; the horses and the asses were pasturing, one man was smoking a short pipe, and skinning a rabbit the while, the queen sat plaiting what seemed to be a girdle of many colours, and the old one was tending a cake in the embers. A young damsel sat there — a beauty such as I had never before beheld, not even in Lancashire, for she was different from them all, though not surpassing — nothing human could do that — but this had a feminine grace, and a faultless beauty of a type which was entirely new to me. A scarlet strap and a short sleeve were the only covering to her shoulders, her neck and arms being entirely bare. Over the front of a laced bodice of various hues, hung a small bib of fine linen, which so far covered her bosom as modesty required. A green kirtle bound her waist and fell below her knees, leaving her legs and feet, which were models of symmetry, as innocent of hose or pumps as they were at her birth. Her complexion was a clear olive, whilst her features I can only describe as being strikingly impressive from their beauty, and much like those which I had seen in the portraits and on the statues of Oriental nymphs and goddesses of antiquity. Her hair, of raven lustre, was plaited and wreathed on her head, where it was bound with ribbons of bright and grave colours mingled, and held by a comb, and thence dividing, fell in graceful locks over her shoulders, and below her bosom. She was on her knees, sipping broth from a china basin, and with a silver spoon. I accosted the party with the usual salutation of "good morning," to which the man and the two women replied. We chatted as I stood there respecting various matters, as the road, the weather, fellow wayfarers whom I had met, and things of that kind, and in the course of our conversation the man informed me that my best way to Leicester would be through Welford, and not through Market Harborough, which was the more common route. After satisfying my curiosity as well as I could consistently with a decent observation, I bade them good-bye, and was coming away when the mistress of the party, or queen, as I may call her, asked me if a mess of broth would be acceptable. I had been thinking before that never had broth smelled so temptingly as this did; I therefore expressed my thankful acceptance of her offer, and taking a seat on the sod I partook of a breakfast such as I had little expected to find at such a table, for besides the broth, the young nymph, by direction of the queen, placed before me bread, cold mutton, fowl, cheese, with mustard, and green onion as a relish, so I laid to as freely and as plenteously, according to my wants, as ever did alderman at a corporation feast. My kind entertainers seemed the more pleased the more freely I partook, and after making a most excellent meal, during which I was neither annoyed by many questions, nor embarrassed by ceremony—for they mostly spoke to each other, and that in a language I did not understand—I again expressed my sincere thanks and pursued my journey, deeply interested by the scene I had quitted, and particularly so by the two amazing beauties I had beheld.

Northampton, a garrison town, was the next place through which I had to pass, and as a recruiting party of marines was stationed there—as my friend the gipsy had informed me, though whether or not they had orders to press he could not tell—I waited outside until the quiet hour when people had all gone home from church, and had got seated at their dinners, before I essayed the perilous experiment of walking through. The wished-for time soon came, the bells had all ceased tolling, and the streets were nearly deserted, when I stepped at a leisurely calm pace, as if in no great haste to be gone, along the clear broad causeway of that neat and cleanly town. Everything seemed to my wish; it was a hot day: the sun glared on the pavement and against the windows; the blinds and curtains were nearly all closed; the doors were open to let in air, and I could hear the children laughing, the mothers scolding, and the knives and forks clattering as the good folks were partaking their happy meal. I envied them not, I only wished in my heart that every soul in the place might be compelled to eat, and never cease eating, until I had walked clear and far away of that burning pavement and blistering flag-road; and in sooth I began to think it certainly would be so, the streets were so quiet, when all at once, pondering as I went, and with my hat pulled over my brow, I found I was approaching a marine, who was crossing me at right angles. I would have given the world if the fellow had only been like the towns-folks, quietly employed with his pudding, instead of being where he was, but I took care not to betray any outward sign of either alarm or dissatisfaction. He was alone, and no other person was in sight, and if he stopped me, and my old protection trick failed, I had nothing to do, but either to out-run him, or knock him down, or both, and so decide the matter. These thoughts, however, and these resolves, which came as quick as a throb, were no sooner present, than, to my surprise as well as satisfaction, the man merely looked at me in an ordinary way, and nodding, said, "Good voyage, shipmate," to which I readily replied, "Good quarters, shipmate," and each passed on.

And now, as the protection which I have once or twice mentioned will not be any more alluded to, I may as well explain, that these documents which were given to apprentices, were no protection at all save whilst the apprentice was on board the ship to which he belonged, or if on shore, was engaged in the lawful service of his master. If the navy was greatly short of hands, as in the expedition we passed in Yarmouth Roads, for instance, not only apprentices were seized despite of their protections, but even carpenters and mates of coasting vessels would sometimes be made free with. In my case, therefore, who was absconding from my service, the document, had it been perused, instead of being a protection would have been a detection, inasmuch as it would have required a degree of ingenuity beyond my command to have shown why I, an apprentice on board a coasting vessel on the North Sea, should be found traversing the streets of St. Albans, or of Northampton, the king's veritable terra firma—instead of being on his other element, the ocean.

This escapade was a great relief to my mind, since having now passed this second garrison town I had not much fear of being interfered with by press-gangs, though, wherever there was a party of marines it was possible that I might be questioned. The weather was, as I have intimated, that of a truly English summer's day. Towards evening, when the heat was mitigated to a joyous coolness, came a breeze that swept odours from the wild rose and the honey-bine. Then, by the hill-sides, or along the valleys, or up the meadow paths, appeared young and happy couples, the lads in their clean smock-frocks, and the lasses in their new pumps, smart caps and ribbons, and all seemingly so full of happy, contented, and hopeful love, that the tears dimmed my eyes as I looked towards them. "Ah!" I thought, "and will not I be walking with one as dear and as bonny as any of them before long." And thus as I wandered forward waned that sweet Sabbath eve, and small indeed was the amount of "cash in my locker," wherewith to procure a lodging, but on I went, and I must have passed some seven or eight miles beyond Welsford, when it being nearly dark, I stopped at a good-looking public house, and after paying for a glass of beer, which took nearly the last copper I had, I asked the landlord if there was not a snug corner in his stable or hay-loft in which I could be allowed to rest till morning? He said the cattle all slept and pastured out, and he had not so much as a lap of straw on the premises; but if I would walk on a couple of miles or so, I should arrive at a place called Wigston, where the yearly feast was being held, and if I only got amongst the young fellows there, I would have all I wanted, and that too for nothing. So thus discouraged in one respect, and encouraged in another, I again commenced my journey, and walked a long way, the eve settling into darkness, and not a glimmer from a house, nor the bark of a sheep-dog, nor any other indication of inhabitants to be seen or heard. I kept on in this way until I became quite tired, and looked in vain for some barn, or outhouse, or cattle-shed, in which I might lay down, but not a vestige of cattle or cattle-shed was to be seen. Not even the tinkle of a sheep-bell could be heard in that vast stillness. At length I thought I espied something like swathes of grass on the other side of a low fence, and climbing over, I found them to be what I expected. I straightway therefore commenced making my bed, and collecting a number of swathes together I lay down on part of them, and pulled the remainder over me until I was pretty well covered, and so, with a bunch under my head for a pillow, and my hat for a sleeping cap, I bade good-night to one star which hung winking above, and in a moment care was no more. When I awoke it was broad day, and the lark was singing overhead. I jumped up, shook off the dewy grass and clover, and thanking God for so excellent a bed, with freedom, I leaped over the fence, and pursued my journey.

It was now evident that unless I could hit upon some plan whereby I could procure sustenance on the road, my travels must soon cease. My last penny had been expended that morning in the purchase of a cake, and I had not a single halfpenny towards carrying me eighty-six miles. As for having recourse to dishonest means, that never entered my thoughts, whilst to beg I could not yet bemean myself. Something, however, must be devised, and as I wore under my trousers a pair of stout woollen drawers, nearly new, I concluded on selling them, if I could meet with a customer; and accordingly I went over the hedge into a quiet little corner, and stripped off my drawers, tying them up in a small pocket handkerchief which I had taken care to preserve. I was so entirely satisfied with this proceeding, so easy with respect to present means of subsistence, that I fell into a profound sleep, and so continued during a considerable time. On arriving at Leicester, I stopped at a clothes shop, at the door of which an elderly female stood, of a very decent appearance. I accosted her, and entering the shop, offered her my drawers on sale. She examined them, and asked how much I expected for them? Well, I said, I should not be very particular, but I thought they would be cheap at two shillings.

"Two shillings!" said the dame—her keen eyes fixed upon me—"Why, young man, I would not give two shillings for all the clothes you have on your back."

I said I was sorry to hear her say that, but how much would she give then.

"You are a sailor I suppose."

"I am, or at least have been," I replied.

"I have a son that is a sailor also," she said. "I wish him a safe return then," I replied.

"Aye, a safe return, with plenty of prize money," she quickly added.

"Be it as you wish," I replied.

"Are you going to see your friends?" she asked.

"I'm going to stay with them I hope."

" Well, I'll tell you what I'll do," said the dame. "I'll just give you sixpence for the drawers, and that's what I call dealing handsomely with you."

"Could you not give me something more, mother," I said, trying to soften her by that tender appellation, though but with small hope of success.

"Not one half-farthing more shall I give, if you talk till night," said the dame, "and if I ever get the money back again, I shall be lucky."

I still chaffered with her, trying to obtain a small advance, but it was of no use, and considering that I might dodge round the whole town and be no better, I resigned the drawers.

"Where's the napkin they were tied in?" she asked.

"It's here I replied," showing it.

"Oh," she said, " I must have that you know, I bid at the whole lot."

My anger was equalled only by my disgust — the little napkin was very dear to me — and taking up the drawers I was about replacing them in the napkin with a view to leave the shop, when judging as I supposed my purpose, she threw down a sixpence, saying, "Give me the drawers: if you were my own son I could not behave better to you."

I first secured the sixpence, and, then putting down the drawers, said, "God help the son who has such a mother as you to come to," and left the place.

My next business was to buy a small loaf, which I soon did, and eat it with a voracious appetite as I went on my way. I proceeded down the street and out of the town without being once annoyed by the appearance of either marine or recruiting party. I passed through Montsorrel and Loughborough without stopping, and took my rest and a draught of porter at a small public house beyond the latter place. After this, towards evening, I met a company of women coming from the hayfield; they were disposed to be merry, and dancing and singing with their forks and rakes on their shoulders, they formed a ring around me. At length one of the youngest of them sung a snatch of a popular song:

> "I will be sure to return back again
> If I go ten thousand miles, my dear,
> If I go ten thousand miles."

They next produced a keg and a basket, and the kind creatures made me sit down amidst them, and partake of their brown bread and hard cheese, which I did heartily, and quenched my thirst with a good draught of their home-brewed ale, after which, with many thanks on my part, and kind wishes on theirs, we separated.

If I could have made up my mind to begging, here had been a fine opportunity for trying my talents in that line on these kind and sisterly beings, but I could not find in my heart to inform them how sorely I was distressed: and though I knew that unless I either solicited relief on the road, or some unforeseen assistance came to hand, I must at least endure two days of horrible starvation and fatigue, I could not humble myself to the act of craving charity. So still cherishing a kind of irrational and gloomy hope beyond hope — whilst my benefactors returned to their cheerful and welcome homes, I advanced into the shades of evening, and the grey and solemn stillness of a summer's night had enshrouded all around when I arrived at the village of Shardlow.

At one little window only could I see a blinking light. I knocked at the door, and it was opened; an old couple who were preparing to retire to rest seemed somewhat alarmed at my entrance, so I hastened to make known to them that I was a stranger on the road, and would thank them to direct me either to a hayrick or a cattle-shed, where I could find shelter for the might. They commiserated the hardship of my lot in being necessitated to ask such a question, and directed me to a stable connected with a public house a little farther on the way, the residents of which would probably be gone to bed. I thanked the old folks, and without much trouble found out the house and the stable alluded to. All was dark and silent around; the stable was quite unoccupied, and not a straw, nor a lock of hay could I find within the place. I tried to make the manger my sleeping berth not without a grateful remembrance of the one at Bethlehem — but I could not fit my shoulders to the trough, and sleep being denied me there, I lay down on the bare pavement below, thinking, carnal though I was, that if the manger once served as a bed for a heavenly Lord, the stones beneath one might even suffice for a wandering sinner like me; and so I stretched my wearied limbs on the floor and fell asleep. In the morning I rose as refreshed as if my bed had been one of down, and leaving my sleeping apartment in as tidy a condition as I found it, I quietly shut the door after me, and continued my journey. I spent my last penny in the purchase of a cake as I entered Derby, and as penny cakes were rather small concerns in those days, mine was quickly devoured.

I passed through the town without stopping, and soon found myself once more amid the beautiful scenery of which our island is so rife. After walking a mile or two I overtook a little crabbed-looking middle-aged man, who, notwithstanding that he limped on one foot, and travelled with a stick, got over the ground rather cleverly. I soon found out that he was a stay and corset-maker by trade, was a great professor of religion, and was going to Manchester, as he said, to pick up a penny in the way of business, and "to speak a word to the heathen," when opportunity offered. And now, I thought to myself, if this man has only money enough about him to carry us both to Manchester, and will undertake to provide for me on the way, I shall look upon him as one sent by Divine providence. I was not long in ascertaining that he had the means to assist me, and then, in return for his communication, I gave him a short history of my adventures, without letting him know the whole truth, and concluded by a proposal that as we were both journeying to one town, we should keep company, and that he should furnish the means for my very frugal subsistence till we arrived there, when I would introduce him to my friends, who would thank him for his kindness, and amply repay him besides. The prospect of turning a good penny on the road appeared, from the manner in which I stated the case, so plain and certain, that the little man assented to the proposal, and we jogged on to Ashborne, where he paid for a basin of milk, and a pennyworth of bread for each, and this was our breakfast. Soon after leaving Ashborne, we fell into company with a private of light dragoons, going home on furlough. At first his presence was not very agreeable to me, but I soon had reason to conclude that he had not, for the present at least, any designs of entrapping me, so we three journeyed together. We now began to mount the hills over which we had to pass to Buxton, and a long, dreary twenty four miles the journey would be, as I was given to understand. The day was very hot, and I required refreshment in order to enable me to support the heat and fatigue, but I found my commissary was not going to be at all prodigal of supplies. In walking about ten miles he paid for one gill of sorry treacle beer only, and shortly afterwards, finding I could not keep pace with my comrades, I sat down on a knoll by the roadside, and they went forward, disappearing over the long moors. After some time, having got a draught of blessed water at a little rill, I made an essay to proceed, and had not gone far ere I arrived at a large inn and posting-house called New Haven. A haven it was indeed to me. I asked one of the stable men for permission to lie down on the hay-baulks, which he civilly granted, and there I remained sleep-bound until far in the afternoon. On awaking I set forward again, quite refreshed and in good spirits, and was the more anxious to get to Buxton since I should then be only twenty-two miles from home, a distance which I thought I should be able to walk with the refreshment of water only, should chance not throw in my way a particle of solid food. Encouraged thus by the consciousness of being almost on the verge of my native county, and of being now traversing the tops of some of those hills which I had so often contemplated from our play-ground at Middleton, I stepped forward with a light heart, over a country of waste and cheerless moors, and of rolling, billowy hills. Though greatly fatigued, as much probably from the heat of the three last days as from the want of food, I continued, with many cheering anticipations, to urge my feeble steps in the direction of my hoped-for resting-place for the night, though God only knew what sort of a resting-place that was to be. Another opportunity now occurred for my asking charity, and I made up my mind to do it. It was a secluded place in the bottom of a valley. I was descending one side, and a gentleman, mounted and walking his horse at a quiet pace, was coming down the other. We met nearly at the bottom, and I looked at him and lifted my hat, but when my hand should have been extended, and the words of supplication should have passed my lips, I could not do either the one or the other, and the gentleman, merely nodding in return to my civility, passed on.

Shortly after this I began to feel sickly; my head became confused, and I sat down merely as I thought to rest and take breath, but I probably fainted, since when consciousness returned night had completely set in. I however got up as well as I could, and again put my now stiffened limbs in motion, and had not proceeded more than a mile ere I became aware that I was approaching numerous habitations, and pressing forward I was soon at the entrance into the village of Buxton.

My first endeavour was to discover, if I could, a stable or outhouse of some sort, in which I could take up my lodgings—the last of the sort which I should want on my present journey. I had not hovered about the street long ere I espied a ladder reared against what appeared to be a hay-loft; so I crept up as daintily as if I had been mounting to a curtained bed of down, and found to my great joy that I was on a boarded floor, well stored with hay. Here, then, was my bed at once, and now all my troubles were over. I was groping about for a place to make my bed, when, as sudden as a flash, I fell through the floor, and found myself lying on my back in a lower place. I was rather confused at first, and scarcely conscious of what had happened, but was soon made aware that something was vastly wrong by screams of murder, with occasional prayers and imprecations. Presently a door opened, and several men entered the place with lights, when I found that I was lying in the stall of a stable, with my legs across the body of a female, who continued making a great noise, and whose dress was not in the most decorous condition. Though shaken by the fall and still confused, I immediately got upon my feet, when one of the men, holding a lanthorn to my face, demanded to know why I brought my strumpet into his stable. In vain I protested that I knew nothing whatever of the woman. He insisted that I did, and that probably I should have laid hands on other game also if I had found anything worth carrying away. To this insinuation I had no reply save a repetition of the assertion that I was innocent, and I added that I only became aware that any living being was in the place by the accident of falling through the hole in the floor above, which I pointed out, and also stated my motive for going there. By this time the woman had risen from the straw, and was busy arranging her dress,

"Why," said one of the men, "is not that the girl that has been in company with the limping fellow and the soldier all night?"

"The very same," said another.

"Oh! I see how it is," rejoined a third—" where is the old fox concealed? he has not been in the tap-room since this woman left it."

"He's somewhere in the place," said one of the men.

"He'll be found not far off," said another.

Instantly they began to search, when a slight noise in the next stall led them to look that way, and they discovered a pair of legs sticking out from under some straw.

Straight that hunting note which is raised on the taking of a fox was shouted by half-a-dozen voices, and seizing the legs, they pulled out my little lame friend, the stay and corset-maker, with whom I joined company that morning.

"Here he is, sure enough," said one of the men, when they had done shouting.

"The old dog bagged alive," said another.

"Well, how has this come about?" asked the owner of the place. "What account can you give of yourselves?" he continued.

Here a scene and a dialogue ensued, which, however diverting it might be to those present, I will take the liberty to omit from my narrative. Suffice it to say, that the landlord cleared the place, locked the door, and put the key in his pocket, the whole of the party, the woman excepted, entering the public house to which the stable was attached, and from whence the greater part of them had issued on hearing the noise. Here several persons were drinking, smoking, and singing in a kind of kitchen or family room, and amongst them, drunk and nearly asleep, was my other fellow traveller of the morning, the young dragoon. The stay-maker was now sadly bantered on account of his adventure, and at last, in order to make his peace with the landlord and the company, he paid for a quart of hot ale and gin, of which I took one or two small glasses, though I would much rather have had something to eat.

After I had sat in this company a considerable time, weary and longing for repose, I espied an opportunity to slip out of the place, and again mounting the ladder to the hay-loft, I made sure of not falling through that time. Quickly was I oblivious of all care, and did not awaken until the morning was far advanced. On descending from my bed I inquired about the soldier and the stay-maker, and being informed that they had started three hours before, I turned my steps through the village and followed them.

Wearily, and rather faintly, though with a good heart, I mounted the hills which enclose Buxton on the Lancashire side, and then, with greater ease, I began to descend the long road down to Whaley Bridge, my only refreshment being now and then a draught of water from the small mountain rills which trickled through their rock channels on the moors. After passing Whaley Bridge I began to ascend, slowly enough, the steep old road to Disley. The day was again very hot, and when I had mounted this hard path of the olden time to a considerable distance, I rested on a stone wall opposite some cottages, at the door of one of which I soon espied an old woman winding bobbins. I asked her for a draught of water, when she immediately rose to oblige me, and brought forth a basin of delicious butter-milk. I thanked her most gratefully, and as I stood leaning against the doorpost, much fatigued, she asked if I could eat some oaten cake, and on my saying I could with pleasure, she invited me to come in and sit down, and speedily presented me with half of a good substantial cake, baked thick and without being riddled. I quickly dispatched the cake, when the old woman—a fine-looking old mother she was—casting on me a glance of womanly feeling said, "Bless me, lad—for thou art somebody's lad, I dare say—thou hast been famished, almost dying of hunger, I'm sure; couldst thou eat another piece of cake?" I said I could, and informed her that this was the first food I had tasted since I left Ashborne the morning previous. She accordingly gave me the other half of the cake, part of which I ate, and the remainder, with some cheese, she made me put in my pocket as a snack on the road.

Blessings on the memory of that kind old woman! I thought she was much like what I remembered of my own mother, only more aged. I stole many a look at her as she moved about the house. Blessings be ever with her memory!

After leaving this cottage, refreshed and somewhat rested, I was soon at Disley, and from thence I passed through Bullock Smithy (now Hazel Grove) and Stockport to Manchester, where I arrived at dusk, and took up my quarters at the house of a friend until night had set in, when I visited my father and other relations, and was received by them with a joyful welcome. I thought it rather strange, however, that they expressed not any surprise at my return, and on further conversation I learned that my kind friend, the little staymaker, had visited them the same day, and had prepared them for my coming. He had made them quite easy respecting my condition, having told them that he had advanced me money sufficient to carry me home comfortably, and that I was coming on at my leisure. The rascal was consequently very well received by them, and went away trebly repaid for what he said he had advanced to me. My father, however, though he abhorred the fraud and the deception, said, "Never mind the money, 'My son was dead, and is alive again, he was lost, and is found.'"

And now, if we would derive a benefit beyond the mere amusement which the perusal of this book may afford, we should here pause and survey that career of life which I had lately been pursuing, and then note down the events which followed from it. The dangers, the hardships which I had undergone, and many of them I have not set down, not liking to amplify on such matters, were only the natural results of a course of parental disobedience, and a disregard of conscientious warnings, which, like good angels, would have turned me from the path of error—of sin—but I would not.

From such a course what could be expected save a retaliation of evil for the evil I had committed; for as surely as night succeeds day, as certainly as death comes after life, so inevitably does good beget good, and sin produce misery. Let the reader then, the youthful one especially, who seeks to benefit by the reading of this book, note what, in my case, followed a vicious irregularity of living; and then, if he would escape providential chastisement, let him, with a steady determination, eschew evil, on the track of which chastisement quickly follows, and is never turned aside.

CHAPTER XXV.
WAREHOUSE WORK AGAIN—
READINGS—CATHERINE.

HAVING now had enough of an unsettled life, at least for the present, I endeavoured to obtain constant employment, and a regular situation, in a warehouse, and shortly I got an engagement in that of Messrs. Hole, Wilkinson, and Gartside, an eminent printing concern, whose works were at Cross Hall, near Chorley, and whose sale warehouse was in Peel Street, Manchester. Here my business was to unlock the warehouse at morning, to kindle a fire in the counting-house during winter, to sweep the floor, to dust down the desks and tables, and generally to make the place tidy and comfortable against the arrival of the book-keepers and my employers. My next morning's job was to sweep the floors of the sale-rooms, to dust the counters, benches, and shelves, to lay all the prints straight, and place them in regular piles according to their several sorts. My own place, the packing-room on the upper floor, was next to be swept and made ready for work; and the like having been done to a small print-room adjoining, I either took a seat in the counting-house until relieved by the bookkeeper, or I remained at my own desk in this upper storey. This desk was a snug concern, or at least so I deemed it. It was furnished with writing materials, convenient drawers and recesses; a ruler, a penknife, a folding-up slate and pencil, and on it were deposited a file, with notes from the sale-room of every parcel of goods which I had to deliver or pack; a book in which every parcel or pack which had to go by carrier was entered and signed for by him; and a smaller book in which were noted down, and duly signed for, every parcel of goods which was delivered in Manchester. Such was the routine of my duty on three mornings in the week, and such the place of retirement which was my own peculiar right when not called to action by the requirements of my situation.

My employers were George Hole, a son of an extensive farmer near Newark-on-Trent, who managed the selling department of the concern at this Manchester warehouse; John Wilkinson, a manufacturer, who attended to the buying of the cloth necessary for the concern; and Henry Gartside, a first-rate practical printer, who managed that branch of the business with great ability. On the mornings of Monday, Wednesday, and Friday, the warehouse was opened at seven o'clock; and on the three market mornings of Tuesday, Thursday, and Saturday, it was opened at six o'clock. By half-past six a large cart, drawn by two stout horses, would be at the door. Before seven, Mr. Hole and Mr. M., the salesman, would have arrived, and would probably find from a dozen to a score of country drapers chatting and walking about in the counting-house, the lobby, and the sale-room. Exactly at seven o'clock the sheets were thrown off the cart, and the delivery commenced. Mr. M. counted the pieces by twenties, and placing them on my shoulder I carried them upstairs, and threw them down on a clean white cloth, which was spread on the floor of the sale-room. A scramble then commenced amongst the buyers which should get the most pieces; sometimes they met me at the sale-room door and tore them off my back; and many a good coat have I seen slit up, or left with the laps dangling, after a struggle of that sort. The pieces having all been delivered in this manner, the old carter drove off to put his horses up, whilst Mr. M. hastened to assist in the sale-room, and I, from a wish to be as useful as I could to my employers, also attended, handing pieces to the customers, and now and then taking occasion respectfully to point out a piece which was a better one than common. For having naturally a taste for objects of a beautiful or striking description, I soon acquired a tolerably correct judgment of prints also; and though I made not any parade of my talent, I had not been accustomed to prints long ere I could form a rather sure guess whether or not a style of work would sell. Such was a print delivery and a morning's sale at a Manchester warehouse in the year 1808.

The pieces which had been selected were left doubled up, piled in lots, and ticketed with the name of the buyer. Mr. Hole and Mr. M. would then go to breakfast, and if a buyer who had missed the delivery came in, I showed him the prints which were left, when he selected what he approved of, gave his name, and I piled and ticketed them the same as the former lots were.

By this time the book-keeper would have arrived, and I went to breakfast, and on my return would be despatched to the post-office for letters. The way-bill of articles wanted for the works was next put into my hand, and I went round to the chemists, the drysalters, the block-makers, the engravers, or to any other parties who had to supply materials to go back by the cart, and ordered whatever was required. I next delivered all lots of prints purchased by Manchester houses, or ordered to be left with them for package with other goods. The cart was next loaded for its return, and by the time that was despatched the old church bell would have dropped ringing one o'clock, and the doors were then locked and we went to dinner. At two o'clock we again opened, and I commenced my afternoon's work by carrying up to my packing room the first lot of prints that, having been entered in the day-book, was ready for being sent off. That lot having been packed, or trussed, and neatly marked — at which feat I soon became no common hand — the other lots were successively made up in their respective forms, and, having been entered in the carrier's book, were duly signed for by him, and sent to their several destinations. By this time it would probably be five or six o'clock in the evening, and the goods which had been ordered for that day having been all disposed of, our employers would retire at tea-time, and at six, after I had carefully raked out the fire, closed the shutters of the counting-house, and walked round the rooms to see that all was right, I and the bookkeeper—if he was present—locked up the warehouse, and I took the keys to Mr. Hole's residence in Faulkner Street, and so terminated my employment for the day.

I have been thus particular in describing the transactions of one market day, inasmuch as that description may suffice for those of any other market day of the busy seasons of spring and autumn, when new patterns and styles of prints were produced in the market; and inasmuch also as that I am rather of opinion that morning sales, like the one I have described, are no longer known in Manchester, nor ever will be again.

I was well satisfied with my situation, and used my best endeavours to please my employers, and to promote their interest in every way which my humble condition permitted. Nor were they unmindful of my exertions, and I had not been long in their service before they voluntarily advanced my wages from eighteen to twenty shillings a week. This was a great encouragement to me, since it gave me to understand in a most pleasing manner that my endeavours were appreciated. I continued those endeavours, and in a short time my wages were increased to a guinea a week.

As spring and autumn were our only really busy seasons, I had occasionally, during other parts of the year, considerable leisure, which, if I could procure a book that I considered at all worth the reading, was spent with such book at my desk in the little recess of the packing-room. Here, therefore, I had opportunities for reading many books of which I had only heard the names before, such as Robertson's "History of Scotland," Goldsmith's "History of England," Rollin's "Ancient History," Gibbon's "Decline and Fall of the Roman Empire," Anacharsis's "Travels in Greece," and many other works on travel, geography, and antiquities. I also enlarged my acquaintance with English literature, read Johnson's "Lives of the Poets," and, as a consequence, many of their productions also. Macpherson's "Ossian," whilst it gave me a glimpse of our most ancient lore, interested my feelings and absorbed my attention. I also bent my thoughts on more practical studies, and at one time had nearly the whole of Lindley Murray's "Grammar" stored in my memory, although I never so far benefited by it as to become ready at parsing. A publication of a different description also fell in my way. Mr. Hole was a reader of Cobbett's Weekly Register, and as I constantly saw the tract lying on the desk at the beginning of the week, I at length read it, and found within its pages far more matter for reflection than, from its unattractive title and appearance, I had expected to find there. The nervous and unmistakable English of that work there was no withstanding. I thenceforth became as constant a reader of Cobbett's writings as was my master himself, and was soon, probably, a more ardent admirer of his doctrines than was my employer. As I generally attended the counting-house when the book-keeper and salesman were absent — unless called out by other employment—I had many opportunities for these perusals. I seldom indeed failed to examine whatever book I found upon the desk, and if I happened to be left to lock up at noon, which would sometimes be the case, I would hasten to the next shop and buy a cold lunch for dinner, thence return to the warehouse and lock myself in, that I might have an opportunity for examining some book which had attracted my attention. And in this way, during nearly all the four years which I passed in the employ of this firm, I continued to examine or to read every book which fell in my way, or which I could readily procure.

Such was the manner in which I was employed whilst with Messrs. Hole, Wilkinson, and Gartside, namely, alertly busy during two months each of spring and autumn; occasionally busy at other times; and with a comparatively small amount of warehouse labour during the remainder of the year. Our early openings gave us a good start of the day; everything was understood and done promptly, and when our neighbours were hurrying and packing to get ready for the carriers, we, having cleared all off, would probably be closing the warehouse. Very rarely indeed did we stay after six o'clock; not unfrequently did we close at half-past five, and sometimes we shut up at five. I then went to my lodgings, got tea, washed and put on some better clothing, and spent the evening either in a country walk or a stroll in the town. Those were some of the most satisfactory days which I had experienced during a long time.

Not unfrequently my evening walks would extend as far as Middleton, for the separation which ensued on my going to sea had not in the least degree diminished my regard for the dear object of my affection, whilst on her part it seemed only to have increased her attachment. Again, therefore, we had our walks through the leas of Hopwood or Middleton. Sometimes, on fine Sunday afternoons, we would ramble as far as the wood-crowned Tandles—ancient fire-hills—and descending by their romantic footpaths into the sunny valley, and thence through the shadowy, mysterious, old Druid-haunted wood, returned to Middleton at the closing of another blessed day, my heart repeating, in reference to the scene in Northamptonshire, "Ah! And have not I been walking, as I thought I would, with one as dear and as bonny as the best of them!"

Having heard that one of my fellow apprentices on shipboard had returned, and was living at Cheetham Hill, I took an opportunity for going over there, in order to find him out. At the door of a small cottage, the site of which is now enclosed in a shrubbery, stood an old woman whom I thought I must have seen before. I looked again, and who should she be but the mother of my once dear Catherine; but oh, how altered! aged, attenuated, and sadly humble in her apparel; humble in the material, but still proud and particular in its cleanness and the formality of its adjustment. I at once determined to speak to her, and as a pretence for so doing I crossed over the highway, and asked her if she could inform me where the person I was in search of lived? With a quick and inquisitive look, which I seemed not to notice, she scanned me over, and said she did not know the person I was asking about.

Lingering a moment till my look met hers, I said, in affected surprise—"Surely I should know your features; are not you Mrs. W. who once lived at a farm in Crumpsall?"

"I am," she replied.

"And will you permit me to ask one question, which I assure you is not prompted by curiosity, but arises from a sincere respect for the person I would ask about?"

Here I heard a slight coughing within the cottage, and the old woman leaned her arm, which was now tremulous, against the door-frame.

"What is your question, young man?" asked she.

"I wish to know how your daughter Catherine is?" I replied.

"Catherine is very poorly," said the old woman; and looking at me again, "does Catherine know you?" she asked.

"She did know me once," I said, "and I think she cannot have quite forgotten me yet."

"I think I know now who you are," she said, with a more satisfied manner.

"Perhaps you do; I have no objection that you should know me," I said. "But pray, where is Catherine then, if she is so poorly?"

"She is here," replied the old woman.

"Might I be allowed to speak to her?"

"Yes," said the dame, "there cannot be any harm in that now. Only"—whispering in my ear— do not speak loud, nor say anything that may fluster her, or put her out of the way."

"God forbid," I said, entering the cottage with a careful step.

Catherine was seated in a low chair near the fire, a pillow was behind her head, and her left arm rested on another, which lay on a white table, on which also were a prayer-book, open, another small book or two, and some fruit.

The moment I entered the room there was a brightening in her eye, and a flushing on her cheek, but instantly, seeming to check herself, she appeared calm, and motioned me to come near.

The old woman placed a chair for me, on that side of the table where her arm lay, and doffing my hat, and wiping my forehead, and eyes also by the way, I sat down, and taking her hand gently in mine, I said—

"Dear Catherine, I am truly grieved at seeing you so unwell."

"Ah, Samuel!" she said, "are you come at last? I did not expect this; I dared not hope for it."

"Why not, dear Catherine?"

"I thought you were too happy elsewhere ever to think of me."

"Indeed, I have been very happy, and very unhappy also but I have never ceased to love you as a sister—as a dear friend."

"That is quite enough," she said, "since I have now no love to bestow, save that for my Redeemer."

"Are you happy?" I asked.

"I am," she replied, "very happy. I know that my time in this world is short, and I am prepared for the change, but I wished to see you, God permitting, and now you are come at last, and I shall have done with things of this world."

"Dear Catherine," I said, "I am glad that I have come then."

She then desired me to state particularly how it happened that I was in the company of the young woman with whom she last saw me at Manchester; and I thereupon narrated the circumstances exactly as they occurred. She then said she was satisfied, for that my account corresponded in every particular with that given by the girl herself. I asked her if she had seen the girl, and she said she had met her one day, some time since, on the road to Manchester. The girl was travelling with wares in a basket, and she having become a customer, led the girl into conversation, and at length asked her if she remembered coming down the Mill Gate with a young man, and being led by him into a cook-shop. The girl, she said, at once acknowledged the fact, and gave the same account of the circumstance which I had done. And now, Catherine said, she had only to ask my forgiveness for having thought wrongfully, and perhaps injuriously of me.

I said I had nothing to forgive her for, but if she wished me to say the words, why then I as freely forgave her as I hoped to be forgiven. She said we had both been sufferers. That dangerous old sibyl in whom she had placed her confidence had misrepresented my actions, and abused her too easy belief. But it was now all over, and she had only to implore me to prepare for the same great change which she had shortly to undergo. Sooner or later I should have to come to the same state, and I should then find it a blessed thing so

> "To have lived that I might dread
> The grave as little as my bed."

I asked her if she was quite prepared for the change. "Oh quite prepared," she said, "blessed be my Redeemer."

She leaned back, rather exhausted. Her mother motioned me not to speak any more. Catherine gave me her hand again. I felt the pressure of her burning fingers, and placing them reverentially to my lips, I intimated that I would shortly come again, and withdrew. On my second visit, with a small present of fruit and confectionery, Catherine was too ill to speak, but she knew me, and held out her hand. Her cheeks kept blushing and paling, and her eyes were almost painfully brilliant. On my third visit she was in her coffin, shrouded and knotted with white love-ribbon, and decked with sweet herbs and flowers. Her mother stood weeping behind the curtain, and the attendants were downstairs, so I touched her cold forehead and pale cheek with my lips, and placing one little memorial on her bosom, I took my last look and came away.

CHAPTER XXVI.
ROBERT BURNS—A WEDDING—A RIOT.

AT the time when I was in the employ of Messrs. Hole, Wilkinson, and Gartside, it was the custom for porters and warehousemen, such as myself, to go round on New Year's Day a Christmas-gifting, to the block-makers, engravers, carriers, and others employed by the firm. On the first New Year's Day of this my servitude, I refused to exercise this privilege, and so lost my Christmas gifts for that year. The porters of the neighbourhood could not comprehend the motives for such an act of disinterestedness and independence; and when we fell into company, which we sometimes did, at Dolly Burton's, who kept an excellent tap at the "Red Lion," in Church Street, I was lucky if I did not hear my self-denial characterised in disparaging terms. They said I could be nothing less than a fool, to miss a legal and honest chance of putting a pound or two into my pocket, for the trouble of a forenoon's walk; and they talked to me so, that, in sooth, I began myself to think I was not so bright about the head as some folks. Accordingly, the next New Year's Day I went with two others on that, to me, distasteful errand, and in about three hours I had pocketed thirty shillings. But I resolved never to go again. There was so much humiliation mixed up with the thing, that though the money was useful, I felt self-reproached when I reflected how it had been obtained. So there was no more New Year's gifting for me.

I think it was about this time that Chatterton's life and poems fell in my way. They interested me very deeply, though I could not help believing that his account of the Rowley manuscripts was scarcely credible. Burns's life and writings next fell into my hands — Robert Burns, the Scottish ploughman, of whom I had heard mention made so often, and yet, strangely enough, had never read one sentence. Well now the poems, and an account of the manner in which this gifted man wore out his life in this world, were before me. And did I not sit down, beside my quiet desk, under the skylight, and read, or rather compress to my very soul, every word of that precious book? Aye, through, and through, and through again did I note it, line by line, and sentence by sentence. And this man, whom methought I saw before me as plainly as if he had stood there, was Robert Burns, the deathless-named, the world-wide famed Robert Burns. There he was, a tall, stooping, lank-haired, weather-browned, dreamy-eyed, God crowned, noble-minded ploughman. And this, too, was of his writing, of his soul uttering; this "Lass o' Ballochmoyle" was one strain of his never-dying melody! If this be really so—-if this be indeed his poetry—what can these sensations possibly be, which awaken within me whenever I read a true poet's verse; these strange and undefined emotions which have brooded over my heart ever since I knew what love and poetry were. If these expressed sensations of the noble poet peasant constituted his imperishable wreath, what could these unexpressed but somewhat identical feelings of mine be, save poetry without the form—a spirit without the body. What then, methought, if I tried to throw them into form? what if I dared an essay to give them utterance in verse? Burns thereat looked kindly—or so I dreamed—and with a sweet, strong voice said encouragingly, "Try mon, and fear not." So I tried, and the result was such that when vanity whispered, "I also am a poet," I knew not that it was vanity; and from that time I became an occasional writer of verse.

So greatly was I pleased with the character of Burns that in accepting him as an example I made a too faint distinction betwixt his genius and his failings, and in striving to emulate the one I sometimes fell into an imitation of the other, which was quite a different thing. My visits to Dolly Burton's became more frequent, after warehouse time, and were occasionally prolonged beyond the limits of sober refreshment. A few clerks, tradesmen, and some of the better sort of porters, used to meet in the little parlour there, and after discussing the news of the town, or of the nation, during which pipes and glasses were replenished pretty freely, and joke and banter were not spared, singing would commence, and a strange thing would it have been indeed had it terminated without

> "Wha first shall rise to gang awa,
> A cuckold coward loon is he;
> Wha first beside his chair does fa,
> He shall be king amang us three."

But then, Mother Burton's ale was of so excellent a tap, and she was so kindly an old landlady, at once discreet and obliging, that we respected her as much as we liked her ale, and there might be something in that also which detained us. But whatever was the cause of our frequent meetings, whether the ale, or the landlady, or the music, or all together, it would be greatly probable indeed, that before we separated a couple or two of our cronies would be in a condition to enact Shanter or Souter Johnny on their way home.

I was not so unreflective as not to perceive to what this course must inevitably tend, and with a view to put an end to it at once, I resolved to marry. This was the more likely to be effected without much difficulty, inasmuch as my courtship had been duly paid, and it was long now since my intended fair had entertained any other expectation than the one I now purposed to accomplish. So one forenoon, when she came to Manchester on an errand, I asked leave out of the warehouse for an hour, and having met her at a place appointed, we proceeded to a goldsmith's shop, and I contrived to fit her neat finger with a ring, worth nine shillings, which she folded in tissue paper, and then in another paper, and next wrapped in a huzzif, tying it round and round with the tape band, and next placed it in a pocket-book which she carefully folded and conveyed to the very deepest recess of her pocket, feeling again, to make sure that it was there. This important business being settled, I helped her to mount her little tit Trim, bade her good-bye for the present, and seeing her off at a trot towards home, I returned to my work, happy in the certainty that when I was wed, I should have a wife who would create for me an ever-welcome home.

The banns had been duly published, the day agreed upon, and all was ready. So I made an appointment with my friend Booth to rise early on Sunday morning, and take a good swim in the river before I went to meet my bride and her friends. Booth and I were up betimes, and as speedily in the water at Sandy Well, luxuriating in the cool element most gleesomely, when what should start us from our enjoyment but the sound of the old church bell ringing seven o'clock, within a quarter of an hour of the very time at which we should have met Mima and her company at Harpurhey. We had been mistaken in the time an hour. So we put on our clothes, and hastened towards the place appointed, but before we arrived there we espied the party coming on the road, and meeting them, we all came to Manchester, in a very good humour, as wedding folks ought to be. After breakfasting at my sister's in Greengate, where I lodged, we proceeded to the Old Church, and lo! when the ring was produced, the bride's finger was so swollen with walking, that the ring could not be passed over the joint. The minister, who was the Reverend Joshua Brooks, seeing that the ring was not placed according to custom, began, as he read the service, to thumb it with his nail, in order to force it over. I was afraid he would hurt the dear little woman, and was about to remonstrate, when he suddenly quitted us, and hastening to one side of the communion rails, he gave a boy who stood leaning against them a smart box on the ear, and then, without saying a word, he returned to us. Meantime, in order to prevent his further annoyance, I had taken hold of the whole of the finger, and held it with the ring on in my hand. But he now attempted to thrust my hand away, and tried to commence forcing the ring up again.

"Let the ring go over," he said.

"It can't go further," I replied, "her finger is swelled."

"It can go further, and it shall go further," said the irritable little being, and I, almost as irritable, said quickly, "It sha'n't go further."

"Oh; very well," then observed he, "stand down, you are not man and wife until I have bestowed the benediction."

"Benediction? indeed!" thought I, "a blessed benediction it must be that has to pass those lips."

However we stood back, and as he had finished the ceremony for us, except the benediction, he went through the same form with four or five other couples, after which the clerk ordered us all to kneel down; we of course kneeled with the others, and the benediction having been bestowed indiscriminately, we rose from our knees, and I suppose each bridegroom did as I did, for there was a sound of kisses in the place.

"How stupid you were," said the reverend personage, when we went into the vestry to sign the registers, and to pay the fees—No, I had forgotten, the fees were paid beforehand—"How stupid you were," said he, "not to let the ring go on the finger."

"The ring was on the finger," I said.

"Yes, but not properly; not over the joint."

"That is not required," I said. "Besides, the finger was swollen, and it was painful."

"But the ring is over the joint now," said he.

"Yes, but not through your endeavours; and whether it were or not you had no right to interfere in the manner you did. The ring was on the finger, and the form of solemnisation does not require more."

" Pho, pho, man," said he, "sign the book; sign the book."

Both Mimi and I signed the book. Thus we were married, and I was happy.

The morning following, I opened the warehouse, and prepared it as usual, and the remainder of the day was given me to keep my wedding on. Mima and I went to Middleton, and whilst we sat at a merry tea party at my uncle's, a being which was dearest to me of any in the world, save my wife, was brought in, and presented. A young girl held in her arms a sweet infant, just of age to begin noticing things. It fixed its good-tempered look upon me, smiled, and stretched forth its hands. — "Bless thee," I said in my heart — taking it in my arms, and pressing it to my bosom—"Bless thee, my dear babe, though my coming has been late, and after long looking for, I will be a kind father to thee. Yes, though a proud and supercilious world may view with contempt the misfortune of thy birth, the more it disparage thee, the greater shall be my love. Bless thee, my little innocent," and I held it fondly, for my heart yearned towards it. Meanwhile, as if its mother had heard what my heart alone spoke to my child and to God, she sat looking at us through trembling tears. I gave the babe to her, saying kindly, "Dear love, be happy. The fault was mine, and it shall be my life's endeavour to repair it."

Soon after this we commenced housekeeping at Manchester, and a brief period having elapsed, my wife and child again returned to live at Middleton, I generally, in summer time, walking over after warehouse hours; in winter visiting them twice or thrice a week, and always spending my Saturday nights and Sundays at home. I was now a settled family man, serving my employers duly, and, God knows, I can with truth say, that I served them honestly also. My greatest ambition was to please them, and to provide for my family, and as I was tolerably successful in both objects, I was as happy as a mortal need be in this world.

It was about this time, that the authorities and some of the ultra-loyal inhabitants of Manchester made their first grand political mistake, which occurred within the sphere of my observation. Charles Wood, I recollect, was Borough reeve that year, and a placard with—if I mistake not—his name appended, was exhibited, calling on the inhabitants of Manchester and its vicinity to meet in St. Ann's Square, for the purpose of passing a congratulatory address to the Prince Regent, afterwards George IV. On the day appointed there was a large muster of people from the neighbouring towns and villages, and the original concocters of the measure, fearing they would not be able to carry it, kept entirely away, and abandoned their intention altogether. The crowd, seeing there was not to be any meeting, formed a ring in the square, and appointed a chairman, and passed some resolutions of a tendency contrary to those originally purposed to be carried. Meantime, groups of people were in other parts beginning to commit excesses. About half a dozen, who from their appearance seemed to be countrymen, accosted a gentleman at the entrance from Exchange Street into the square, and after some opprobrious expressions they laid hands on him, and then began to strike him with sticks which they carried. He tried to escape into some of the shops, but the doors and windows being mostly fastened he was disappointed. The men continued striking him; his hat was knocked off, and on his head, which I saw was a little bald in the front, he received several blows. My feelings and partialities had hitherto been all on the side of the populace, but I could not witness this cowardly outrage without feelings of indignation and disgust. Pushing in amongst them, "For shame, men," I said, and warding off two or three blows, I received several on my arms and shoulders. At that moment, some one in a shop, opening the door, as if to see what was the matter, the gentleman slipped in, and the door was again closed and bolted in an instant.

Just then a great shout was set up near the Exchange, and the whole party hastened off in that direction, I following leisurely. When I got there a number of fellows were throwing chairs, tables, and benches through the windows above the post office, and the furniture being quickly broken up, the fragments were used in smashing the lamps, and front windows of the building. Another party of the mob were in the large room, breaking and destroying everything that stood in their way, or that excited their spirit of mischief. Fragments of tables and chairs were hurled through the windows into the street, and thence back again; the costly chandeliers were shivered to atoms, and at length, a heap of straw was piled up and set on fire. At this juncture the police and a party of the Cumberland militia arrived; the fire was extinguished, and several of the rioters were taken into custody. A troop or two of the Scots Greys soon afterwards made their appearance, and began clearing the streets, when, it being then warehouse time, I hastened to my work.

CHAPTER XXVII.
A CRITICISM—MIDDLETON FIGHT—A PARTING—CONCLUSION.

IN the exercise of my talent for verse-making, I had so well pleased myself that at length I determined to test the merit of one of my productions by offering it for publication, in the Manchester Gazette. The office of that paper was then at the top of Hunter's Lane, and William Cowdroy was the editor; a gentleman of whom I had a very high opinion, for, though he was rather satirical, and at times, somewhat crusty with his correspondents, he on the whole, evinced an encouraging spirit; at all times he exhibited a quick and just perception, and to his judgment, therefore, was this piece of mine submitted. It was a description, in verse, of my first visit to Oldham, and described in an ironical strain the interior of a cottage at Priest Hill, and scenery in the immediate neighbourhood. It was in the Lancashire dialect, and commenced as follows :—

" 'Twur on a Sunday afternoon,
I don'd me shoynin' Sunday shoon,
An off I seet wi' Jim an' Jack,
We beawnc'd to Owdham in a crack."

After the description of the place, which was certainly doggerelish, it concluded with this stanza:—

"An' neaw yon meawntuns hee and far,
  Curtain'd the god o' day;
Gone to the west his feyery car,
  An sunk his blazin ray.
Wi evening mild, we tripp'd the plain,
An' merrily hied us whom again."

I put it in the letter box, and on the Saturday following a note to correspondents desired the writer to call at the office. Accordingly, on an evening of the week following, I, in a state of mind betwixt doubt and assurance, called, and was shown into a room, where I awaited the appearance of the literary Solon as if death or fate had depended on the issue. At length he came, a man about sixty years of age; of middle height and somewhat fat and fussy; his complexion was a little rubicund; his nose, with spectacles on it, somewhat snubby; his eyes, as he looked under or over the glasses, grey and piercing; and his general appearance and manner that of one possessing power, and disposed to use it in his own way.

"Well, young man," said he, holding his head back, and looking at me, "what is the business you are come upon?"

I said I was come about a piece of poetry. "What poetry?" asked he.

"It was a piece entitled 'A Trip to Oldham,' and the writer was requested to call at the office."

"Are you the writer of that?" he asked. I said I was.

"And how the d—l could you expect that I should give it a place in my paper?"

I said I hardly did expect so much as that, but I hoped to obtain his opinion as to its merits.

"Well, then, my opinion is that it has no merits," he said.

I said I was but a young hand at verse making, and if he would state whether it was the subject, or the manner of treating it, which rendered the piece objectionable, I should feel obliged.

"Oh! both are objectionable; it is trumpery doggerel throughout. Here is your paper, and I hope you will never offer me any more such." Saying which, he took up the candle, and went out of the place, leaving me to grope my way down the lobby and out at the door as well as I could.

Such was the first reception which my verses met with from a Manchester editor. Sorely indeed were my expectations disappointed, and sadly humbled was my ambition, yet I was not disheartened. "This being a failure," I said to myself, as I was going down Hunter's Lane, "I must e'en try to do better the next time, as many a poor genius has done before me. And notwithstanding what the critic has said, I am as certain as I am of my own existence that there are redeeming passages in the poem. He does not understand it. It is written in a rude dialect. He is testy and out of humour. And besides, he is no Solomon after all." Thus I criticised the critic, and settled the matter, in my way.

One afternoon we were astonished and alarmed at the warehouse by a report which had come into the town that the power-loom manufactory of Messrs. Burton and Sons, at Middleton, had been attacked by a numerous mob, with the intent of destroying the machinery, and that several of the mob had been shot dead, and a number wounded. As soon as we had locked up for the evening, I, of course, hastened off to Middleton, and on my arrival found the report to be true.

About two o'clock on the afternoon of this day (the 20th of April) the inhabitants of the town were surprised by the appearance of numbers of men, many of them armed with sticks and bludgeons, who simultaneously arrived in the town from various districts of the surrounding country. Several provision shops in the upper part of the town were entered and plundered of bread, cheese, bacon, and groceries, and in some instances plunder was prevented by presents of money. The mob seemed to arrive from all parts at once, and the smaller parties having formed into one main body in the turnpike road, the whole proceeded to the lower part of the town, and there joined another large crowd, which seemingly had been waiting for their arrival. In this year—1812—there had been much destruction of machinery in various parts of the manufacturing districts of the kingdom, and when the infatuation spread into Lancashire, the power looms of Messrs. Burton seem to have attracted the early attention and hostility of a great portion of the hand-working operatives, who, by means of secret delegations, held frequent private meetings for the purpose of concertina measures for the stoppage or destruction of the obnoxious machines. Of these proceedings the Messrs. Burton were probably informed, since a number of their weavers, dressers, and overlookers had been for some time drilled to the use of firearms within the mill. A piece or two of small ordnance were also placed within the yard, opposite the main entrance, and such other precautions had been taken as were deemed necessary for the defence of the place. These measures were superintended by Mr. Emanuel Burton, who was greatly respected by the workmen, and had inspired them with a portion of his own spirit of resistance.

On the report reaching the factory that the mob was coming, the works were stopped, and all the hands, save those detained for the defence of the mill, were sent home. The mob, after a short delay in the market place, proceeded to the bottom of Wood Street, where the factory was situated, and halted in front of the building, and a score or two of boys who led the mob set up a shout, and began to throw stones and break the windows. A number of discharges from the mill followed, but as no one seemed to have been hurt another shout was set up, and the cry went round, "Oh! they're nobbu feyerin peawther; they darno shoot bullets," and the stone throwing was recommenced. Other discharges from the mill now took place, and some of the mob who had experience in such matters remarked that the crack was different, and that ball was being fired. A moment only confirmed this opinion, for several were wounded, and three fell dead, on seeing which the mob fled in all directions. In a short time a troop of the Scots Greys were in the town, and they were quickly followed by a company of the Cumberland militia. The streets and lanes were then cleared, after which the horsemen returned to Manchester, and the militia took up their quarters in the mill. The number of the wounded on this unfortunate occasion was never truly known, but it was soon ascertained that four persons, all young men, had been killed. Joseph Jackson, sixteen years of age, and David Knott, aged twenty, both from Oldham, were killed at the end of Chapel Street; John Siddall, of Radcliffe Bridge, aged twenty-two, was killed lower down the street; and George Albison, a young man from Rhodes, was wounded whilst going along the highway, and shortly after bled to death, there being no surgical aid promptly at hand.

On my arrival the streets were all quiet, the doors closed, and the alehouses silent. People's minds were, however, sadly agitated, and fierce denunciations were uttered against "Burton and his shooters," whilst very little anger was expressed against the men who had plundered shops. In the coat pocket of one of the killed was found a half-pound of currants, the fruit, no doubt, of such plunder.

I state these things because they are facts, and not from any feeling which I now have, one way or the other, except for truth; though at the time I entertained perhaps as strong a dislike towards the "shooters" and their employers as did any man in the town. My dear wife and child I found safe at home, but greatly was I alarmed, and exceedingly thankful, when I learned that my wife, in her curiosity to watch a mob, had gone down the town, and, with another thoughtless woman or two, had stood at the window of a cottage nearly opposite to the factory, within range of the shot, and only a few yards from the spot where one man was killed. I gave her a lecture for so doing, the first perhaps since our marriage, and being convinced of her folly, she promised never to transgress in that way again, and I daresay she never has.

The morning following this eventful day I went to my work at Manchester, as usual, and in the afternoon we were again startled by the intelligence that a mob larger than that of the day before had visited Middleton, and had burned the dwelling of Mr. Emanuel Burton and those of several of his workmen to the ground. On my way to Middleton that evening I met individuals on the road who were returning to Manchester with fragments of picture frames and mahogany goods in their hands. The mob had indeed been desperately bent on destruction that day, but, more wary than on the day preceding, they had divided their forces, and whilst one strong party threatened the factory, and by that means detained the militia at that post, others went to the houses of certain of the workmen who had defended the factory the day before, and not finding them at home, had piled their furniture in the street, and had destroyed it by fire. In this manner the furniture of one cottage at Back-o'th'-brow, and that of two others at the Club houses was destroyed. The mob, it should be understood, was on this day armed with guns, scythes, old swords, bludgeons, and pitchforks. A party of colliers from the neighbourhoods of Oldham and Hollinwood carried mattocks, and with these tools were in the act of knocking the end of a house down, when they were called off to another place. For whilst these outrages were in progress at Back-o'th'-brow and Club houses, another party of rioters set off towards Rhodes, and it was to aid these latter that the colliers were called away. The house of Mr. Emanuel Burton, at Parkfield, was the first object which attracted their vengeance. It had been abandoned by the family, and the mob immediately ransacked the cellars and larder, the younger ones crunching lumps of loaf sugar or licking out preserve jars, whilst the older hands tapped the beer barrels and the spirit bottles, or devoured the choice but substantial morsels of the pantry or store-room. This part of the business having been accomplished, the work of destruction commenced, and nearly every article of furniture was irretrievably broken. Amongst the rioters were two sisters, who might have been taken for young Amazons, so active were they in the pillage, and so influential in directing others. To some of those around them they were, however, known only as "Clem" and "Nan," the two tall, dark-haired, and handsomely formed daughters of a venerable old weaver, who lived on one of the borders of the township. These two were in a room, the windows of which were hung with light muslin curtains, and a sofa, with a cover of light cotton, was also in the same room. Nothing further in the way of breakage remaining to be done, and these two being the only ones in this room, "Come," said one to the other, "let's put a finish to this job," and taking up a shred which lay on the floor, she lighted it at the fire which had been left burning in the grate. In a moment the sofa was on fire; the sofa set the curtains in a blaze, and sofa and curtains communicated the flames to the floor and window, and at the expiration of probably half an hour not a beam nor a board remained unconsumed in the whole building.

The next place intended for destruction was the mansion and farmstead of Mr. Burton, senr., at Rhodes, and only a very short distance from the scene which has just been described. A part of the mob was already hovering about the grounds, and some individuals had advanced into the yard and begun operations, when a tumult and a clatter of hoofs caused them to look around, and they beheld the Scots Greys close upon them. Their flight and dispersion were the work of an instant, and this valuable property was saved.

Whilst the Greys were dispersing the mob at Park House and Rhodes, others of the same regiment, assisted by the Militia, were clearing the rioters out of Middleton, which they did speedily and effectively. In the performance of these services, however, greater severity was exercised than had been the wont of these two corps on former occasions. A man named John Nield, from Oldham, was shot through the body by one of the Greys whilst attempting to escape near Alkrington Hall; another man was shot by one of the Greys, and left for dead, near Tonge Lane; a woman, also, who was looking through her own window, was fired at by another of the same party, and a bullet went through her arm. But a serjeant of the Militia earned deathless execration by shooting an old man, named Johnson, from Oldham. Johnson had never been nearer to the mob or the factory than the Church public house, where he had sat in the kitchen with the family, and had smoked his pipe and drunk a glass or two of ale. Towards evening, when it was supposed that all the disturbance was over, he strolled into the churchyard, and was standing with his hands in his coat pockets, reading the inscription on a grave-stone at the steeple end, when a serjeant and private of the Militia, having ascended the Warren, caught sight of him from amongst the trees; the serjeant went down on one knee, levelled, fired, and killed the old man dead, the ball passing through his neck. A number of shots were fired at the soldiers during the pursuit, but none of them, I believe, were wounded, except from casualties with their horses. A number of persons were made prisoners during the riot, and subsequently many left the country for a time. The two Amazonian damsels escaped seizure, and few only of the real leaders were ever prosecuted; whilst several who had as little to do with the outrage as I had myself were, on the information of a bad, half-crazed, but artful doxey, named Kent, lodged in jail, tried, found guilty, and sentenced to long imprisonments.

And now, friend reader, I have to return to my own affairs, and to relate an incident, which, next to my grandfather's rejection of Madam Ann Bamford's overtures, and my father's refusal to let me learn Latin, had probably a greater influence in determining my subsequent condition than had any other event of my life. I allude to the circumstance of my leaving the employ of my old masters, in Peel Street, and to my preference of a country residence with domestic employment, which consigned me at once to a life of independence, with alternate ease, exigency, and poverty.

Our young gentleman, Mr. M. the salesman, having been recently married, and become a housekeeper, it happened that he wanted a load of coals, and as I was always glad to render him a service, I undertook to get him a load of real Oldham Black Mine. We had been very slack at the works of late, and the cart had often returned almost without any load, and as no intimation had been given me of a change in that respect, I went out after breakfast, although it was a market day, and bought the coals for Mr. M., and saw them delivered and paid for. On my return to the warehouse, the cart had, to my surprise, been waiting to be loaded with grey goods. On my meeting Mr. Hole in the passage, he looked displeased, and asked where I had been? I told him, and he said I was neglectful; that I ought not to have gone off when I knew the cart would have to be loaded, and if I could not attend to their business better I had best look out for another situation. I merely replied that I had not been wilfully neglectful, for that I did not expect the cart would have to be loaded that day; and so I went to work, and had the cart loaded and off in quick time. Those expressions of my employer sunk deep into my mind: they sorely wounded my feelings. I pondered them over and over, trying to discover some ameliorative meaning in them, but as I could not disguise or qualify their intention, I told Mr. M. at the week's end that I understood Mr. Hole's words as a notice to leave, and that I should accordingly do so at the expiration of a month.

I am not assured that Mr. M, said anything in my favour to my employer respecting this business, though I daresay he would not omit so fair a course. Nothing, however, was said to me, until the month was out, when Mr. M. said they were not yet suited with a man, and it would put them to great inconvenience if I left at that time. I accordingly stopped another fortnight, and as they were not yet prepared, I stopped another week and then left the situation.

As trade was now going well, work for the loom was readily obtainable, and good wages were given. After, therefore, I had made up my mind to leave, I turned my attention to employment of this sort, purchased looms, bespoke work for myself and wife, who had become tolerably handy at the business, so that when I left Messrs. Hole and Co. I was in a degree pledged to become a weaver.

I should, however, mention that, pursuant to my habit of versifying on nearly every occasion in which my feelings were interested, I had composed a couple of stanzas on this momentous event, which stanzas, on the day of my departure, I wrote on the slate on my desk, and left them there. They were as follows:

"To-morrow's sun beholds me free,
   Come night, and I no more will own
A master's high authority,
   Nor bend beneath his angry frown;
But to my native woods and plains
I'll haste, and join the rustic swains.

Gay printed 'fancies,' 'plates,' nor 'chintz,'
   No more with wonder shall I view,
Nor criticise the various tints
   Of pink or azure, green or blue,
Save when I pluck the flow'ret sweet
That clasps my lonely wandering feet."

A farewell, I may surely be allowed to say, quite poetical, and sentimental enough for a hard-fisted warehouse porter.

Well! on the Tuesday after I had left, I went to Manchester about the work I was to have, and as one warehouse which I had to call at was in Watling Street, and another was in Marsden's Square, I must go past my old warehouse or take a circuit, and I chose the direct road. When I got into Peel Street, old Bob, the carter, who was never very active, was sadly hobbled in the loading of carboys and other unhandy articles, and as I stopped to inquire how he was, he asked me to lend him a hand, and I did so. My place had not yet become occupied by another, and Mr. M. seeing me helping about the door, called me in, and asked me where the scissors were with which we used to cut patterns? So I found them, and he desired me to take them to Mr. Hole, who was upstairs in the sale room, and that I did also. Mr. Hole, on seeing me, was quite free, and asked very kindly how I was, to which I replied in that tone of becoming respect which I never could suppress when treated with proper regard. He sent me upstairs into the smaller print room for some pattern shreds, and taking a passing glance at my little recess and the desk, I noticed that the slate was removed, an intimation to me that the place had been overhauled, and my verses probably discovered. I was therefore the less surprised when on my return to the sale room Mr. Hole asked me whether or not I had got another situation? I said I had not got another. He asked whether I had any expectations of one, and I replied that I had not yet made any application. Because, he said, "You are qualified for a more respectable situation than the one you have had with us, and if you think proper to look out, and apply for one such as I have alluded to, I will give you a recommendation, with which you will not need to be ashamed in asking for one highly respectable; and as you are at present disengaged, if you choose to come back and stop with us until something more befitting you offers, you will find everything agreeable as heretofore." I thanked him in terms of fervent and sincere gratitude; stated to him what were my views relative to present employment, and said that should I have occasion to change my plans, and to revert to the prospects which he had opened before me, I would, with every sentiment of grateful respect, hasten to avail myself of his kind assistance.

He said he was afraid I was acting on a mistaken view of what was most conductive to my welfare, and he should be glad if I did not regret it hereafter.

I said I hoped I should not, and that at any rate, for the present I should be happy with my family.

And so, with mutual kind wishes, we parted.

And here, for the present at least, must the reader and I part also. A narrative of the course of my life from 1813 to 1816 may perhaps engage my pen on some future day. Meantime, the reader may be given to understand, that having, on my leaving Manchester, secured plenty of material for the loom, my wife and myself working in one place, she soon became an expert weaver, and we were as happy, probably, as two human beings of our condition could be; our little girl, the light of our eyes, and the joy of our hearts, playing beside us. Afterwards we went to reside with my wife's uncle and aunt, she assisting the old people in the house and shop, and I, on the recommendation of Mr. Hole, taking the situation of putter-out to weavers at Middleton, for Messrs. Dickinson and Wilde. Afterwards they offered me an engagement at their warehouse in Manchester, which I declined. Subsequently, for a short time I was engaged in the bookselling or publication business; and, in 1816, was a member of a Committee of Parliamentary Reformers, and secretary to the Hampden Club, at Middleton. Should the reader, during any leisure moment, wish to hear my narrative resumed, he may consult my book entitled "Passages in the Life of a Radical," and if that does not suffice, but he wishes for further acquaintance, he may peruse my "Walks in South Lancashire," which I purpose shortly to resume. Those walks may perhaps lead us to "The End," after which some abler hand will probably take up the task of marker for history, which I have so imperfectly performed.

Lightning Source UK Ltd.
Milton Keynes UK
UKOW02f2114301016
286494UK00001B/45/P